Christianity and National Integration

CHRISTIANITY AND NATIONAL INTEGRATION

Edited by

O.L. Snaitang

Merostar Rani

SYNOD COLLEGE
Shillong–793002, Meghalaya (India)

&

AKANSHA PUBLISHING HOUSE
NEW DELHI-110002 (INDIA)

AKANSHA PUBLISHING HOUSE
4649-B/21, Ansari Road
Darya Ganj, New Delhi - 110 002
Ph.: 23263193 / 9811582579 / 09435116718
Fax: 011-23263193
Email: ektabooks@yahoo.com
www.akanshapublishinghouse.com

Christianity and National Integration

First Published 2009
ISBN 978-81-8370-200-3

PRINTED IN INDIA

Published by Akansha Publishing House, New Delhi and Printed at Mehra Offset, Delhi.

Contents

Foreword

Christianity is an Asian religion that originated in Israel due to the works and mission of Jesus Christ in the first century. It first came to India through St. Thomas, one of the disciples of Jesus Christ in about A.D. 52. Though this ancient religion appeared to have remained confined to Kerala, it was a strong and vibrant church. The spread of Christianity in India is the result of the works of several Catholic and Protestant mission societies and missionaries from the 16th century onwards. Though the overall percentage of Christianity in the country is still below 3%, yet it has made tremendous contributions in nation-building through education, humanitarian activities, language and literature. Despite those, its role in promoting national awareness and interests among the people requires further through academic investigation. It is in the light of this that Synod College organized a national seminar on "Christianity: National Integration" on the 14th and 15th of October 2008 and invited scholars, academicians, students in this field to present papers and share their views on this theme.

This book "Christianity and National Integration" is a compilation of papers presented in the above-mentioned national seminar. It will be a useful source of information to the students working in this field and I believe will contribute in furthering an in-depth study, examination, discussion and research on the extent to which Christianity has played in

National integration and nation-building in India especially in the nineteenth and twentieth centuries. The papers have highlighted the contributions of the Indian Church in various fields in the country in spite of the problems and challenges it faces from various quarters. Notably education, health care and humanitarian services were the prominent contributions that Christianity has made to the society in our nation.

The publication of this book is a humble and modest initiative of the college in this vast field of the role of Christianity in national integration. I hope it will serve as a source of valuable information to students of the subject and provide interesting materials for a reader in general.

I also congratulate the Seminar Organizing Committee for the laudable effort in organizing this national seminar and the editors for the effort in bringing out the papers in the form of a book.

Dr. D. Wanswett
Principal
Synod College

Introduction

India is a pluralistic and multicultural nation that encompasses to its fold numerous faiths, ideologies, ethnic groups, languages and many others. Its unity and diversity is unique and it has set an example to several developing and developed countries. The nation's integrity, however, rests on mutual understanding, cooperation, respect and responsibility among these different identities. Christianity, as one of these identities or forces, is very much an integral part of India. Though its overall percentage is till the recent past below 3%, Christianity is nevertheless actively participated in building the nation through a wide network of educational schools, colleges and universities, health services, promotion of indigenous literatures, upliftment of women, working for the general welfare of the downtrodden and victims of injustices, rural reconstruction and continuous participation in life building activities. Its services have been to all manner of people.

Many scholars from India and abroad have given sufficient attention to the study of the history of Christianity in India. While much ink has been produced on its presence in the country, there have however negligible studies on its role and contribution to national integration. Lack of in-depth academic research has mostly resulted in misunderstanding and misinterpretation.

In this connection Synod College, Shillong sought to address to this lacuna through an in-depth study and discussion among academicians of the country. After giving serious thought and planning to this pertinent subject, the College decided to hold a national seminar. Following that, a two day National Seminar on the general theme: *Christianity: National Integration* was held at Synod College Auditorium, Shillong on 14th – 15th October, 2008. Shri P. A. Sangma, former Speaker of Lok Sabha and currently Chairman, Meghalaya State Planning Board, Shillong was its Chief Guest and his well prepared Inaugural Address is included in this book.

Among those who attended and presented papers were Dr. James Massey of Delhi, Dr. Kranti K. Farias of Mumbai, Dr. Marina Behera of Bangalore, Arunava Banerjee, Richard R. N. Bajpai and Pranab Puitandi—all from Bankura, West Bengal and others from Northeast India. Papers that have been presented were at least of high quality, broad based and informative.

In his paper on *National Integration and Christianity: An Analysis of National Integration with Special Reference to the case of Christians and the Role of Education,* Dr. James Massey brings out a comprehensive overview on the subject and raises pertinent issues on the questions of racial domination, divisive and captive educational system. In view of the flaw in the systems, he comes out highly with suggestions that India is urgently in need of citizens' solidarity, faith commitment for the liberation of the poor etc., and responsibility of educators to eliminate caste-class principle of education. Dr. R.D. Lyngdoh provides continuity to the subject through her presentation on the *History of Christianity in India.* Her paper dwells on the social and cultural milieu in the Indian situation, the beginning of Christianity and meaning of Christianity in Indian context.

While these two papers set the tone of describing the subject, it was Dr. Marina Behera and Dr. Snaitang who attempted to touch most specifically upon the subject - Christianity in its historical setting and perspectives. Whereas Dr. Behera brings out the discussion on Christianity in Indian historical background, Dr. Snaitang traces its presence and role in historical perspective.

Closely related to this discussion, Archbishop Dominic Jala provides further significant findings from his presentation on *Christianity: Role in National Integration.* It is another concise but lucid paper that brings out the realities of Christian presence even in the midst of divisive challenges. While underscoring the value of human persons, he calls upon promoting a civil society. Tejdor Tiewsoh's *Christianity: National Integration* is also informative and contextual as he brings out a comprehensive summary paper by touching upon India's historical setting, pointing out anti-national agencies and explaining the role that Christian churches have done on the people irrespective of caste, class or creed.

H. Iangrai devoted his paper on the *Contribution of Christianity to Nation Building.* While tracing its origin to St. Thomas in the first century A.D., he highlighted the areas that Christianity had played actively then and continues to do so till today.

The *Social Role of Christianity in India* was another related significant subject and this aspect was presented by Arunava Banerjee of Bankura Christian College, West Bengal. He clearly stated the contribution that Christianity has made through education in bringing about enlightenment, liberation and constructive service to the nation.

Richard R.N. Bajpai who tried to examine the topic entitled *National Integration: Role of Christian Educational Institution* from a broad perspective but given his knowledge on the contribution of Christian educational institution he narrowed down his paper by underscoring on value-based education.

While the above presentations were at least general and macro in nature, it was Fr. Sabastian Karotemprel who provided a regional study by bringing out his well researched paper on North East India and dealt with harmony and national integration through culture and development.

Another significant regional presentation came up highly from Dr. Kranti Kiran Farias who has concentrated thoroughly on the role of Christians of South Kanara in national integration. Pranab Puitandi too who has taken up a case study on the role and participation of Wesleyan Methodist Missionaries in Bankura brought out significant factual information on their contribution in areas of health services and education.

Dr. M. Rani's monograph presentation on the life and political role of Rev. J. J. M. Nichols-Roy was also important. As a Christian and ordained minister of the Church in Shillong, Rev. Nichols-Roy took active part in both the state and national politics. Dr. Rani recorded well about Nichols-Roy's contribution to the integration of the hill areas of the Northeast with India.

In her paper, Dr.M.W. Lyngdoh Nongbri gave a brief writing about culture and discussed the interface of Christianity with culture from the sociological perspectives.

Last but not the least, another presentation was from Dr. D. Marngar. His paper on the *Genetical Concepts of the First Biblical Man and Woman on Earth* though appears to have been outside the purview of the main theme of the Seminar but insofar as it was presented in its scheduled session and recorded in the proceedings of the said National Seminar, it was thought appropriate to include it in this collection in the larger interest of academic information and inquiry in the subject.

These papers that have been collected in this volume are in our views relatively scholarly and academic but neither the Synod College nor the publishing partner is responsible for authenticity of opinions expressed, correctness of historical information or accuracy of data. However, we strongly believe that even in the midst of debates and discussions on this subject, several articles of this book will serve as an eye opener to scholars, social workers, political leaders, theologians and students for further study and research. We also look forward that the outcome of such venture will bring about mutual understanding, academic dynamism and constructive building measures for the unity, integrity and development of the country.

Editors

August 15, 2009

Our Contributors

1.	Arunava Banerjee	–	Lecturer, Department of Political Science, Bankura Christian College, Bankura, West Bengal
2.	Dominic Jala	–	Archbishop, Shillong Diocese of the Catholic Church.
3.	D. Marngar	–	Lecturer, Department of Zoology, Synod College
4.	H. Iangrai	–	Lecturer, Department of Education, Shillong College, Shillong
5.	Kranti Kiran Farias	–	President, Church History Association of India, Mumbai
6.	James Massey	–	Former Member, National Commission for Minorities, Govt. of India and Director of Dalit/ Sulbaltern Studies Centre, New Delhi.
7.	Marina Behera	–	Faculty, United Theological College, Bangalore
8.	Merostar Rani	–	Coordinator, Internal Quality Assurance Cell, Synod College

9. M.W. Lyngdoh Nongbri	–	Programme Manager, World Vision, East Khasi Hills, A.D.P.
10. O.L. Snaitang	–	Research Fellow, Indian Council of Historical Research.
11. P. A. Sangma	–	Former Speaker, Lok Sabha.
12. Pranab Puitandi	–	Selection Grade Lecturer, Department of History, Bankura Christian College, West Bengal
13. R.D. Lyngdoh	–	Lecturer, Department of Zoology, Synod College, Shillong
14. Richard R. N. Bajpai	–	Principal, Bankura Christian College, West Bengal
15. Sebastian Karotemprel	–	Faculty, Sacred Heart Theological College, Mawlai
16. Tejdor Tiewsoh	–	Assistant Regional Head, RZIM, Life Focus Society, Shillong

1

Christianity: National Integration*

—P.A.Sangma

Dr.D.Wanswett, Principal, Synod College Mrs.P.R. Lyngskor, Vice Principal, Synod College distinguished guests, Members of the teaching and non-teaching fraternity, dear students

I am honored to be associated with this National Seminar and I thank the Synod College for having invited me to grace this inaugural session. As you are aware of I am no stranger to this institution. I have been associated with its academic engagements on a number of occasions in the past. I commend Synod College once again for having chosen a theme that appropriately reflects upon our spiritual and social well being. As a faith, Christianity has been under relentless provocation in recent times and it is important that we address these concerns on two dimensions, as followers of Christ as well as citizens of this amazing nation, India.

In this multi-religious and multi-cultural nation, Christians constitute just under 2.5 per cent of the population.

---

*Inaugural Address in National Seminar

Numerically we are small in number but the faith that we profess has been a moral as well as a spiritual force of India. It is amazing to witness the dedication we offer to our faith through our committed devotion to observing the services and practices associated with it. We are indeed a spiritual country and God has not forsaken us in our search for Him.

Christianity came to India in the first century when St. Thomas arrived at the Kerala coast in 52 A.D and by the third century there were Christian settlements in Kerala. Historically, Christianity came to India well before it went to Europe. Since then Christianity has shaped the nation with its core foundations demonstrated immeasurably in the fields of education, health care and social service amongst other basic empowering resources. Today India prides itself in being one of the largest reservoirs of human resource in the world and Christians and Christianity have contributed tremendously to this. Many of the people (people of other faiths) who lead India today have at some point of time been tutored under Christian educational institutions. What will happen to the educational foundation of this country if these Christian educational institutions decide to close down? The thought is shattering! And of course, let us again be reminded of the savior of the 'poorest of the poor'. Mother Teresa's commitment, dedication and service to the call of the Lord with utmost humility exemplify the tenets of our faith. Pope John Paul II had this to say, "*Mother Teresa marked the history of our century with courage. She served all human beings by promoting their dignity and respect, and made those who had been defeated by life feel the tenderness of God.*" Similarly the then Prime Minister of India Inder Kumar Gujral called her "*an apostle of peace and love.*" These glowing tributes paid to her reflect the core foundations of Christianity.

It is a common perception to say that Christianity is a western religion. This is factually not true if we look at the history of Christianity. Addressing the St. Thomas Day celebration in New Delhi on December 18, 1955, Dr. Rajendra Prasad the then President of India, said: "*St. Thomas came to India when many of the countries of Europe had not yet become Christian, and so those Indians who trace their Christianity to him have a longer history and a higher ancestry than that of Christians of many of the European countries.*" Like Judaism and Islam, Christianity has its roots in the Middle East. However, its spread was distinctly towards the west where through the Church it developed a close association with the existing empires and later on, with the nation-states of Europe. What is true is that over the centuries it was the westernized form of Christianity that was introduced to India through the pioneering efforts of missionaries. Throughout the 18th and 19th centuries missionaries across denominations made important contributions to social progress in India and much of the modern influences in Indian society can be attributed to the role of Christianity in India. Christian missionaries helped in establishing schools and colleges all over India and also spread the message of faith and goodwill in the country. Christianity and its teachings have influenced many a social reformer in the country including Mahatma Gandhi.

As a highly accommodative faith Christianity has considered the local needs of such a diverse nation. What we have seen in the recent past is the Indianisation of Christianity, "a vital act of creative thought and practice." Names of churches and Christian denominations have lost their western flavor to this process and instead we have the Church of North India and the Church of South India. It has been a most common sight to observe that priests especially of the Catholic church wearing a long cassock. However, today this dress has been replaced by a saffron garment. Similarly the internal arrangements of a church have also been altered. I have attended services where priests do not use an altar or pulpit but sit cross-legged to conduct mass and Indian music is played with a *harmonium* and a *tabla* (instead of the usual musical instruments). These are but few of the numerous instances in our practices that have experienced the remarkable Indianisation process.

In Meghalaya we have a living example in father Sylvanus Sngi Lyngdoh, fondly known as father *Sngi*. His life and dedication to the Lord has exhibited an extraordinary range of spiritual activity- an evangelist, a teacher, a writer, a multi linguist and a faith healer. He has been a pioneer in cultivating an inevitable link between Christianity and the traditional Khasi faith. Among the Garo community, the *Wangala* dance, a post harvest thanks giving ceremony, is undoubtedly the biggest traditional festival. It was for a time banned by the church as it was considered 'pagan' and 'anti-Christian'. Through determined efforts we have been able to revive it today for the simple reason that it is very much a part of our tradition and culture. In fact the use of traditional drums in church congregations in the Garo hills has now become a routine practice. The Christian faith has been able to permeate the tradition and culture of various communities through this accommodative process of Indianisation.

Another concern which has to some extent been the cause of misunderstanding between some elements of the two religions in India, Hinduism and Christianity, is the issue of conversion. The Indian Constitution does not prohibit conversion for it has granted us the fundamental right and freedom to profess and to propagate the religion of our own faith. Similarly the apprehension that conversions are taking place on a big scale is also not true as numerous Census Reports of India have provided abundant statistics to confirm so. The census data in India shows that among the major religions in India Christianity has the lowest growth rate. The percentage figures available clearly indicate that the Christian population is on a decline. (In 1981 Christians constituted 2.43% of the total population, in 1991 they constituted 2.34% and in 2001, 2.30% of the total population). Looking at these statistics I can firmly say that the Christian population in India constitutes less than 2.5% of the total population even after almost 2000 years of Christianity in India. Should this be a cause of worry for our antagonists? Despite the documentary proof of Christianity being a minority religion in India and hence the fear of conversion and ultimately consumation of Indian society being unfounded, what is important to note is that conversion is a matter of one's personal conviction which one exercises as a responsible citizen of this country. It should be practiced on the core foundations of secularism and freedom of religion as enshrined in the Constitution of India.

In concluding, I once again thank the organizers for this noteworthy opportunity to interact with you. I am confident that this seminar through its subsequent sessions will evoke powerful responses on the various issues associated with the theme especially of the admiring contributions that Christianity has made and continues to make to this nation especially as a vehicle of integration.

Thank you

2

National Integration and Christianity:

An Analysis of National Integration with Special Reference to the Case of Christians and the Role of Education

—*James Massey*[*]

Introductory Remark

First, I would like to place on record my sincere thanks to Synod College, Shillong, particularly to Dr. D. Wanswett, Principal of the College, Dr. M. Rani, Coordinator of The Internal Quality Assurance Cell and Rev. Dr. O. L. Snaitang, Joint Coordinator of the seminar for inviting me to present this paper on the subject 'Christianity and National Integration'. I have changed the title to 'National Integration and Christianity', because it is in this order that I will be dealing with the proposed topic here.

The Rev. Dr. (habil) James Massey is the Director of Dalit/ Subaltern Studies Centre, New Delhi; Former Member, National Commission for Minorities, Govt. of India; Privatdozent, the faculty of Protestant Theology at Johanan Wolfgang Goethe-University, Frankfurt am Main, Germany and Secretary of the Board of Theological Education of the Serampore College (University).

I would also like to add a personal note about my credentials that allow me to speak on my given subject. I am not a 'politician' as some of my friends think I am, because of my former position with the National Commission for the Minorities (Govt. of India). In fact I served on that Commission by virtue of my being an Indian Christian. Therefore whatever I will be sharing with you on my given subject, I will be doing as an Indian Christian.

Then speaking strictly in the technical sense, I cannot be called a theologian as well. However, to present my credentials, I would like to use both these titles for myself – particularly that of a 'theologian': but that I would like to do with a qualification. I would like to say that 'I am an organic theologian', that is to say, I belong to a specific area of theology, which in some circles is termed as 'the theology of the subaltern people', or more particularly 'the Dalit theology'. Since both of these theological expressions fall within the category of 'Political theology', I could be called a 'Political theologian'.

Now what is a 'Political theology'? The articulation of this type of theology begins with the ground realities of 'this world' instead of the 'other world'. Here the attempt is made to address the issues of world-significance and of great practical importance, which are related not just to human beings, but to the whole inhabited world. This theological expression is broad in its ecumenical sweep, because it deals with common issues that are supposed to be the concern not only of the Christians, but also of all people (even those who belong to other faiths or no-faith)[1]. The important characteristic of political theology is that it is always inclined towards the rights of the people who are at the margin, at the periphery or at the level at which they are always considered 'outcasts' or 'outcastes'. It is biased because both God of the Bible and Jesus Christ were on the side of these groups of people (Exodus 3:7-8; Luke 4:18-19). It is against this particular background that some reflections are offered here on the subject of this paper. I shall therefore request that these reflections be received by keeping in mind this background.

The discussion of this paper will be divided under the following sub-heads: 'Historical Background of National Integration', 'National Integration in the Indian Context', 'Major issues related to National Integration', 'Christians and National Integration', 'A Divisive and Captive Education System' and 'India Demands from its People: Solidarity, Commitment and Responsibility'. The paper ends with very brief concluding remarks.

Historical Background of Indian National Integration

The historians present here will agree with me that the importance of history is not only as a record of the past, but also in its potential to reveal to us our identity as human beings. Such revelation of the past not only informs the people of a nation how they reached to their present state and regained consciousness but also initiates in them a process either to bring further change in their situation for betterment or to preserve what they have inherited from the past. But then, there are always some people who will avoid talking about the past, or even if they talk, they will limit their talk about the past to a certain point of history that would suit their interest. This is also applicable to a large number of our Indian leaders - political and non-political - belonging to the power block or to the dominant groups. Of these, the former are afraid if they will go beyond certain point of history they will lose their power, and the latter are concerned more to maintain the status quo.

What is being said here is also true with many of those who are concerned with the question of national integration– particularly the dominant groups, communities and the leaders of these communities — because when they talk about valuing or preserving the rich Indian heritage of 'composite culture' which according to them is 'ours', they project that view in such a way as that heritage had always been there from the time immemorial. This is the first myth, which should be dealt with, if we are to talk about a genuine or an authentic national integration. It is here that our historians can help us.

Our country has lived now for more than six decades as United India, but this period of six decades was not always happy in our life as a nation. It is because the vast majority of the Indian citizens (above 80%) always felt of their being in an alienated state. These constitute the subaltern groups belonging to tribal, adivasis and Dalits communities (including the Scheduled Castes), the Other Backward Castes (OBCs) and the religious minorities. There is a kind of mistrust and impatience, which has gone deep down into the psyche of these people. One force behind such a state has been the caste based oppressive treatment, which they have met for centuries now. This truth has been revealed even in many of the Government sponsored commissions' reports like that of the Mandal Commission.[2]

The freedom of India and her Constitution which became effective on 26th January 1949 certainly created a hope for change in the mind of these communities by recognizing their neglected past and offering them number of corrective measures (articles 14, 15,16,17,19, 21, 25, 30, 244, 244A. etc.,). But in spite of all these constitutional measures, not much has changed. Discontentment, instead of stemming out, is in fact on the increase. One has to read the book like *India—A Million Mutinies Now* by V.S. Naipaul,[3] which tells how most of the subaltern communities have reached a point of war-like stage. Why and how has this happened? It not only poses a problem for national integration today, in fact it has actually created a "danger and possibilities of disintegration". I agree with Dr. Debi Chatterjee, when she says: "India appears under threat, and the fears of its balkanization loom large. To tackle the multifarious problems, the State authorities have time and again negotiated with, and in some cases even signed agreements with representatives of the disgruntled sections of the population. In the long run, these, however, have proved to be futile exercise."[4] To understand the dynamics working behind this problem of our country we have to look into our past history.

Historically India was never a nation-state or a united-state in the present sense. It was a sub-continent or region having many small independent kingdoms, followed different administrative systems, languages, cultures, customs and even had different ethnicities. In the Indian sub-continent possibly the largest Hindu empires that existed were of Ashoka (273-232 BCE), Samudra Gupta (400 CE) and Harsha (420 CE), which did not cover even the half of today's India. Meanwhile number of invaders - first, Turks and then Moghuls came and plundered the region. Even today Dalits and Adivasis do not hesitate to claim that they are the earliest indigenous inhabitants of this region, now known as Indus and Harrappan Civilization (3500 BCE). Dr. Chatterjee gave a quote from Karl Marx's writings in which he summarized the past history of India in these words: "The paramount power of the Great Moghul was broken by the Moghul Viceroys. The power of the Viceroys was broken by the Maratthas. The power of Maratthas was broken by the Afghans, and while all were struggling against all, the Briton rushed in and was enabled to subdue them all."[5]

This quote gives a clear idea that prior to the coming of the British, the region called today 'India' had neither a single administration nor a government. In other words, it was neither a state nor a single nation. It was during the British colonial rule, that for the first time India came under a single united administration and it became one unit; but still, not a nation. Because it was not the interest of the British to construct a single nation-state, they in fact encouraged the divisions, because that was the only way for them to control India and rule the same.

But at the same time we cannot deny the fact that the seeds of nationhood had been sown, which later on after Independence helped India, to become the present nation-state. However, during the freedom movement and the various dialogues and table conferences, many differences surfaced, which became sharper later. One such difference was between the Indian National Congress and the Muslim League, which finally resulted into the partition of the subcontinent into India and Pakistan. The predicament of the Scheduled Castes was similar whose representative Dr. B. R. Ambedkar raised question again and again like "What would power transfer to upper caste Hindu elite mean for India's untouchables?"[6] It was under such circumstances that today's India was born on 15th August 1947.

So we see, that the real process of national integration and state formation including 'nation-building' began after our country's independence from the colonial rule in 1947 and efforts to that end are still on. But then what this process actually means?

National Integration in the Indian Context

According to the authors of *Pluralism, Minorities, National Integration, Problem and Prospects* the process of nation-building and state formation, especially in a plural society like India, "In its dichotomous presentation of 'self' and 'others' the mediating space between the two is either overlooked or deliberately ignored. It is probably this space in which the federal nation building seeks to establish a federal nation without delegitimizing either of them, yet constructing a cohesive political community with composite national cultural identity. The process through which a cohesive federal political community with minimum value consensus is created may be referred as national integration."[7]

The Constitution of India spelled out in detail the principles behind the process of national integration. If one goes very carefully through the contents of the Constitution particularly parts I, II, III, IV and IVA, which contain Fundamental Rights, Directive Principles of State Policy and Fundamental Duties respectively, one will find the following important aspects of this process: *one*, the process of state formation by bringing in the territorial and institutional integration, which actually leads to state formation; and *two*, the process of nation-building, which actually involves the process of citizenship building based on civic consciousness instead a narrower consciousness. Here the civic consciousness is built on the universal principles referred to in the Preamble of the Constitution, which include *justice* (in the areas of social, economic and political); *liberty* (in the areas of thinking, expression, belief, faith and worship); *equality* (in the areas of status and opportunity); and *fraternity* (which is to assure each individual the dignity and will help in maintaining the unity and integrity of the nation).

So the process of national integration proposed in the Preamble of our Constitution and its implementation in truth is supposed to lead to establishing a 'just society' in which every Indian citizen irrespective of caste, religion, language, race, gender etc., will enjoy the equal human dignity as well as equal citizenship. But has India achieved this goal or made a sincere move towards this end? In order to get an answer to this question, we have to look into some of the major issues related to the national integration in India.

Major Issues related to National Integration

It was the President of India, late Dr. Sarvapally Radhakrishnan, who once said: "National Integration is not a house which could be built by mortar and bricks. It is not an industrial plan too which could be discussed and implemented by experts. Integration on the contrary, is a thought which go into the hearts of all the people. It is the consciousness which must aware the people at large."[8] A notable expression here in this statement is '*a thought which must go into the hearts of all the people*', which makes a point clear that the national integration is indeed a process not a time bound project as understood by many of the planners both at regional and national levels in India. It may be true with the territorial and institutional integration which India has succeeded up to some extent by bringing in its physical federal structure, princely states after our Independence in 1947 which actually was part of the process of the state formation. But here the other side of the national integration is not covered, which has to do with the change of hearts. This we call the 'emotional and psychological integration' and this actually is the way to achieve the sustainable national unity and national integration. State formation is only one aspect of national integration, because the other aspect of the same is 'nation-building', which only takes place with the change of the 'heart'.

Prof. Humayun Kabir points to 'mental reservation' as one of the obstacles in bringing about such integration. Often various groups belonging to religious, linguistic or regional forces are listed as opposing factors to such integration, Prof. Kabir explains, "if we carefully analyze their attitudes, we will find what they oppose is not integration but the loss of their identity."[9] In my study of Punjab Militancy between 1985 -1995 I reached the same conclusion that the Sikh struggle was for their identity.[10] The similar views I heard about the Nagas and indigenous groups of Manipur and Tripura in a three days conference which I attended in Guwahati, during July 2008.

It became very clear to me that the major issue that underlies behind the struggles of various North Eastern hill communities (tribals) is the question of identity. My observation further got clarified through my readings of some of the writings of North East Indian writers. For example Ms Patricia Mukhim writes: "The so-called separatist tendencies amongst some of the NEHA tribes were initially only attempts on their part to define their socio-cultural identity vis-à-vis the others in the new circumstances of independence."[11] While giving comments on Ms Mukhim's views, Dr Pristilla Lyngdoh, even makes the same point clearer by saying: "No effort is made for an emotional and psychological integration which is urgently required. Moreover, for most tribes in the North East, the experience of being an integral part of a nation is relatively recent and their difficulty in absorbing this fact needs to be sympathetically viewed. It is against this historical and geo-political background that the problems besetting the region have to be viewed and analyzed... What is needed for the tribals of the North East is the sense of right direction and preservation of their tribal identity. Integration is not acculturation or assimilation, but the sense of belonging and coming within the national mainstream without losing the tribes' cultural identity."[12] Dr Lyngdoh's views could be applied to many other parts of India.

Political and economic interests are also contributory with the religious and the faith factors and play major role against the whole concern of the national integration. Again, as Prof. Kabir says, "Unless economic and political interests are mixed up with a man's (sic) faith there is no reason why there should be a clash between his religious and his national loyalties."[13] A number of examples can be given in support of such views. For example, 1984 Hindu-Sikh riot in Delhi, in which more than 3500 Sikh were killed. Or the recent riots of Jammu and Kashmir over a land transfer issue to Amarnath Shrine, which till August 10th 2008 many lives and over Rs. 10,000 crores lost, at all front. It happened when political interests combined with faith took precedence over the national interest.[14]

Related to the issue of faith taking precedence over all the national loyalty is the question of majority and minority issue, which right from the freedom movement days and all through the last four decades of India's freedom continues to be a major challenge to national integration process. In this regard in my work entitled 'Minorities and Religious Freedom in a Democracy' (2003), while recognizing the key role of religious freedom in nation building, I pointed out:

> "The Constitution in real sense provides a balance between India's national unity and its cultural, religious, and social diversity. The framers of the Constitution were aware that there would be tensions between majority and minority communities that majority community may believe that a separate identity of minorities will endanger national unity. And also minority groups may feel threatened and fear that their identity would be lost in the process of assimilation by this majority. Strangely enough, during the second half of the twentieth century, such tensions and fears have become more pronounced."[15]

This statement was based on the first hand experience which I went through as a member of the National Commission for Minorities, Government of India from 1997-1999. During this period I investigated many such cases which were the result of the growing up tensions between the majority religion and minority religions. Unfortunately this tension is still on the increase today. The examples of which are the recent happenings in the states of Orissa and Karnataka, which include attacks on Christian worship places. Here in this situation, the statement made by India's first President the late Rajendra Prasad during St. Thomas Anniversary Celebration in December 1955 has considerable relevance. Dr. Prasad actually gave the assurance to all those who inhabit this country that "we do not look for conformity to faith, but expect loyalty from every individual who happens to be a son or daughter of this country—not loyalty to dogma or any faith, but loyalty to the country."[16]

The last point which I want to add is related to the majority population of India particularly representing those who have been historically victims of the caste based social order of India, which include: the Dalits, Adivasis, Tribals and the Other Backward Castes. Among these groups of people, even the religious minorities can be included, because majority of the membership of these minorities had the origin either of Scheduled Castes or Scheduled Tribes or OBCs. Now the regaining of peoplehood or the lost elements of the humanity is to be one of the main bases of the nation-building process of India. Because nation building process is supposed to enable space to all in very spheres of India as a 'nation'. Here again I would like to refer to Prof. Humayun Kabir who said that "the surest way of achieving national and emotional integration" is "To work for an India in which all languages, all religions, and all communities, in a word, all interests and aptitudes will find ample scope for expression and fulfillment."[17] This statement was made by Prof. Kabir on April 16 1958, when he was the minister of Scientific Research and Cultural Affairs of India. Now about fifty years has passed when this statement was made, but has anything changed during this period of half century?

One answer to our question is found in V. S. Naipaul's work (a reference to which has already been made) which he completed in 1990. His book is based on his travel experience in India for a number of years and is based on his first hand experience of encountering face to face different groups in different parts of India. His conclusion that was stated towards the end of his work is most relevant for the discussion of this paper. He said:

> "Independence was worked by people more or less at the top; the freedom it brought has worked its

> way down. People everywhere have idea of who they are and what they owe themselves... The liberation of spirit that has come to India could not come as relief alone. In India, with its layer below layer of distress and cruelty, it had to come as disturbance. It had to come as rage and revolt. India was now a country of a million little mutinies."[18]

To what did V.S Naipaul refer as " little mutinies"? If our historic mutiny of 1857 was a demand for 'freedom' then these 'little mutinies' representing various communities are involved in asking 'equal spaces' in every spheres of the life of the country, which include political as well as social and economic too. But it seems that this key demand still has been awaiting to get fulfilled, even after 61 years of country's independence. About the danger of such delay Dr. B.R. Ambedkar did warn on the 25th November 1949, a day before finally our Constitution was adopted. His warning came as a part of his closing address to the Constituent Assembly of India, as the Chairperson of the Drafting Committee, when he said:

> "On the 26th of January 1950 we are going to enter into a life of contradictions. In politics we will have equality and in social and economic life we will have inequality. In politics we will be recognizing the principle of one-man one vote and one vote onc value. In our social and economic life, we shall, by reason of our social and economic structure, continue to deny the principle of one-man one value. How long shall we continue to live this life of contradictions? How long shall we continue to deny equality in our social and economic life? If we continue to deny it for long, we will do so only by putting our political democracy in peril. We must remove this contradiction at the earliest possible moment or else those suffer from inequality will

> blow up the structure of political democracy which this Assembly has so laboriously built up."[19]

His emphasis is poignant when he points out that with the acceptance of the Constitution in our political life we have accepted the principle of equality, but in social and economic life inequality not only continues to prevail, but continues to increase. Finally he adds that if this contradiction continues; "those segments of Indian society which are victims of this contradiction will blow up the structure of political democracy". This answers the question why India, now has "a million little mutinies". With this poser I want to move to the second part of the Paper's subject, 'The Christians and National integration'.

Christians and National Integration

I will divide the discussion of this section into two sub-sections, 'Christian participation in Nation-Building' and 'Christian community with identity crisis'. In the former Christian contribution made in positive terms in different forms is being discussed and in the later what went wrong because of which they today are faced with an 'identity crisis'.

Christian Participation in Nation-building

When we talk of the Christian contribution either to national integration or nation-building, without any doubt I will say, the Christian community was indeed in the forefront right from the beginning, since the independence of our country in 1947. Their efforts in this direction was reflected in a four year study programme (from 1956 to 1960) undertaken by the National Christian Council of India (NCCI) and the Christian Institute for the Study of Religion and Society in order to see how the Christians and the Christian churches can take active part in building a new India, while working together with other faith communities at the same time. One of the main objectives of this study was: "To work out the elements of a Christian understanding of certain crucial issues in the political, economic and social development of modern India."[20] The outcome of this four years study was published in 1960 under the title *Christian Participation in Nation-Building*. This classic document still is a guiding source for those who would like to understand the nature and method of Christian participation in the whole issue of national integration as well as in nation-building. Many of the Christians including myself owe our understanding of the nation-building to this document.

Besides the Christian efforts like the one mentioned here, the contributions of both the Christians and Christian missionaries were most important in the whole area of language and literature. For example in my language Punjabi, most of the development of modern Punjabi literature, we owe to Christian missionaries of Punjab. The first Punjabi Grammar, first Punjabi vocabulary book (*Sabad kos)*, the first Punjabi dictionary and various forms of literature were prepared and introduced by the Christian missionaries. Even the pioneer research in the Punjabi *Gurmukhi* script we owe to one of the first American Presbyterian missionary E. P. Newton.[21] Language is not only a means of communication, it actually is a vehicle to carry forward the culture. Such contribution was not limited to the Christian missionaries alone, but it goes to the credit of the native Christians as well, which in fact is less recognized truth in our various local Indian contexts, but certainly it is one of the areas where Indian Christians have made a considerable contribution.[22] Here we must note that language and literature is one of the distinguished marks of a healthy nation, which actually is the most important part of a process of nation-building.

There is another area of Christian contribution, which may be taken as an indirect contribution in bringing a kind of renaissance, which led to a social reformation among the major faith communities, which include: Hindus, Muslims and Sikhs. It actually came in response to Christian preaching when a large number of people belonging to different faith communities started converting to Christianity. These were the people whom, these faiths had ignored for centuries. Here I am referring to various ex-untouchables or today's Dalit communities. The best examples were the formation of Hindu organizations like *Brahmo Samaj* (1872) and *Arya Samaj* (1878), the purpose of which was not only to check the influence of Christianity, but also to question the evils of caste and other similar practices within their fold. *Sanatan Dharam* (1887) and *Dev Samaj* (1887) were the other similar examples in Punjab. The Christian missionary movement also awakened the Muslims and one important result was the establishment of the famous *Ahmadiya Movement* (1889) in Punjab. Again it came into existence mainly to protest against Christianity and the success of Christian proselytization. Among the Sikhs, number of reforming movements came into existence. These movements included *Nirankar movement*, *Namdari* or *Kuka movement* and others, the purpose which included to check the preaching of Christianity in Punjab and to weed out many social evils which had come to stay among the Sikhs. The most important Sikh movement was the *Singh Sabha* movement, which was started during the 19th century. The main purpose of this movement was to create an awakening among the Sikhs and introduce social reform through education.[23]

Before moving to the discussion of the next sub-section, I must refer to what Christianity specifically has contributed to the life of hill communities in the North East region of India. North East India shares with the rest of the country, the contribution of Christianity in the areas of education, literature and medicine. But on two points North East part of our country stands special: *One,* the Christian values have brought basic changes in the total outlook of the hill communities. One concrete example of such change can be seen when a practice like 'head-hunting' got vanished. About this Ms. Mukhim expressed nicely, "In a tribal society there is a close tie between the religious, cultural, social and political institutions. A change in one invariably affects the other. Christian values are founded on love of neighbour, peace and harmony".[24] *Two*, the building and maintaining of the identity, about which Ms Mukhim again says, "Christianity provided an ideology that helped the tribal people maintain their identity in the face of serious erosion of their traditional, religious, social and political institutions."[25]

Christian Community with Identity Crisis

However, there is another side of this coin too, which in fact to some extent flaws–and certainly slows down–the Christian participation in nation-building. This cannot be perceived by Christians if they do not bring change in their outlook towards the services they have rendered to the society till now. They consider themselves the best service providers in the country in the areas of education and health. But this myth gets easily shattered when we look at some of the views expressed by churches or church bodies

In the Indian context, the identity of the Indian Christians or Church can be described as a 'community of the poor' or 'the church of the poor or marginalized', because the large majority of the membership of the Church comes from poor and marginalized communities belonging to Dalits, Adivasis, Tribals, OBC and other weaker sections. According to one rough estimate about 15,000,000 out of a total of 25,000,000 Christians in the country are Dalits alone. But if we add here the number of the Christians of Tribal and OBC origin, this number will be very high. It will be more than 80%. But inspite of this naked reality, the Christians/Church continue to project their image or identity as elitist. The final report of the Inculturation Commission and Conclusions of the Jesuit Conference of India has been very explicit about the image or identity of Jesuits (a most important Roman Catholic Order), when it says:

> "The society's massive investment of men and resources in the educational apostolate in India makes it inevitable that the Jesuit image is mainly derived from our men in education and from our educational institutions. A large urban thrust doubtless characterizes Jesuit educational service in the country; its favoured medium of instruction is English, and the sector of the human community served by it is comparatively the more privileged one. Whether we like it or not, all these factors combine not only to project an elitist image, values of the 'upper ten' to the point of successfully obscuring truly evangelical values while uprooting and alienating us from the values of the majority of our people."[26]

The same truth is also recognised by the Church of North India (a major Protestant Church). In one of the reports of the CNI Synodical Programme "Towards an Understanding of Mission", it says:

> "Despite the majority of the membership of the Church consisting of the marginalized, it has been primarily serving the interest of the elite and upper ten per cent through the educational, medical and other institutions,... The Church also generally reflects the culture and values of the dominant systems."[27]

It is interesting to note here that what the above two Indian Christian Church traditions have realized now, Dr. B. R. Ambedkar realized about 60-70 years before them and stated the same very clearly. But it seems that his challenge went unheeded by the Christian Church in India at that time. In his essay on 'The Condition of the Convert', Dr. Ambedkar said:

> "It is necessary to bear in mind that the Indian Christians are drawn chiefly from the Untouchables and, to a much less extent, from low ranking Shudra castes. The social services of Missionaries must, therefore, be judged in the light of the needs of these classes. What are those needs? The services rendered by the Missionaries in the fields of education and medical relief are beyond the Ken of the Indian Christians. They mostly benefit the high caste Hindus... If this is so then the money and energy spent by the Christian missionaries on education and medical relief was misapplied and do not help the Indian Christians. The Indian Christians need two things. The first thing they want is safeguarding of their civil liberties. The second thing they want is ways and means for their economic uplift."[28]

What these views and statements confirm is that: the Indian Church, both theologically as well as sociologically, is 'the Church of the Poor or marginalized'. But somehow the Christian community or the Church still continues to present her 'elitist image' or 'elitist identity' by all means. This is the contradiction or crisis of Christian identity with which the Christian or the Church in India has been living. Therefore it has failed either to make any real impact on the poor in general and Indian Christians in particular. She has also failed to fulfil their needs, still less fulfil her own faith commitment. This crisis has also lowered the participation of Christians in the nation-building in India as a whole. In our discussion of the next section we will find a still deeper problem related to this issue with reference to education system followed in our country.

A Divisive and Captive Education System

After looking into the main issues faced by the process of national integration in general in section IV and followed by the discussion on the 'Christian and national integration' including nation-building in section V, here in this section we will look into the issue of education which is supposed to be the key in forging the emotional and psychological integration. Education is also supposed to be the foundation, on which a nation is in real sense can be built. It indeed is the surest way of nation building. Education is also a common concern for all the citizens of India including the Christians. It is important to see where does our present education system stands today?

How it is ironical that in spite of our awareness about the role of education in the development of a modern India, we have been able to achieve so little in that area during these sixty one years of our independence. The framers of our Constitution had stated their concern for the universalization of the elementary education in Article 45 under the Directive Principles of State Policy, saying "The State within a period of ten years from the commencement of this Constitution shall endeavour to provide, free and compulsory education for all children until they complete the age of fourteen years." It is to say that by January 1960 (i.e. ten years after the adoption of the Constitution in January 1950) all the Indian children upto the age of 14 should have received elementary education. But it did not happen.

To find an answer to this question, one might examine the reasons behind a number of discussions and planning that had taken place different levels till we finally had in 1986 a new 'National Policy on Education, 1986'. According to this National Policy a core syllabus common to all schools was to be developed, higher education was to contribute to the national development, formal and non-formal technical education was to be devised, evaluation system re-modified, degrees delinked from jobs in selected areas, the status of teachers was to be maintained, teacher's education overhauled, planning for education decentralized and resources through donations to be raised. Besides these main feature in the Education Policy 1986 special emphasis was laid on removing the disparities in order to equalize educational opportunity for those sections of our society that have been denied equality so far, viz, women, Dalits, indigenous communities (tribals), other backward classes, minorities and the handicapped. A special concern for the universalisation of primary education and adult education by 1990 was also stressed. Though in principle this policy on education was right in spirit, but the fact is that even to-day more then 50% population is illiterate and more then 75% is without quality education.

Why is this so? Why is it that inspite of our best intentions we are unable to catch up with any education target and the 'education' just does not percolate down to the grass-roots of our society. One basic reason behind this failure we may find in a study conducted by Ms. Pushpa M Bhargava. As reported in *Indian Express* during April 1993 in her analysis entitled 'A Divisive Hierarchy: Haves and Have-nots of Education' she points that Indian education is by and large a hereditary affair. "For about three to five percent of population — education would run in the family, with everyone, no matter how capable or incapable, going through high school to a college and finally ending up with a job," she wrote. "For the remaining 95% education under-privileged even literacy is a struggle, leave aside education.... It has been calculated that no more than 50,000 to 1,00,000 people from the hereditary non-educated move every year to the status of the educated ones.... For all practical purposes, therefore, a section of people has simply replaced the British within the hereditary educated class. Lack of education means lack of awareness and lack of ability to assimilate information even if one has access to it. Lack of education is also equivalent to economic deprivation ... Our present system of education tends to keep the majority equally backward." Now if this will be the speed of the education then how many centuries will take us to reach our goal? But why is our education in this state? Again the answer lies in the history of our education system.

A cursory look at the history of education in our country will confirm that we never cared to utilise education to lay the foundation on which the structure of our society could be erected. Instead we used it to enjoy privileges and to rule the masses. Right from the Vedic period to modern times, education had been a "hereditary affair" — preserve of the handfuls, denied to the majority.

Covering rather a long span (1500 B.C. to 700 AD.), the Vedic period promoted the Brahmanic educational traditions. Its entire education system was caste-class oriented. Education was available only to the members of three upper castes—*Brahmins, Kshatriyas* and *Vaishyas*. In fact the whole right was only being enjoyed by Brahmins, who could educate themselves and teach others also.

During the Medieval period, with the arrival of the Muslims (A.D. 700 - A.D. 1700) education of the masses suffered further setback because of two main factors. One was the introduction of Persian as the new official language of the country. Previous to it education was imparted in Sanskrit and vernaculars. The shift in language - particularly from vernaculars - alienated the lower classes from the educated and the ruling classes.

In the British period (A.D. 1700- A.D. 1947) two forces worked side by side to influence our education system: the British rulers and the Christian missionaries. They influenced not only the education system during their span of time, but also our present education system in the post-Independence period. Both had objectives before them, which certainly was not to uplift the down-trodden masses. The British policy included the special education plan for the children of the Indian Chiefs for whom they opened separate schools even under this policy the education imparted at various government run schools *were not directed towards the spread of literacy among the masses.* Government policy as such created an eagerness among the upper classes for English education which would fit them for the government posts. The objectives of the European missionaries with regard to education was also similar to that of the British government.

Sixty one years have gone by since the Britishers have left India. Given this historical background, our first step '— the concern for the education for all, enshrined in our Constitution — is certainly a positive and a very big step forward towards making of modern India. But beyond this proclamation, unfortunately, we could not achieve much and education remains 'a hereditary affair' even today It is because, for all practical purposes the British rulers were simply replaced by a section of people akin to them and with similar priorities.[29]

India Demands from its People: Solidarity, Commitment and Responsibility

It was "we the people of India" after "having solemnly resolved" decided "to constitute into a Sovereign Socialist Secular Democratic Republic" with a pledge that together we will secure to "all its citizens" justice, liberty, equality and fraternity in all areas of their life as well as we will assure the "unity and integrity of the Nation". The first part of the pledge to secure all citizens justice and equality in all areas of life is what we call core of the 'nation-building', and to keep intact the "unity and integrity" is what we meant by the 'national integration', The discussion of this paper clearly revealed that we the people of India are still far away from achieving the goals set out in the Preamble of the Constitution on the both end. Therefore, it is this demand for a response, which we are supposed to give individually as well as collectively as citizens of India. Here I am making a few suggestions, which I feel are common to all of us. These are suggestions addressed to the three sections of the people of India, *First*, people or citizens as a whole for 'citizens' solidarity', *second*, the Indian Christian community for her 'faith commitment' and *third,* to those who are responsible for education means 'educators' for their 'responsibility'.

Citizens' Solidarity

The citizens' solidarity is one of the most important means which can enhance the spirit of national integration in a country like ours, in which each citizen is having more than one identities because of different faith, different culture, different ethnicity, different language, different ideology and at the same time living in different region. Because of such varied contexts, in order to maintain 'the unity and integrity' of India as a nation, the Constitution has endorsed the principle of 'unity in diversity'. To make this point clearer, our Parliament through an amendment has added in the Preamble along with 'secular', the expression 'democratic'. These principles have already been discussed in this paper. Here our concern is how we the citizens of India can together work in order to implement the agenda that was put forward in the Preamble of our Constitution. One way to do it is, by enhancing 'citizens' solidarity', which means we as citizens of India have to commit ourselves to the good of other. Here 'other' is important, because our most conflictual situations arose from the notion of 'others' and 'us' which start demanding a shift in position or to enter a pot set on the fire, where one loses one's identity. But the principle of solidarity does not put such demand or ask for a change or for a conversion. Its unconditioned commitment to take the other person's place even to the point of death. This is the meaning of the expression 'solidarity'.

I use the expression "to enhance" because the "citizens' solidarity", is already there, but it goes many times unnoticed. Majority of us experience such 'solidarity' in our 'work place'; in our 'community life'; where 'we live'; in 'our village' or 'town'; at common time of 'celebration of religious, cultural or national festivals'; and in our 'inter dining' and other such number of occasions. This process is 'on' all the time at all levels and between all the people in our country. What I ask here is to enhance and make more visible this solidarity. This is one of the important factors on which we can build our nation without demanding from other the dissolution of his/her individual identity.

Faith Commitment

What has been suggested about the 'citizens' solidarity', is applicable also to Christians or Church in India. In fact they as citizens of India have to be part of the citizens' solidarity. It may become easy to do so, if as Christians they are willing to re-examine their faith commitment. They also have to re-look their present definition of Community or Church, which presently as a people, a congregation is supposed to be created by God around the Word and the sacraments, with an essential order. But this definition need to be re-looked, if they are going to fulfill their faith commitment as Christian Community/Church as people of God who has been placed in the world in order to become instrument of transformation (John 17:18). If this is true then the mission of the Church is essentially to a world, which only will be carried forward by the lay members of the Church, who are working in various secular areas of the world. Therefore the emphasis on the ministry for the ordinary or lay Christians have to be placed at the forefront and ordained Christian ministers' role will be to equip these lay persons as God's people for the mission of establishing the reign of God on this earth (Ephesians 4:12), which actually means a human just society based on the principle of 'justice and equality'. Here we see a close proximity between the biblical vision of God's reign on this earth (Isaiah 11: 1-9) and our constitutional vision of a 'just society' as described in the Preamble of the Constitution. So the call for every Christian here is to support the democratic system of our country, not only because this system was adopted in the Constitution of our country, but also because this system falls nearest to the Christian understanding of human being, the world and the political order derived from the law and love of God as revealed in Jesus Christ.

The Christians as a faith community also have to take up the concern of average Christian as well as citizen and work for their social and economic upliftment. Also they have to re-look into the role of their institutions and other organised programmes, because most of the Christians run organized programmes and the various institutions continue to support the values of the dominant and the rich small sections of our society. The Christian community/Church cannot fulfill her faith commitment by keeping silent or by saying that their responsibility is limited only to religious matters and has nothing to do with political, economic and social issues. This kind of understanding of mission suits the powerful very well, both within the Church and outside it. The present call to the Christians as a whole or the Church and the various institutes (educational, medical, social services etc.), is to rededicate for the good of the poor some of their works.

The Christian community indeed if she wants to follow the example of her Lord, who 'became poor' for the sake of the poor of this world (2 Corinthians 8: 8-9), if she wants to become the bearer of Good News or a partner in the establishment of a 'Just Society' in the world, then this is the only way for her to enter into a process of an 'authentic imitation of Christ' or 'authentic solidarity' by which she will able to play an effective role in the whole process of national integration as well as nation–building.

Educators' Responsibility

The education is indeed the best catalyst of change in any given society. Its role is also considered essential for a full development of human personality. But here as seen in our discussion of section VI of this paper, the right to education, for centuries was limited to a small minority of people in our country. For centuries, the large majority of Indian citizens did not have the right to education, and were condemned to bare existence. Therefore the task of introducing them to the world of education is very essential, but not enough. It is true that after our independence, we are able to introduce our masses to the world of education, but it is also true that we have not gone beyond that introduction. Now what is the reason behind this block?

The answer to this question is very simple and clear that we as Indian citizens are able to achieve our freedom from the colonial rule, but our education system continues to follow all the set norms of colonial rulers of different times including the caste-class based education policy. Based on this policy we have in every village, in every town, in every locality of metro cities, government-run schools for the masses by which we are able to introduce at least our part of the population (may be 50%) to the world of education. Then we also continue to have schools and other institutions for the privileged classes, which today might cover about 25% population (traditional upper 10% plus about 15% new class of middle class). In truth today these 25% upper and middle classes are the target groups for the benefits of so-called development, which actually is part of a new 'economic world order' given to us by the process of globalization. Now what about the remaining 75% population of India? Should we continue to offer this larger part the Indian masses, the education in the 'vernaculars' or local languages in order to make them better 'nationalists' or 'citizens' and only see they get education to fit them for their position of life, but keep them away from the quality education, which could have given them social and economic quality as well. Unless this will happen, we will continue to be away from building a real nation.

Now what is the answer to our problem, which indeed is related to the whole education system in India, and here comes the responsibility of the educators. I am using here the expression 'educators' to cover not only to those who provide formal or non-formal education, but to cover all those Indians who are responsible for the present education at all levels including the Government sector which include the umbrella bodies like Human Resource Development Ministries, Planning Commission, University Grants Commission etc. and also the various groups who consider themselves part of the Indian civil society including Christian community/Church.

A call here for the educators is to work towards abolishing a principle of 'two tumblers' practice, which traditionally was used to perpetuate our caste based untouchability and in some parts of India still continues. The same principle is introduced in our education system by the colonial rulers, by having two types of schools, one for the masses - ordinary schools mostly run by our Governments in local languages; and other public-schools for the privileged classes or those who can afford, mostly run by the private sectors of business groups in English medium. As long as such division will continue in our country, the pledge that was given to the masses on 26th November 1949 by the Nation for equal opportunity in all areas of life including education (part of Preamble of our Constitution) will continue to be a thing of the past. Can we the members of the community of educators take this issue to those who are in power in different places and tell them to 'get away with this 'two tumblers policy' from the education system of India, so that all citizens can enjoy the equal right to receive the quality education which in real sense can transform the life. This will be a possible way to building a strong India as a 'Nation'.

The second part of the responsibility of the educators is actually related also to the same, that is, if we are genuinely interested to make our education system relevant and equally available to all the citizens of India, then the first step will be to dismantle the inherited colonial education system, which in the case India is having a number of layers of colonization and replace it with an alternative policy based system, which is indeed a very challenging task. The models of such alternative systems are available within the country, specially what was proposed by Mandal Commission in 1980 while discussing the issue of upliftment of the backward classes of our country. Also there are models available, which were used in South America based upon the writings and experience of the well known educationist Paulo Freire. But first there is a need to create a 'will' among our policy makers with regard to the change in education and I believe the role of the educators' community is pertinent in this regards.

Concluding Remarks

At the close I only would like to add that whatever I have said here, it came from personal experience as a citizen of India, as an Indian Christian and as one who also is part of the community of educators. So this whole discourse I have addressed to myself as well.

NOTES AND REFERENCES

1. Alister Key (Ed.): *A Reading in Political Theology*, SCM, Founder, 1975, p. XI
2. *Mandal Commission Report of the Backward Classes*, Along with Introduction, Akalank Publications, Delhi, 1990, p. 19.

3. Naipaul, V.S.: *India: A Million Mutinies Now*, Minerva, Calcutta, 1991.
4. Chatterjee, Debi: *Sociology of National Integration*, Calcutta, 1993, p. 1
5. *Ibid.*, p.2.
6. *Ibid.*, p. 3.
7. *Ibid*, pp 94, 95.
8. Quoted in: Bahrawaj, K.K.: *Combating Communalism in India*, New Delhi, 1993, p. 13.
9. Kabir, Humayun: "Problems Relating to National Unity", in *Report of Seminar on National Integration, April 16-17, 1958*, University Grants Commission, New Delhi, 1961, p. 11.
10. Massey, James: "Sikh Identity in the Context of Punjab Issue", in *Current Thoughts on Sikhism* edited by Dr. Karak Singh, International Institute of Gurmat Studies, Ludhiana, 1994, pp. 6, 11-17.
11. Mukhim, Patricia: "Christian Impact on North East India and National Integration", in J. Puthenpurakal, (ed) *Impact of Christianity on North East India*, Shillong, 1996, p.71.
12. Lyngdoh, Dr. Pristilla: "A Response to Patricia", *Ibid*, p. 82.
13. Kabir, Humayun: *op.cit.*, p.14.
14. *Hindustan Times*, New Delhi, Wednesday, August 13, 2008, p. 10.
15. Massey, James: *Minorities and Religious Freedom in a Democracy*, CDS & Manohar, New Delhi, 2003, p. 96.
16. Quoted in: *Ibid.*, p.10
17. Kabir, Humayun: *op.cit.*, p.16.
18. Naipaul, V.S.: *Op.cit.*, p.517.
19. *Constituent Assembly Debates*, Official Report Lok Saba Secretariat, Vol XI, 14-11-1949 to 26-11-1949, New Delhi, p. 979.
20. Devananda, P.D. and M.M. Thomas (Eds.): *Christian Participation in Nation-Building*, Bangalore, 1960, p.VI (Preface)
21. See for detailed information and discussion: Massey, James: "Presbyterian Missionaries and the Development of Punjabi

Language and Literature", 1934-1984, In *American Presbyterian's in India/Pakistan,150 Years, Journal of Presbyterian History*, Volume 62. Number 3, Fall 1984, pp. 258-261.

22. See for Punjabi Christian's contribution: Massey, James: "Christianity and Culture: their relationships in the 19th and 20th Centuries Punjab", in *Religion and Society*, Volume XXXVI, No. 4, December 1989, CISRS, Bangalore, pp. 30-32.
23. See for discussion on Renaissance Among Hindu, Muslims and Sikhs: *Ibid.*, pp. 26-28.
24. Mukhim, Patricia: *op.cit.*, p. 66.
25. *Ibid.*, p. 67.
26. Aixala, J.: *Jesuit Formation and Inculturataion in India Today*, Anand, 1978, p. 17.
27. CNI Synodical Programme – 'Towards a Holistic Understanding of Mission Consultation' in *Church: A Community in Mission for Justice, Peace and Integrity of Creation.* (15-17 November, 1993) A Report, New Delhi.
28. Ambedkar, Dr. Babasaheb: *Writings and Speeches,* Vol. 5, Education Department, Government of Maharashtra, Bombay, 1989, pp. 452-53.
29. See for detail discussion on 'Education for All' in Massey, James: *From Truth to Truth-Journey Through Faith*, New Delhi, 2008, pp. 196-2006.

3

History of Christianity in India

—R. D. Lyngdoh

Introduction

The history of Christianity requires thorough studies in order to get the clear knowledge of its presence and role among the people. The topic itself is vast and wide and many difficult understanding of the ideas may crop up. One may fail to produce the correct perspective too. Several attempts have been made by many scholars to investigate into the history of Christianity in India (Appasamy, 1942; Perumalil and Hambye, 1972; Laing 2002) and there arose problems of producing authentic records. It offers a lot of solution to the problem; some of them contradict with each other while the rest are in complementary with. It needs more time and devotion to many information. The setting of Christianity helps to reflect on the correct perspective of the Indian quality as a whole. The teachings of Jesus Christ are relevant to all people and all nations. His teachings such as equality, liberty, justice and peace are also relevant to Indian context. The fundamental rights as envisaged in the Indian constitution (Gupta, 1983) speak clearly on the basic principle of the democratic concept of Governance. These fundamental rights were already conceived in the mind of Jesus Christ when He preached about the kingdom of Heaven. This topic can be looked upon as one of the vital factors of the integration of Christianity into the National mainstream of India.

This paper is divided into the following schematic arrangement:

(i) The social and cultural milieu in the Indian situation.

(ii) The beginning of Christianity.

(iii) Meaning of Christianity in the Indian Context.

(iv) Conclusion.

The Social and Cultural Milieu in the Indian Situation

The religion of India is pantheistic in nature. Many Hindu scholars say that Hinduism believes in one god but with many manifestations. The pantheistic conception with each god has its own separate identity and responsibilities. Somehow, in decades the emergence of the conflicting areas of human personality which to some extent creates a variety of differences in human relationship. Most Hindus are religious minded performing regular rituals. Many of them are still searching for a more secured and stabilised life. As Gandhi quoted, "There are innumerable definitions of God, because his manifestations are innumerable...... But I worship God as Truth only. I have not yet found Him, but I am seeking after Him. I am prepared to sacrifice the things dearest to me in pursuit of this quest. Even if the sacrifice demanded my very life. I hope I may be prepared to give it." (Norman, 1790).

In the Indian society, the caste system is prevalent from time immemorial till today. There are altogether four castes viz., the Brahmins, the Vaisyas, the Kshatriyas and the Sudras. Brahmins are the teaching and priestly community; the Vaisyas are the trading and commercial community including the artisans; the Kshatriyas are the army community that look after the defence of the country; the

Sudras Sommunity who serve the other three communities. Sudras are the lowest community. For many generations, these communities have been living as separate identities. Mahatma Gandhi, the Father of the Nation in the 1920's and 1930's had strongly advocated the new trend of thinking that all people in India should love equally without any discrimination. In the 1940's the Gandhian movement for abolishing the caste system had gained momentum. After India attained its Independence, the Government in both the central and the state legislatures had passed the law that all castes, races, communities and tribes should live in an ideal equality and that all people should attain the same rights in living all over India. Nowadays, in some pockets of influences there is a wider acknowledgement of the necessity of living equally as enshrined in the Constitution of India. But in other pocket of influences, the system of caste inequality is still being used in the widespread manner. India is a land of many diversities. There are many tribes, races and communities that exist in various parts and corners of the country. Along with these wide varieties there are also many cultural systems. Each tribe and ethnic group has its own culture in a very limited space. But all these ethnic and cultural groups are trying to integrate into one bigger stage culminated into the Indian culture.

The Beginning of Christianity

The history of Christianity in India is as old as Christianity itself. People hardly acknowledge Christianity as the religion of self-inborn phenomenon; but holds that it is the foreign mission of the Western church also as Western Christianity. Many scholars are of the opinion that Christianity had the origin from the apostolic time. Thomas came to India and settled in the South till his death. He died as a martyr at the 'Little Mount' near 'St. Thomas Mount ' and was buried at Mylapore near modern city of Chennai (Firth, 1983).

"Christian" means the one that follows Jesus Christ. Thomas was one of those who had walked hand in hand with Jesus. Christ has said to his disciples (including Thomas): "Go to the world and preach the Gospel wherever you go". Thomas landed at Cranganore in South India in 52 A.D. Here, Thomas had brought the message of Christ– the message of salvation. Therefore, I would like to share a thought in this; don't we think that this is the first hand knowledge of Christ and His teaching that we Indians received from Thomas himself; the one who had seen, lived and was with Christ? If we go and find out the origin of Jesus Christ, we will find that He belonged to Asia. Hence, we can claim Christianity as the Indian religion. Neil (1984) too was of the opinion with the Indian apostolate of Thomas. Therefore, the foundation of Indian church goes to Thomas.

In 1510, Goa was taken over by the Portuguese empire and their primary aim was trade and commerce. Along with their trade objective they had brought Christianity with them and tried very hard to build a strong Christian population and made the conversion of the people of those places. Conversions were encouraged in different ways e.g., inter-marriages between Portuguese and Goans, books etc. In 1614, the British East India Company opened its office in Bombay and in 1662, the Portuguese gave Bombay King Charles II of England for marrying a Portuguese princess. With the coming of British to Bombay, the Christians in that particular region were exposed to their teaching and became a more literate community. Going together with the government measures, the British missionaries were also able to draw more Indians to Christianity in the propagation of the teaching of Christ. Further, the British government had given protection to the civil rights of those who adopted Christianity such as child sacrifice; they also did declare the ban of "Suttee". In 1664, Jean - Baptiste Colbert, the French Minister of Finance succeeded in establishing the first viable French company known as the French East India Company. The company got its factory established at Surat and acquired a foothold in Southern India by acquiring Pondicherry in 1674. In short, the European powers came to India for commercial purpose but they also preached the Gospel to local people and got them converted to Christianity. Amongst the five European powers viz. Great Britain, France, Denmark, Netherlands and Portuguese that came to India, the Portuguese were most enthusiastic to convert Indians into Christianity.

The Meaning of Christianity in the Indian Context

The Christianity and its doctrine are very relevant to the Indian context. The main teaching of Jesus Christ is based on divine love and this divine love should be manifested in the human love. The Gospel of Jesus Christ, which Christianity peaches, is about love. When love conquers the human mind it makes one to set aside all kinds of selfishness and narrow-minded considerations.

As India is a land of many contradictory elements that sometimes have gone to an extent of some irreconcilable attitudes, the Christian tenet of God's love in highly pertinent speaks volumes of facts for moulding India towards its perfect goal. In the light of the religious social and cultural background of India, as we know; Christianity does mean a lot to the country for the pursuit of the just treatment of all communities. Christianity has had a great influence on the life of Gandhi. His words were almost Biblical. His ways and techniques were always conformed to Christianity. Jesus has always been the role model of Gandhi's life. There are many things we could find that Mahatma Gandhi was so much influenced by the teaching of Christ especially the Sermon on the Mount. One quotation of Mahatma Gandhi goes like this, "There is nothing to prevent us from profiting by the light that may come from the West. Only we must take care that we are not overpowered by the glamour of the West. We must not mistake the glamour for true light." (Norman, 1970)

The teaching of Christ speaks about love (Mark 12:30-31), unity (John 17:21), equality (John 13:16), freedom from evil (John 8:31-34), justice (Luke 18:1-8), peace (John 20:19), co-operation (Galatians 6:2), truth (John 14:6) and light (Mathew 5:14 -16) (Douglas, 2003). In India people were always bound to many malpractices; due to their beliefs (religious or traditional) that led them to many sorrowful effects e.g., "Child sacrifice", "Suttee" etc. The coming of the Gospel had helped them in every way trying to put an end to their ways and customs; had enlightened the people to acknowledge the Gospel even though, they may not be completely became Christian but was acceptable by many of the Indians in the different ethnic groups, e.g., traditionally, tribals live a life of fear of demons and terror of social oppressors. They set Jesus as the victor over these demons and liberator from social evils. Further, Christ as a Victor brought them in the understanding of the natural life cycle in a life of a person viz. life, death, resurrection, ascension and second coming of Christ. Jesus remains forever as a Mediator between God and man. He is the one who could be touched with the feeling of one infirmities.

Jesus exhorted his followers to be salt of the earth and the light of the world. The secular world is God's world–the one that Christ came to redeem and is committed to man's stewardship. The psalmist says, "The Heavens are the Lord's but the earth He hath given to the children of man" (Psalms 115:16). The message of Christian Gospel is self-supporting, self-controlling and self-propagating (Renwick and Harman, 1989). India is a land of diversities where there are many conflicting elements in which they have been binding into a broad spectrum of a well-knit society. One of the main drawbacks of the Indian society is the presence of caste system. The caste system has cropped up so that a number of divisive elements are trying to raise their heads to create so much differences of ideas, beliefs, works and even the menacing segregation between man and man. The message of the Christian Gospel plays a very essential and dynamic role in bringing about the unity, justice and peace in the country.

Conclusion

India is a land of a conglomeration of diverse cultures and beliefs. Jesus came to offer unity, peace and harmony to all people belonging to different caste, tribes and ethnic groups. He has given the authority to his disciples to preach the Gospel to the end to the world. All the disciples obeyed His command to proclaim the message of love (Mathew 28:19). Further, Jesus was an Asian and He asked His disciples to go to the world and to tell the people and preach the Gospel of God's love to all nations. I would like to end up this paper by putting it in the way to say that, Christianity is not to be considered as belonging to a foreign origin, but it should be a part of the Indian life.

REFERENCES

1. Appsamy AJ. 1942, *The Gospel and India's Heritage*, Society for Promoting Christian Knowledge, New York: The Macmillan.
2. Douglas A. 2003, *One Hundred Bible Lessons: Basic Bible Doctrines*, GLS Publication, Mumbai.
3. Firth CB. 1983, *An Introduction of Indian Church History*, The Christian Students' Library. The Christian Literature Society Publication.
4. Gupta DC. 1983, *Indian National Movement and Constitutional Development*. Vikas Publication, Delhi.
5. *Ka Centenary History Ka Balang Presbyterian ha Ri Khasi–Jaintia naduh 1841 haduh 1940*, Khasi Jaintia Presbyterian Publication.
6. Mark Laing JB. 2002, *The Indian Church in Context: Emergence and Growth*.
7. Neil S. 1984, *A History of Christianit in India Beginning to A.D. 1707*. Cambridge University Press.

8. Norman Cousins. 1970, *Profiles of Gandhi*, Indian Book Company Publication, Delhi.
9. Perumalil CML. HC. and Hambye SJ. ER. 1972, *Christianity in India: A History of Ecumenical Perspective*, Prakasham Publication, Aleppey, S. India.
10. Renwick AM, Harman AM. 1989, *Ka Jingiathuhkhana jong Ka Balang (The Story of the Church)*, Ka Khasi Jaintia Presbyterian Synod Publication.

4

Christianity in Indian Historical Perspective

—O.L.Snaitang

India in Ancient Cultural Background

India is a large country bounded by the seas and Sri Lanka on the south; Pakistan on the west and Myanmar on the east and China, Nepal, Bhutan and the Himalaya ranges surround the entire long northern stretch of the country. Though its inhabitants belonged to different ethnic groups, India enjoyed a pride of a single geographical compactness. The land witnessed the presence of hills, plains, valleys and deserts. Rivers, rivulets, and waterfalls are found in most parts of the sub-continent. The country is also famous of beautiful peacocks, tigers and rhinoceros. Natural forests and vegetation, and others have added beauty to the country. India had also changing accounts of human history.

Dalits and tribals were in most probability the first who inhabited the country.[1] Though this argument had gone into controversial debates in numerous fora well even to the recent past but what had officially been established was by the discovery of disappeared cities at Harappa and Mohenjodaro through Sir John Marshall's archaeological excavation in 1922-23.[2] The findings subscribed to the presence of non-Aryan indigenous inhabitants. Though dalits and tribals were nomads but the discovery of the lost cities might have testified to their settlement. Their occupation that had led to the establishment of cities would have been long. It was perhaps for the sake of general health and peaceful habitation that had made the indigenous people to opt for a stable and settled life. Settlement therefore came after people's realization of the importance and value of human beings. By settlement means concentration in agriculture, cultivation, farming and trade.

Social life and relationship were important elements in the ancient society.[3] There was an evolution of clans and kinship relations. These characteristics were distinctive development in the social order. They also made them different from other animals. Their distinctive nature was also in such a way as to make them recognized who was from the same clans and who was not. At the same time these social distinctive institutions were introduced to evolve a spirit of equality and respect. Again, ancient society witnessed collective decision and responsibility, cooperation, sharing of natural resources, community development, mutual caring and united protection against the enemies.

Nature was regarded as important part of human beings. Though the indigenous people did not seem to have believed in pantheism, they nevertheless looked at the nature or the mother earth with a sense of belonging.[4] They did not leave it as it was but introduced certain measures in order to save it from inhuman exploitation. As a result, primary societies witnessed the introduction of community lands, sacred groves or dedicated forests, so that people's utilization of land would be under the control and moderation of respective indigenous machineries.[5]

Indigenous people believed in a democratic political administration.[6] Its state functioned under the electoral process in which adult members could take part. The state council was the highest body in terms of making laws, administration and served as a judicial court of justice. The chief was a titular head and belonged to the accepted dynastic family. He was the dispenser of administration and justice but the supreme deciding power was with the council. Members of the council were elected from respective founding clans, villages and sub-ethnic enclosure within the community.[7] Its duty was to look after the security, law and order, collective well being and unity.

However, there were other developments that had a place in the ancient people culture on the negative side.

First, *Loss of written script:* The indigenous people did not give importance to a written culture.[8] This attitude could have emerged because of their being materialistic and egoistic in addition to their devotion and commitment to benefited agriculture, pastoral and farming. It was also a question of survival and so saw written culture as immaterial. Besides that, as lands and forests were collectively owned and as there were equal distribution for use, the indigenous people did not anticipate any set back whether on their profession or habitation. They gave importance to a spoken word. As a result, primal people remained illiterate. While illiteracy was not a problem in ancient primal setting it was in due course an element of backwardness.

Secondly, *Emergence of unintelligible dialects*: It was not just loss of alphabet and illiteracy but the indigenous people preferred to divide the once common spoken language. Why did they do so one found it difficult to answer, however, I assume that people wanted to exercise their free will and looked for an independent life.[9] The development was an indication of maturity and long time of existence.[10] Though the people could have become proud of their long history and maturity but it just contributed towards weakening their culture. Rise of a new dialect means creation of a separate identity.

Thirdly, *Rejection of someone's domination:* Indigenous people were different because of their sensitivity to their individuality, clan identity, family unity and freedom. It was because of this perception that resulted in the creation of independent kingdoms, languages and separate of sub-ethnic society.[11] Differences became evident even in lifestyle, dresses and manners.

Fourthly, *Difference in religious practices:* Religion was a vital and internal part of people's cultural life. Indigenous people did not believe in idolatry. They did not have priestly hierarchy. Though their religious belief and practices were common they did not seem to have kept it in tact in the course of their history. Religious divisions were seen in areas of worship, sacrifices and festivals. In short, religion was reduced to a clan and at a most to a sub-ethnic level of a given self-enclosed kingdom.[12] Traditional religion lost its unifying power. Its universal nature was over a long successive period of time reduced to a micro clan or limited clustering level of villages.

Fifthly, *Superstitious belief:* Another negative development among the indigenous people was superstition. It was an unreasonable imagination on certain things that gripped people's mind and attention and placed them on fear, fatalistic and misfortune. While this belief system was related to nature and environment, it had some relation with human beings. Relationship with human was negative as it tended to produce suspicion, condemnation and counter-response.

Sixthly, *Development of inhuman concern:* Besides the rise of superstitious belief, there developed among the indigenous people some kind of inhuman concern that jeopardized people social relationship and unity. Three instances are in order, viz., headhunting, slavery and taboo. One, *Headhunting*:[13] Certain tribal groups like those who lived in Nagaland, Arunachal Pradesh, Mizoram and elsewhere were in the ancient period practicing cutting of human head and people respected this practice. The person who did it was placed in high honour and women would prefer to marry someone who had had the distinction of cutting many heads.

Two, *Practice of slavery:* Certain groups of people, like the kings in Mizoram, practiced what was known as the *bawi* system, i.e., the system of maintaining slaves.[14] People were employed in this job that in most cases remained for life because of being in debt trap or captured. Be that as it may such developments was rather uncalled for in what would have been society of mutual respect and help besides sharing of resources.

Three, *A religious taboo that prevented social help:* Some people's groups like the Khasi-Jaintias had perceived religious understanding that did not make them sociable when a neighbour became victim to unfortunate accidence, like tragic death, unnatural death of child delivery or death by committing suicide.[15] People believed in the presence of *ka tyrut* (god of unnatural death) and were always afraid of its attack if someone was helping the victims. There was no immediate service in such cases except those who belonged to the same family.

These negative social developments have not just affected the people but threatened the unity and integrity of the nation.

Changes Following Aryan Invasion and Rule

Though certain divisive and inhuman feeling had developed among the indigenous people, they were however people, who believed in freedom, equality and work culture. Classification of service in terms of which one was hnourable and who was not in their social set up appeared to have been a non-existent.

History is proof that people of Aryan roots have come to India from central Asia.[16] In other words, the findings from the archaeological excavation and study of the Harrapan and Mohenjodaro civilization did not give any signs of the presence of Aryan culture in the centuries well before at least a millennium and half BC. These groups of people were culturally advanced had invaded India. Their mighty army, wisdom, wealth and religion could easily defeat the simple agricultural people. The tribals were pushed to the jungles, dalits placed outside the Aryan social order and made them servants and the Dravidians who inhabited the Deccan region were also driven that they had to move southward up to the South. Following the Aryan rule, indigenous people experienced displacement, alienation, classification and oppression.

The invaders did not seem to have a sympathetic spirit or human concern for the primal people. Conquest resulted in occupation, rule and expansion. In this situation, indigenous people lost their land and habitation. Their life was in due course pushed out of the new imposed social order.[17]

Again, the imposition of social distinction and institutional means had over a period of time resulted in alienation and outside domination. In a traditional unsophisticated world, the new power introduced a well designed polity, economy, religion, and education. Under the new dispensation, the primal peoples were outside human social order.

Closely related to this inhuman development was the introduction of the new religion. Aryan religion did not come to offer the good news of God's salvation of the unsaved and poor indigenous peoples. It did not offer hope for the present or for the future. Rather, it had come with strict imperialistic motive that produced judgment, exclusion and subjugation. Dalits and tribals were regarded as monkeys or ravanas and treated as chamals.[18] The new religion is synonymous with domination and oppression.

Caste system was a non issue in ancient primal society. The invaders put it as a determining rod to differentiate and subjugate the indigenous citizens. The law of karma though is part of the larger Hindu philosophy, is however, disastrous on its application on the indigenous people.[19] Karma believed in rebirth or transmigration of souls and someone's next life is determined by the present one's action or works. In this connection, the sufferings and plight of dalits and tribals were seen as God's judgment because of their doings and so they deserved so. Such interpretation made the dalits and tribals to accept so and looked at their situation as self-defeating and in the process placed them upon perpetual slavery.

These new socio-religious codes were suppressing mechanisms to oppress the primal peoples. It was through these means that had made them to assert that their religion was superior and final and regarded others as inferior or sinful. Justification was evident not just in their attitude but actions alike. Aryans who believed in their religious purity did not regard other's faiths as faith at all. In other words, Aryan religion lent credence to the efficacy of caste and karmic belief system. The plight of the dalits or tribals was well seen under the new imposed social order as the outcome of their bad deeds and so the divine judgment.

An Overview of Indian Christian History

History of Christianity in India is a long history but may well be seen in six traditions, viz., Syrian tradition, Catholic History, Protestant Christianity; Churches of indigenous origins, Christianity of Pentecostal tradition and non-denominational Christianity. However, given the limited time of presentation I will try to touch upon the first three traditions.

St. Thomas Syrian Tradition:[20] Christianity in India is as old as Christianity itself. It was believed that St. Thomas of the first century had labored in India. He had established churches and ordained priests. However, while a strong Syrian Christian community had well been founded among the native Indian in what is known today as Kerala, its spread and subsequent impact on the larger Indian-continent is virtually negligible. The Nestorians that have undertaken major missionary adventure in the region and Asia are so far remained confined to Thrissur in Kerala.[21] Therefore, it is not an exaggeration that major Christian presence and influence began after the imposition of the Portuguese and Danish colonial powers.

Catholic Christianity:[22] European colonial powers, viz., the Portuguese, the Dutch, the French, the English and others intruded into this region for economic and political interests. It was they who brought significant changes among the indigenous cultures and promoted Christian intrusion. The Portuguese's main interest was in achieving monopoly in trade and control of coastal stations. They were instrumental for bringing the Catholic mission as early as the mid 16th century. The Catholic mission that began its missionary operation in the region by the 16th century came along with the Portuguese colonial authority in Goa, India. The Catholic ministry could well be seen in three dimensions, viz., evangelization of the downtrodden among the Parava fisher folk of Tamil Nadu and in the Mukkavars of Kerala,[23] the conversion of Syrian Christians[24] and inculturation.[25] From a humble beginning, therefore, the Catholic Church has over a period of time spread to other regions the sub-continent and Asia.[26]

Protestant Christian Movement: Like the Portuguese, the Danes too looked for economic profit and began to control certain strategic maritime stations, like Tranquebar in Tamil Nadu and Serampore in West Bengal. Though the Danish colonial officers came to India without taking any Christian priests with them, the King of Denmark played a significant role for imposing the Protestant mission in India.[27] It was in their colonial territories that Protestant Christianity could set their missionary stations.

While the Portuguese and the Danes were interested in making profitable trade in the region, the British were somewhat different. Their interests were comprehensive in that they wanted to control not just trade but went inside the interior and took control of the political empires. They brought administrators, soldiers, technicians, arms and ammunitions.[28] They invaded the native princes and established their own empires. The presence of colonial power had brought about political change in the sense of promoting political unity; they were also instrumental for introducing railways, posts & telegraphs and democratic institutions. Be that as it may, however, colonialism represents exploitative vision, negative attitude, materialistic aggression, domination, rule and exhausting of resources.

Protestant missions too, like the Catholic mission, came side by side with the colonial powers. The first Protestant mission too came to India under the direction and supervision of the Danish colonial flag and established permanent mission at the Danish colony of Tranquebar. While the British authority denied permission to the missionaries, William Carey could begin his influential missionary service in a Danish colony at Serampore.[29] Several other Protestant mission agencies began to enter south Asia and started working among people of low origins. The nineteenth century witnessed large turn out of dalits and tribal population to Christian churches.[30]

Christianity and National Integration

It is a fact that Christian Missions and missionaries have

come to India because of their faith in Jesus Christ, the Bible and service. But their attitude to the people and nation had never been negative.[31] National integration is used here in a loose and flexible manner meaning understanding the unity and integrity of the land and people, having a passionate heart for the value of human persons, identifying and searching for the poor, orphans and victims in the society, helping the downtrodden and the marginalized for liberation, growth and development, building a harmonious community, justice and peace and leading the citizen forward.

Given a treatment on this topic, it is necessary and important to provide a working definition on the word 'culture'. The Latin original "kultura" meaning "to cultivate" has a far progressive, integrative, inclusive and procreating connotation. In this sense, the content of the system remains the same but not its form. Culture, therefore, is a universal system and a complete whole and it exists on the cohesive connectivity of components like polity, social structure, economy, religion, language and literature, art, aesthetic, biodiversity. These components are interrelated and contributed to the totality of culture. In this dynamic, moving and mutable set up there is a continuous learning, relearning, reforming and adjusting. It is never a fixed system save its content meaning existence and identity.

Christian attitude towards people's culture was mixed.[32] While it approved most cultural component like polity, social structure, language, literature, agriculture, art and many others, it did not have positive attitude towards religion.[33] Religious elements like traditional belief and practices were in most cases no longer entertained in a Christian community. By this it does not mean that Christianity did not respect other religious faiths. It did show greater respect but insofar as its belief system functions on a different pattern, therefore, those who willingly accept Christian faith have to abide by its religious order and discipline.

Christian role in national integration can also be understood by its activities viz., the creation of standard language and literature, promotion of indigenous literatures like Bengali, Maharathi etc.; development of educational institutions right from the nursery level up to the higher College and University degree levels; introduction of wide network of clinics, dispensaries, hospitals and medical colleges; provision of indigenous leadership; raising the standard of the marginalized and downtrodden people; fighting against poverty, illiteracy and against caste distinction; taking care of the aged, orphans, the disabled and the poor; providing relief and rehabilitation; caring the mother earth, nature and environment; starting education for girls and women; rural reconstruction; career guidance and training for young people and communal peace and harmony.[34] Hence, Christian attitude and their participation and involvement have in the process contributed to Indian civilization and human culture.[35]

Given the above mentioned areas that Christianity had contributed to national integration and nation building, it is appropriate to endorse that Jesus Christ brings the good news of peace and non-violence.[36] Christianity becomes a religion that gives hope to the sinners through repentance, faith and new life but it condemns all sorts of sinful acts. It fights against hypocrisy, injustice and corruption. A system that entertains corrupted practices is not Christian by Biblical principle. These teachings are among the contributing factors towards the larger Indian civilization.

However, it is rather unfortunate that the post Independence India especially in states with majority of Christian population and leadership, there appeared significant demonstration of unfair means even in public places. Besides that, the country witnessed the growing rise of uncivilized, barbaric, inhuman and genocidal spirit among section of India's population. The intolerant spirit seemed to have ruled certain groups of people. The present carnage in Orissa, Karnataka, Assam, J & K and elsewhere has shown to the outside world the inclination of certain groups of our society towards culture of bloodshed.

NOTES AND REFERENCES

1. Cf. R. C. Majumdar, *Ancient India* (First published 1952, reprinted 1994), pp. 19-28. Read also James Massey, *Roots: A Concise History of the Dalits (1991),* O. L. Snaitang, "In Search of a Tribal History" *in Asia Journal of Theology* (October 2004), pp. 398-411.
2. Read John Marshall, *Mohenjo-Daro and the Indus Civilization: Being an Official Document of Archaelogical Excavations at Mohenjo-Daro Carried out by the Government of India Between the Years 1922 and 1927,* Vols. I & II (First published 1931, reprinted 2004).
3. Dr. K. Thanzauva who had studied the Mizo social life discovered the potential communitarian life of this primal people. Though his research has reference to a single primal community, it however serves as a model that might represent significant similarity among most of the ancient primal peoples in India. See K. Thanzauva, *Theology of Community: Tribal Theology in the Making* (1997).
4. A. Wati Longchar, "Dancing with the Land: Significance of Land for Doing Tribal Theology" in *Doing Tribal Theology with Tribal Resources* (1999), pp. 117-126.
5. Read J. J. M. Nichols-Roy, *Land Laws in the Khasi States* (1956).
6. Hamlet Bareh, *Khasi Democracy* (1964).
7. Cf. O.L. Snaitang, *Christianity and Social Change in Northeast India* (1993), pp. 12-18.
8. Read a folk story in Mrs. Rafy, *Khasi Folk Tales* (First published 1920, reprinted 1985), pp. 137-139.

9. See O. L. Snaitang, "Ki 'Tientnat Khasi" *in Ka Thwet Jingstad* (September 2006), pp. 45-46.
10. *Ibid.*, p. 45.
11. Cf. H. Lyngdoh, *Ki Syiem Khasi bad Synteng* (First published 1938, reprinted 1964).
12. For further information, read Sujata Miri, ed., *Religion and Society in North East India* (1980).
13. B. C Gohain, *Human Sacrifice and Headhunting in North Eastern India* (1977).
14. See J. Meirion Lloyd, *History of the Church in Mizoram* (1991), pp. 152-155.
15. For relevant information, read O. L. Snaitang, *Christianity and Social Change ...*, p. 33.
16. Cf. John Marshall, *op. cit.*, pp. 599-648.
17. For further description, see G. S. Ghurye, *Caste and Race in India* (First published 1932, reprinted 1990), pp. 13ff. Read also R. C. Majumdar, *Ancient India...*, p. 32.
18. An example of such treatment, read Nirmal Minz, *Rise Up, My People and Claim the Promise* (1997), p. 8.
19. O.L. Snaitang, "In Search of a Tribal History", *op. cit.*, p. 404.
20. For an in-depth study of the Syrian tradition, read A. M. Mundadan, *History of Christianity in India Vol. I* (1984). Also compare George Nedungatt, *Quest for the Historical Thomas Apostle of India: A Re-reading of the Evidence* (2008).
21. Mar Aprem, *Nestorian Missions* (First published 1976, reprinted 1985).
22. For more information, see E. R. Hambye, *History of Christianity in India* Vol. III (1997); L. Fernando & Gispert-Sauch, *Christianity in India: Two Thousand Years of Faith* (2004). Read also S. Pampackal, *A Short History of the Catholic Church in India* (2007).
23. Cf. I. Lawrence *St. Francis Xavier* (1998).

24. C. B. Firth, *An Introduction to Indian Church History* (First published 1961, reprinted 1983), pp. 89-98.
25. *Ibid.*, pp. 110-123.
26. Read S. Karotemprel, ed., *Heralds of the Gospel in Asia* (1998),
27. E. A. Lehman, *It Began at Tranquebar* (1956).
28. For specific illustration, read F. S. Downs, *Christianity in North East India: Historical Perspectives* (1983), pp. 28ff.
29. Cf. J. T. K. Daniel & R.E. Hedlund, eds., *Carey 's Obligation and India's Renaissance* (1993).
30. J. W. Pickett, *Christian Mass Movements in India* (1933).
31. See O.L. Snaitang, *Christianity and Social Change...*, op. cit., pp. 121ff.
32. *Ibid.*
33. *Ibid.*, pp. 126-132.
34. See Samson Prabhakar, ed., *Towards a Culture of Peace in South Asia* (2004).
35. For recent but comprehensive studies on these aspects, read C. Aerath & G. Menachery, eds., *Christian Contribution to Nation-Building: A Third Millennium Enquiry* (2004); A. Thumma & A. D. Sahayam, eds., *Christian Commitment to Nation Building* (2006).
36. Cf. L. Fernando & Gispert-Sauch, *Christianity in India, op. cit.*, pp. 38-54.

5

Christianity in Indian Historical Background

—*Marina Behera*

Introduction

Today we often hear comments or come across writings that claim that Christianity in India is more a Western, European, or "colonial" religion. But the fact is that Christianity had existed in India much before the European colonial powers had established their rule in India. We have the St. Thomas Christians living in the Malabar Coast (present day Kerala) who claim that it was St. Thomas who brought the Gospel to India in the 1st century.

In such a scenario, it is well to be reminded of the words of Dr. Rajendra Prasad, former President of India, who, at the St. Thomas Day celebrations in New Delhi on 18 December, 1955, said, "Remember, St. Thomas came to India when many of the countries of Europe had not yet become Christian, and so those Indians who trace their Christianity to him have a longer history and a higher ancestry than that of Christians of many of the European countries."

The title of this presentation then rings true in more senses than one—Christianity in India has always been present in the various historical developments of the land, and in many ways it has always remained in the background, pushed to the corner and almost ignored because of this misconception that it was the Europeans who had introduced the religion to the country.

The implications of such an attitude towards Christianity in India today are becoming more and more evident. Increasing attacks on Christians in the name of conversion are thinly disguised excuses for attacking a religion seen as foreign; for better or for worse, an education in Christian institutions is seen as desirable not only for the excellence in education thus imparted but also because Christian institutions are regarded as the inheritors of the legacy of a British system of education and so are identified with a more 'western' or progressive system of education.

This presentation will attempt to examine three aspects of Christianity in the Indian historical background that will remind us of the role Christianity has played in the events that have helped shape our nation. In doing so, it is hoped that we will revisit the ideas that we have held so far and either re-affirm or come to a better understanding of these ideas.

This paper will thus examine firstly, the relationship between colonialism and Christianity in India. Secondly, it will look at how Christianity had influenced Indian society, particularly with regard to the renaissance in early 19th century society in Bengal. Such as choice has been made as Bengal was the foundation province of the British Empire in India and as a result, the initial spiritual, cultural and intellectual awakening among Indians took place here because of the interaction with western ideas. Thirdly, the paper will comment on the role Indian Christians played in the nation's struggle for freedom particularly with reference to the recurring accusation that Indian Christians played little or no role in the freedom movement as they saw British rule as beneficial for the country and especially for the spread of Christianity in India.

Colonialism and Christianity

Like all the colonialists that were to follow them, it was trade that brought the Portuguese, the first of the European powers, to India during the 16th century. Along with trade, their purpose was to also promote the spread of Christianity among those who came under their rule. The French followed the Portuguese in helping the missionaries to propagate Christianity. The French and the Portuguese were Roman Catholics while the Dutch, the Danish and the British who came later, were Protestants.

The approach of the missionaries, both Catholic and Protestant who worked in India from the 16th century was conservative and apologetic. This attitude was one in which they appreciated and exalted their own religion while looking down on the religions of the others. This attitude, as Mundadan points out, "sees the work of missionaries and evangelism in terms of military operations, to be described as advance and retreat, triumph, struggles, lines of defense, plan for attack, as if we were waging a war against believers."[2]

Mission and colonialism interacted in different forms and at different levels i.e. the mode of their interaction differed from mission to mission. The degree and extent of the interactions or conflict between mission and colonialism largely depended on the colonial power.[3] When we examine the attitudes of the Roman Catholic colonial rulers and the Protestant colonial rulers in India and their dealings with the Indians, it was never uniform.

In contrast to the Roman Catholic Europeans, the Protestant trading companies were not missionary minded. They felt that mission work was harmful for their trade and that such activities would jeopardize their trade and profit. Though all of them maintained chaplains to serve their own people, mission work among the natives was generally not encouraged.

We also find that the levels of impact of the various colonial powers on Indian society were different from one to the other. Dharmaraj points out that "Portuguese domination and their effects were not felt equally by all the Indian people living in the sub-continent. But British conquest deeply altered Indian society and transformed it to the core."[4] The impacts of the others were also only confined to their small settlement or enclaves. This may be because all the other colonial powers, apart from the British did not have an empire like them.

Missionary expansion was in some cases, facilitated through its association with the governing agencies. We see evidence of this under the Portuguese and the British. But did the missionary readily welcome this association with the Government agencies and thus risk being identified as a tool of foreign power? Because of the protection the government offered and the development it promised, missionaries gladly accepted identification as members of the political power.[5] Grant, going on the same line says, "Many missionaries fought hard to retain their detachment from the colonial power, but others too readily accepted the status that was thrust on them as members of the ruling race."[6] As political control advanced, the missionaries were prepared to welcome it and cooperate with the Government if they were convinced that its policies would benefit the people.

Thus we have example of William Carey who readily accepted the post of a lecturer at the College of Fort William in Calcutta, in return for the helping hand of the British Government. He believed that such an opportunity would facilitate missionary work.[7] One cannot overlook the serious implication that such a move makes Carey a part of the colonial establishment, whether directly or indirectly. The freedom and protection that the colonial powers gave to missionaries in some instances was quickly availed of by the missionaries. We see evidences of these under the colonial powers which ruled different parts of India at different times.

The missionaries during the 19th and 20th centuries generally saw British rule as a part of God's beneficent plan for India. The Board of Foreign Missions urged its missionaries during this period to work in close harmony with Government officials, many of whom it believed were friendly to judicious efforts to effect India's intellectual and moral renovations.[8] Medical works and education were the areas in which mission and colonial structures were most closely integrated. As a result, the Government found that nobody else could be more reliable educators or health officers than the dedicated missionary force.

However it must not be understood that missionaries in India were wholly dependant on the colonial power for their activities or that they were willing to let their mission become subservient to the dictates of the real politics of the time. As Dena says "Christian missions and colonialism were the two movement opposed to each other fundamentally. They were two distinct institutionalized entities drawing their inspirations from opposite conceptual extremes. Therefore, the interconnections between them were more in the nature of highly temporal processes which was solely determined by the principle of expediency."[9]

Missionary movements, though initially dependent on the territorial expansion of the colonial powers, after a certain stage, played an important role in stabilizing and consolidating the positions of the colonial Governments in the captured territories. However we must not overlook the laudable work carried out by the missionaries, many of whom used the influence of the colonial power to bring about substantial, important and positive change in Indian society.

There were however drawbacks because of the manner in which missionaries cooperated with the government because they viewed the local people and their customs from a superior position. One of these was that the majority of the Indian population quickly interpreted the Christianizing efforts of the missionaries as westernizing efforts.

One of the outcomes of mission work under colonialism was the perception of missionaries as 'vendors of goods'. In this context Shourie comments, "they came to adopt the usual techniques of vendors; the exaggeration common in advertising wares, targeting the section that would be most vulnerable, or receptive, using not just dialogue but allurement and violence."[10]

The relationship between missionaries and colonialism has not always been cordial. The interests of the missionaries and the colonial rulers often clashed. A majority of the Government officials of all the Protestant colonial power were in favour of religious neutrality, though some concession had been made at the later stage. They were more comfortable trading with the Indians rather than meddling in their religious and social life. The missionaries often criticized the colonial policy and missionaries in turn were often viewed as disrupting the peace of the colonial rule. However we must not forget that mission and colonialism were closely linked in humanitarian services, notably in the fields of education, health and medicine.

Christianity and the Renaissance in 19th Century Bengal

The early 19th century was a period of stagnating traditional culture and society at very low ebb, in fact a state of decadence condemned by most modern Indians like Raja

Rammohon Roy, et al. On the other hand we have a still traditional society in the throes of the creative excitement of modernizing itself, of emerging as a new nation, remaining thoroughly its own and rooted in its culture, yet taking its place in the contemporary world. The 19th century was the pivotal century, which saw the initiation of this process that brought about an enormous transformation in the religious, social, economic, political and cultural sphere.[11] It was also a period of spiritual, cultural and intellectual renascence among the educated Indians.

This transformation was effected by several circumstances. We have the total impact of the British East India Company, which influenced Indian life through many channels. This forced the people to adjust their lives to the new circumstances thus effecting a continuum of social change.[12] We also have the influence of Christianity on Indian society. Bengal was the first to undergo significant British influence. By the early 1800's a crystallization of different reactions to western influence could be seen.[13]

According to Kopf, "What develops in nineteenth-century Calcutta is a two-sided process of acculturation, or the merging of interests and identities by representatives of civilizations in encounter."[14] Bengal, the foundation province of the British Indian Empire, was the epicenter of the earthquake of western ideas. At the intellectual level, as Edwardes comments, "Western ideas—and even the actions of the British Government- supplied a means for reinforcing Hinduism and, to a much lesser extent, Islam. The challenge posed by Christianity, as well as the ethical content of its teaching, had profound effects. So, too, did the rediscovery and translation of the Sanskrit classics by European Orientalists, a byproduct of the administration's desire to know more about the customary law of the Hindu."[15] Thus the early 19th century was the period of reawakening which was characterized by the historical rediscovery and reinterpretation of the Indian past, the beginning of the linguistic and literary modernization of several Indian languages, and the transformation of Indian society under the impact of the West.

The prominent British missionaries in Serampore who worked in India during this period, showed a positive attitude to Indian culture and religion. Their cultural philosophy was to revitalize and modernize Indian culture and languages and let Christian values be assimilated into the cultural complex of India.[16]

The Serampore missionaries attempted studying the popular culture and popular languages of India with this aim of revitalization and modernization.[17] At the College of Fort William Carey openly advocated a "vernacularist" position on cultural revitalization. Although he shared little of the enthusiasm of his other colleagues for the basic values of the Hindu high culture in the revitalization of the Bengali society, he also played an important role in advancing popular revitalization. With regard to this Carey and his associates had stated:

> From every plan therefore which embraces the progressive improvement of the whole population of India, we must carefully exclude the idea of universally rendering English the channel of instruction. The great mass of people can receive improvements only in a language familiar to them; and English will never be as familiar as their own native language.[18]

The Serampore missionaries did not seek to make India after their own British image or likeness. They sought to accommodate Protestant Christianity to Indian culture instead of the other way round. As a result they tried to avoid any sense of racial superiority in their dealings with Indians.

The appreciation of the Orientalists and the Serampore missionaries for the ancient values of India and their emphasis that Hinduism and Hindu society could be revitalized from within, created a viable atmosphere for the new intelligentsia in Calcutta to come into positive interaction with the Western and Christian traditions and to search for a new spiritual and cultural identity for Indian society.[19]

Educated Indians had acquired a deep interest in English literature as well as in Western science and Western political ideas. The first effect was to encourage Indians, in particular Bengalis, to write in English themselves. Within a very short period in the 19th century, English came to be looked upon as the new *lingua franca*, the common speech of the educated throughout India.[20]

The desire to imitate English models in an Indian language also first showed itself in Bengal. With the introduction of the printing press, poetry was freed from the oral tradition and from religious or quasi-religious subject matter. This freedom from past forms encouraged experimentation and, in the decade following 1830, there was considerable innovation and adaptation in verse form. Missionary activity resulted in the preparation of textbooks and translations of the *Bible*. The Baptist Mission at Serampore under the guidance of Carey produced a large number of grammars and translations of some of the Sanskrit classics. The majority of the books translated, however were of European, and specifically, English origin.[21]

Carey and the Bengali Brahmins' effort towards the development of Bengali literature in the College of Fort William had an important socio-cultural and intellectual effect. Under Carey's encouragement, these scholars went further in transcending their traditional limitations and in experimenting in creativity with new literary forms.[22]

Another well known missionary in Bengal during this period was Alexander Duff, who arrived in Calcutta in 1830 and who struck out in an entirely different direction from the Serampore missionaries. He considered English to be, to all India, the channel for the Christian learning of the Western world. The effects produced by Duff's labours are: (a) Inrush of Western culture to the upper class of the native society (b) The Western idea of materialism as well as the introduction of the idealistic moral principle in Christianity (c) The Christian presentation of life was held against that stream of nonreligious culture which was then unfortunately rushing in upon India (d) A western pattern of education policy was formulated which formed the basis of the modern University education.[23]

The Serampore missionaries brought to the attention of the public as well as to their political rulers, cases of infanticide, Sati, the ill treatment of lepers and instances of slavery, through the first Indian newspapers, which they founded– *Samachar Darpan* (in Bengali) and *The Friend of India* and the first Indian Periodicals *Dig-Darshan* (in Bengali).

Azariah has rightly commented, "Two factors that brightened the prospects for the abolition of *Suttee* were the relentless and selfless work of the Christian missionaries, and the sign of progressive spirit among the natives best expressed in the person of Raja Rammohun Roy."[24]

Christianity and the Indian Freedom Movement

One of the greatest challenges Christians faced during the struggle for Independence was manner in which Christianity was closely identified with the British. It is in this regard that terms such as "colonial", "colonialism" and "colonialist", in relation to Christianity, Christian mission, or even to all things Christian, has been used for categorically demonizing or epitomizing evil and exploitation, or for categorizing anything deemed to be "anti-national."[25]

Use of the term in this way against Christians in India may not have started with Gandhi. Yet ever since Gandhi attacked Bishop Vedanayagam Azariah in 1937 and called his action, in attempting to evangelize by bringing the gospel to outcaste Malas and Madigas of Dornakal, "anti-national," the term has been used to implicate Indian Christians as being alien, anti-national and unpatriotic, or subject to forces from outside of India.[26]

Perhaps the most glaring and most enduring consequence of missionary work under colonialism has been the quasi-identification of Christianizing with Westernizing.[27]During India's colonial period, the alliance of the Indian Christians with the western missionary societies made the Hindus suspect Christianity as a danger to the nation. This suspicion still lingers. Shourie giving a Hindu perception of the work of Christian missionaries in India says that, "it has the most direct bearing on our denationalization.... In large part no doubt because of the thoroughness with which the colonial design came to be carried out i.e. Macaulay's design to create 'a class of persons, Indians in blood ands colour, but English in taste, in opinions, in morals ands intellect.'"[28]

Well into the 19th century, Indian Christians were fast becoming aware of the fact that their faith which now defined their collective identity was being viewed by their fellow country people as something foreign. They also felt the practical difficulty of being proud of their 'Indian-ness' on one hand and the identification of their religion with the colonial ruler on the other. Lal Behari Day was conscious that after the revolt of 1857 Indians' hatred for Christianity "is more intense than before, simply because they regard Christianity as the religion of the Europeans".[29] Brahmabandhab Upadhyay lamented: "our Hindu brethren cannot see the subtlety and sanctity of our Divine religion because of its hard coating of Europeanism".[30]

The conflict thus caused in the minds of the educated Christians, many of whom were converts from the high castes, along with the superior attitude of the western Christian missionaries as well as Rammohun Roy's and Keshub Chandra Sen's assertions that Indian Christianity should be free of western influence in worship and organization gave rise to the National Church Movement in the 19th century. This movement mooted the idea of a "national Church" or an "Indian Church" in the place of Western denominations of Christianity. It was the first manifestation of Indian Christian self-awareness as distinct from Western Christian Missions and Western denominations.[31]

In the early years of the Indian National Congress, Indian Christians enthusiastically supported it and attended its conferences. At the Madras session of the INC in 1887, there were 35 Christians out of a total of 607 registered delegates. Some of the prominent Christians at the 1887 session were R.S.N. Subramania, a Christian barrister and Municipal Councillor from Madras, Kali Charan Banerji, a prominent leader of the Bengali Christian community who was also an eminent scholar, a brilliant orator and a highly respected Indian Christian in Congress circles and Madhusudan Das a lawyer who later became a Deputy Magistrate in Orissa.[32] It is interesting to note that in 1887, when, for the first time a small conference of Indian Christians from different parts of the country was held in Madras in connection with the National Church Movement, many who attended this meeting were also delegates of the INC meeting for its 1887 session. This was the most powerful manifestation of Indian nationalism. They discussed subjects such as unity and self-support among Christians.[33]

As a result of the World War I, the British Government began to rethink its policy on the entry of non-British foreigners including missionaries into their colonies, including

India. One of the outcomes of such a policy was the introduction of the Memoranda.[34] Attempts were made to use the Memoranda to prevent the Indian Christians, especially those under the employment of the missions from taking an active part in the National Movement.[35]

Citing the Memoranda, the Government sought to use the missionaries to control the political activity of Indian workers employed by the missions. For example, the Basel Mission was running educational institutions in Mangalore and Udupi. Some students from these schools took part in demonstrations during the Civil Disobedience Movement. As a result the District Collector of Kanara annoyed with the mission authorities, told them that "he would withdraw registration and grants if such things would happen again."[36]

The Government issued a warning to the governing bodies of all recognized educational institutions that received government grants (this meaning most missionary schools) as well as all local authorities and school boards that no member of their staff or establishment should be permitted to take part in political agitation directed against the authority of Government.[37]

When the Non-Cooperation Movement started in 1920, there were Indian Christians in the whole of India who took part in it. Though we do not have sufficient data regarding their numbers, it will be safe to assume that such a number would have been quite considerable. Such a deduction can be arrived at when we notice the attitude of Christians towards the freedom struggle as mentioned in the letter that S.K. Datta (1878-1942), Principal of Foreman Christian College, Lahore, wrote to J.H. Oldham: "...I have been talking to a number of friends, Christians mostly, who are much concerned by the present situation. As a matter of fact, more and more of us accept the teaching of Gandhi...". [38]

Further, S.K. Datta, in his Presidential address at the All- India Conference of Indian Christians held at Lucknow between 27 and 30 December 1922 made a reference to some of the Indian Christians who had suffered imprisonment as a result of their political activities.[39] Statements such as these indicate the active role Indian Christians played in the different movements that made up the struggle for freedom.

During the Civil Disobedience Movement, Christians in Bombay from various denominations formed the Nationalist Christian Party. In its first resolution the community said that it "emphatically demands for India the right for self-determination and is of the opinion that the immediate grant for self-governance alone will satisfy her political aspiration".[40]

There were Indian Christians who were members of the Indian National Congress and were actively involved throughout the Freedom Movement. These included Rajkumari Amrit Kaur, S.K. George, George Joseph, J.C. Kumarappa and H.C. Mookerjee who were also close associates of Gandhi, while others such as S.K. Datta, V.S. Azariah, K.T. Paul, B. Ralia Ram and Augustine Ralla Ram while not taking an active role in politics, nevertheless were strong supporters of the freedom movement.

Following the 1937 elections under the new act of 1935, Azariah said, "We ought to have the privilege of voting in the General Electorate, and all the members so elected ought to be guardians of our interests as well as those of any others; we are one with our non-Christian brethren." [41] His stand was that Indian Christians were not different from any of the other religious communities in the country and therefore the Christian community had no reason to be treated in any discriminatory manner.

The Student Christian Association and women such as Pandita Ramabai and Nikambe also were involved in the Freedom Movement.

Conclusion

This paper has briefly tried to put a historical perspective to the role Indian Christianity has played in Indian history. In this attempt, it has looked at the relationship between Christianity and colonialism, the role Christianity played in the revitalization of 19th century society in Bengal and finally the role Indian Christians played in the nation's struggle for freedom.

It is quite obvious that Christianity in India, while striving to overcome the popular idea that it was introduced with the European colonial powers, must also show itself as effective and active in nation-building not only as part of the legacy of having taken an active part in the struggle for freedom, but also in terms of encouraging more effective leadership based on Christian principles.

This is essential because a paper such as this, presented in a seminar that attempts to look critically into the role that Christianity in India can play in national integration must now look to the future and ask the question, what next? We know that Christians played an active role in the struggle for Independence: but does that mean that we only remain comfortable in the fact that we run some of the best educational institutions in the country? We also know that our hospitals provide excellent and affordable healthcare to millions in the country: but do we then become complacent in the knowledge that the Christian community in India is among the most literate in the country?

Our historical moorings in this country, the legacy that we have inherited as having played an active role not just in the fight for our nation's freedom but our contributions in various fields since August 1947 demand that we now look at how else we can contribute to national integration. Could one of these ways be a more active role in the administration of the country and not just in the regions that we belong to?

Are Christian educational institutions in a position to have a more active say in the manner in which various syllabuses are designed and implemented so that education can more effectively address the needs of the country in terms of employment and character-building?

These are some of the various questions I believe this seminar needs to look at. It is good to be reminded of our past, to know where we are coming from. It is only then that we can plan where we need to go. The Christian community in India needs to take challenges such as these into consideration if it is to more effectively contribute to national integration.

NOTES AND REFERENCES

1. Quoted by A.M. Mundadan, *History of Christianity in India*, Vol. I, From the Beginning up to the Middle of the Sixteenth Century (up to 1542), Reprint 1989 (Bangalore: Church History Association of India, 1984), 9.
2. A. M. Mundadan, *Indian Christians Search for Identity and Struggle for Autonomy* (Bangalore: Dharmaram Publications, 1984), 186-187.
3. Lal Dena, *Christian Mission and Colonialism* (Shillong: Vendrame Institute, 1988), 1.
4. Jacob Dharmaraj, *Colonialsim and Christian Mission; Postcolonial Reflections* (Delhi: I.S.P.C.K., 1993), 21.
5. Dena, *op.cit.*, 4.
6. J.W. Grant, *God's People in India* (London: Cox & Wyman Ltd., 1959), 5.
7. E. Daniel Potts, *British Baptist Missionaries in India 1793-1837: A History of Serampore and its Missions* (Great Britain: Cambridge University Press, 1967), 175.
8. J.C.B. Webster, *The Christian Community and Change in Nineteenth Century India* (Meerut: The Macmillan Company of India Ltd, 1976), 125.
9. Lal Dena, *op.cit.*, 12.

10. Arun Shourie, *Missionaries in India: Continuities, Changes, Dilemmas* (New Delhi: ASA Publications, 1994), 15.
11. For details see J.T.F. Jordens, "Hindu religious and racial reforms in British India", in *A Cultural History of India*, edited by Gerald H. Anderson, (N.p: McGraw Hill Book Company, 1961), 365.
12. *Ibid.*
13. *Ibid.*, 366-367.
14. David Kopf, *British Orientalism and the Bengal Renaissance: The Dynamics of Indian Modernization 1773-1835*, Indian Edition (Calcutta: Firma K.L. Mukhopadhyay, 1969), 5.
15. Michael Edwardes, *British India 1772-1947: A Survey of the Nature and Effects of Alien Rule* (London: Sidgwick and Jackson, 1976), 136.
16. David Kopf, *op.cit.*, 80, 93.
17. For details see *Ibid.*, 71, 146ff, 155, 251.
18. "Desultory Thoughts on the Introduction of English into India", in *The Friend of India*, Quarterly Series, II/VIII (1822): 532.
19. George Thomas, *Christian Indians and Indian Nationalism 1885-1950: An Interpretation in Historical and Theological Perspectives,* Dissertation zur Erlangung der Doktorurde der Evang- Theologischen fakultat der Universitat Hamburg, Frankfurt m Main. Bern. Cirencester, 1979, 27-28.
20. Michael Edwardes, *British India 1772-1947: A Survey of the Nature and Effects of Alien Rule* (London: Sidgwick and Jackson, 1976), 136.
21. *Ibid.*
22. David Kopf, *op.cit.*, 112.
23. Sunil Kumar Chatterjee, *William Carey and Serampore: Source Materials on the Missionary Activities in India*, 2nd enlarged edition (Sheoraphuli: Laserplus, 2004), 84, 85.
24. Isaiah Azariah, *Lord William Bentinck and Indian Social Reform* (Thiruvalla: Christhava Sahithya Samithy, 1997), 89.
25. Robert Eric Frykenberg, ed., *Christians and Missionaries in India: Cross-Cultural Communication since 1500 with Special Reference to Caste, Conversion, and Colonialism* (Grand

Rapids, Michigan/Cambridge, U.K.: William B. Eerdmans Publishing Company, 2003), 7.

26. *Ibid.*, 7.
27. Mundadan, *History of Christianity...*, op.cit., 521.
28. Arun Shourie, *op.cit.*, x.
29. G. Macpherson, *Life of Lal Behari Day, Convert, Pastor, Professor and Author* (Edinburgh: N.p., 1900), 98. Cited by George Thomas, *op.cit.*, 64.
30. B. Animanada, *The Blade: Life and Work of Brahmabandhab Upadhyaya* (Calcutta, n.d. (1947), 74. Cited by George Thomas, *Ibid.*
31. George Thomas., 66
32. For more details see D. Arthur Jeyakumar, *Christians and the National Movement* (Calcutta: Punthi Pustak, 199), 93.
33. *A Collection of Papers Connected with the Movement of the National Church of India* (Madras: N.P., 1893), 76-77. Cited by George Thomas, op.cit., 81.
34. The Memoranda was a policy agreed upon by the Government of India and the Missionary Societies in Great Britain and Ireland regarding the entry of enemy and alien missions in India. The Memoranda issued in 1919 were revised in 1921. The Memoranda had three parts i.e. part 'A' applicable to British missionaries as well as those who came through the Foreign Missions Conference of North America. Part 'B' dealt with Roman Catholic societies. Part 'C' was intended for missionaries who came from countries who were not viewed as friendly to the British Empire. See D. Arthur Jeyakumar, *op.cit.*, 13, 18, 97, 98.
35. *Ibid.*, 8.
36. *Ibid.*, 141.
37. "More Missionary Neutrality", *The Christian Century*, April 20, 1932, 501. Cited by George Thomas, *op.cit.*, 195.
38. George Thomas, *Ibid*, 122.
39. *Ibid.*
40. Asghar Ali Engineer, ed., *The Role of Minorities in the Freedom Struggle* (Delhi: Ajanta Publications, 1986), 165.

41. V.S. Azariah, 'Christians and the New Government', *Young Men of India*, Vol. L, No.3, March 1938, 73-74. Cited by Arthur D. Jeyakumar, *op.cit.*, 127.

6

National Integration:
The Social Role of Christianity in India

—*Arunava Banerjee*

"National Integration is not a house which could be built by mortar and bricks. It is not an industrial plan too, which could be discussed and implemented by experts. Integration on the contrary is a thought, which must go into the hearts of the people. It is the consciousness which must awaken the people at large."

Dr. Sarvapalli Radhakrishnan

The concept of national integration is easy to understand but difficult to define. The concept is much wider and the term 'integration' is used to cover an extra-ordinary broad range of political phenomenon. The problem of integration varies from one country to another. Hence, the solution to the problem cannot be uniform. There is also no perfect model of national integration in the world. Every modern state does what it can do to inculcate a sense of national identity and so to foster national unity.

The problem of integration arises when the ability of the organized society to order relationship among people seems to be failing, when its institutions are faltering, the transmission of its values from one generation to another is breaking down and the framework of expectation is being shaken. National integration implies the observance of divisive movements that would balkanize the nation and the presence of attitudes throughout the society that gives preference to national and public interests. In fact the concept of national integration covers a vast range of human relationship and attitudes– the integration of diverse discreet cultural identities and the development of a sense of nationality; the integration of political units into a territorial framework with a government; the integration of the rulers and the ruled; the integration of the citizen into a common political process and finally the integration of individuals into organizations for purposive activities. Most essential component of national integration is the emotional integration of people. National integration implies a sense of belonging, a feeling of togetherness of unity.

India is the homeland of variety and diversity not only in physical features and climatic conditions, but also in respect of language, religion, manners, customs, traditions and folk ways, in the patterns of living prevalent among different sets and localities. Sociologically India comprises different strata of people living as contemporary patterns of life widely different in their value-structures, norms and behavior. Ethnically India is a laboratory of many races and their intermixing. Culturally and linguistically, the variants are much more pronounced. People living in Kashmir, West Bengal, Kerala and Rajasthan, for example, depict different cultural attributes and regional aspirations. In terms of religious communities, India has seven major segments: Hindus, Muslims, Christians, Sikhs, Jains, Buddhists and Parsees. But against the background of this highly diverse and segmented social fabric, the key note to integration is unity in diversity in which both the component are equally valid and mutually interdependent. Rabindranath Tagore regarded the unity of India as the 'unity of spirit'. The first National Integration Council, in its first conference held in 1961 has stated, "The foundations of our national life are common citizenship, unity in diversity, freedom of religion – secularism, equality, justice – social, economic and political and fraternity among all communities".

It is a fact of Indian political life that even after sixty years of Independence the vast majority of the population does not feel integrated with India. Jammu & Kashmir is in great turmoil. The emotional integration of the people of Nagaland, Mizoram, Manipur and Meghalaya is far from deep. There are so many factors, which have inhibited the development of an integrated society in India. Following are the factors that are threatening Indian unity and solidarity- 1] Religious orthodoxy, 2] Varieties of castes, 3] Linguistic Jingoism, 4] Social and economic insecurity, 5] Provincialism, 6] Lack of education, 5] Faulty Economic development and unbalanced growth of population, 6] Erosion of Indian traditional and cultural values etc.

Making Sense of Christianity

Christianity is a monotheistic religion centered on the life and teaching of Jesus of Nazareth as presented in the New Testament. Its followers, known as Christians believe that Jesus is the son of God and is the Messiah. To Christians Jesus Christ is a teacher, the model of a virtuous life, the revealer of god and most importantly the savior of humanity who suffered, died and was resurrected in order to bring about salvation from sin. Christians maintain that Jesus ascended into heaven and most denominations teach that Jesus will return to judge the living and the dead, granting everlasting life to his followers. Christians call the message of Jesus Christ the gospels (Good News) and hence label written account of his ministry as gospels. Like Judaism and Islam, Christianity is classified as an Abrahamic religion. In spite of important differences of interpretation and opinion, Christians share a set of believe that they hold as essential to their faith. Christianity began, as a Jewish sect in the eastern Mediterranean and by the 4th century had become the dominant religion within the Roman Empire. During the Middle Ages, most of the remainder of Europe was Christian, with Christians also being a religious minority in the Middle East, North Africa and parts of India. Following the age of discovery through missionary work and colonization, Christianity spread to the America and the rest of the world. Christianity has played a prominent role in the shaping of western civilization at least since the 4th century. At the early 21st century Christianity has between 1.5 billion and 2.1 billion adherents, representing about a quarter to a third of the world's population.

Short History of Christianity in India

The emergence of Christianity in the religious atmosphere of socio-cultural India is significant enough. Christianity appeared long before the appearance of Islam in India. Like Islam, Christianity also arrived in India in a peaceful way. St Thomas and St Bartholomew were believed to have been the pioneers who took active participation in preaching Christianity since the first century. St Thomas became paying attention in preaching Christianity in Kerala and for his active performance Christianity gained its importance, dignity and popularity in 17 districts of Kerala. Many churches were set up in Kerala and the number of converted Christians became more or less one lakh. According to the famous Greek Stoic philosopher Paentaenus there was also the presence of large number of Christians in the coastal region of Malabar. During the period when St Thomas was in probably Punjab,

St. Bartholomew could have come to the western region of India and dedicated himself to the task of preaching. At that time Kalyannagari, a place near Bombay became the centre of the Indian Christians.

The followers of St Thomas, known as 'Nazrani" attained like the Hindu Brahmins a very high status in the classified social structure of India. They were very conscious to uplift their high social rank and dignity in the society. Like the Brahmins, they also believed in untouchables. Usually they tried to convert the members of the royal family and the people of high social ranks into Christianity. The 'Nazrani' Christians were the primitive and bigoted Christians in India.

In 1552 St. Flancis Xavier, a famous preacher came to Goa. During that period, a large number of Christians resided in Goa. There were fourteen Churches and more than a hundred priests in Goa. The contribution of De Menzes, an archbishop was very important in the expansion of Christianity in the coastal region of Malabar. He tried to isolate the converted Christians from the influence of Hindus. In 1605 Roberto de Nobili, an Italian Jesuit padre worked in Madurai and with the help of his followers he became successful in his mission of converting the local citizens into Christianity. They converted almost 1.5 lakh of the Indian populace into Christianity at the end of seventeenth century. Roberto de Nobili adopted adroit strategy in exhibiting his mine, manner, attitude, behavior, mode of eating, clothing, discrimination in class-consciousness etc. keep good relation with the local inhabitants. He had profound interest and knowledge in Indian language, such as Tamil, Sanskrit etc. He used to discuss about religious matters with the Hindu sage and saints. He could do so for his erudite knowledge in Hinduism and philosophy. However, he was to confront of criticism made by the cognate priests for his unconventional system of campaigning Christian religion.

Furthermore, the Christian preachers received adequate moral and financial support from colonial powers, like Dutch and Portuguese. Subsequently the preachers became more enriched and gritty in demonstration the sermons of their religion. The priests and bishops of different countries visited India in different times. They would come in groups or units and devoted themselves to various kinds of social services. As the consequence, they could formulate a religious atmosphere and at the same time, they got much opportunity to enlighten the Indians with the nature and benevolence of their religion. It is significant to inform that the Christian Missionaries were initially associated with the common people, but later on, they had been alienated from the mainstream of the Indian populace due to their relation with the colonial powers. However, they kept on their preaching activity and converted many Indians into their religion. Largely the tribes of Jharkhand and most states of northeast India were converted.

If we critically examine the history of the development of Christianity in India, we come to know that it never became a hindrance to the social and cultural progress of India. On the other hand, it enlightened the social, cultural and economic status of India from various aspects. At present Christianity becomes a part and parcel of our society. Though it appeared very silently, it has cherished luxuriously in the socio-cultural atmosphere in India, and, therefore it flourished full-fledged with its roots and branches. More or less Christianity influenced the Indian society and vice versa. Now we can neither separate it from our society, nor avoid it as a foreign religion. It has now become an inescapable and inevitable ingredient of our Great "Sovereign, Socialist, Secular, Democratic, Republic".

Social Role of Christianity in National Integration

National integration, by definition, is a national objective.

It cannot be viewed as just an elitist affair. It means that it cannot be confined to the efforts to the efforts of a particular group or class—whether social, economic, political, intellectual or religious. To achieve national integration, a nation-wide endeavor is essential. But it is a fact that the institutions, functions, attitudes and means of Christianity in India have obviously played a positive role in promoting national integration.

The importance of massive public education in the task of nation-building cannot be overstated. In the long established nation-states, public schools serve as agents of political socialization. They try to inculcate attitudes and dispositions that should support state authority over and against traditional demands of the family, tribe or caste and promote acceptance of technology over traditional methods of production. They also open out the minds of the young scholars into a wider cultural consciousness. The historical contribution by virtue of which the Methodist Mission has left an indelible mark on life of the Indian people is the spread of modern education. The Methodist Church in North India provincial Synod has done much work in educational field. Under the leadership of the Church, so many schools and colleges have set up. The mission has also paid special attention to the spread of women education. The opportunity of training in technical work has extended to the boys and the girls. The Missionaries believed that evangelicism and literacy programme should go hand to hand because the common people of other faiths would not be able to understand the inner appeal of the Gospel unless they were literate. To them evangelicism included campaign for eradication of illiteracy. The Mission emphasizes on value-based education in the sense that it should make the person aware of purpose of life. Swami Vivekananda personified two main principles of education— 1] Divinity of man (man is divine spiritual being) and 2] Oneness of the Universe (there is a unity running through this universe). The Methodist tradition also emphasizes the universality of grace: the vast unfathomable sea of God's goodness and truth streams the whole creation reach, enough for all enough for each. The Methodist church in Britain holds the following statements as their principles of mission-

1) telling the good news of Jesus,
2) calling people to faith in Jesus Christ and to Christian discipleship,
3) caring for individual people and communities,
4) sharing in the task of education and social and spiritual development struggling for a just world,
5) being alongside the poor,
6) becoming friends with people of different cultures and faiths,
7) caring for the earth,
8) building partnerships with other churches and other groups who share some of their mission aims.

Economic stagnation sharpens conflicts and intensifies competition and social antagonism, while economic development encourages integration process transcending traditional, communal and regional differences. It is therefore, that economic development for raising the standard of living has become the national object of all developing countries including India. But because of the faulty economic development and unbalanced growth of population; the Indians have not been able to make headway in the right direction. There is a strong feeling among the intellectuals of this country that economic development in India has marginalized the dalits, tribes and religious and linguistic minorities. We can justifiably proud of the contributions that the Indians Christian community has made a positive and definite role in the development of caste and tribal people. For the economic improvement of the Santals and Bauries, so many schemes have taken. The Methodist Mission has also played a crucial role to enable people to get rid of the scourge of leprosy to a considerable extent.

Conclusion

In conclusion, we can evidently say that Christianity has greatly contributed to the nation. It is true, that the main objective of the Mission is preaching and converting people into Christianity but its work did not remain confine to religious-spiritual area, but also covered the secular fields—educational, medical, vocational, social and corporate. Expanding education, being friends of the poor, making faith on humanity and universalism, Christianity in India has obviously played a positive role in nation-building process.

7

Christianity: National Integration

—*Tejdor Tiewsoh*

Introduction

Once, a tourist after visiting many parts of India, was asked to share his thoughts about the people of India. Interestingly, he said that he met the Telegu, the Tamil, the Gujarati, the Malayalee, etc. but did not meet an Indian. India is a conglomeration of a number of cultural and distinct communities, and the reality is that we tend to identify ourselves more with our own cultural and linguistic communities rather than with the national one. Dr. Bareh, an eminent Khasi scholar and leader states: "the truth is that traditionally all of us, to whatever community we belong, whether tribals or non-tribals, were isolated from each other, each living his own life. We have begun to think of ourselves as one nation only recently".[1] Interestingly enough, it is only when India plays cricket against Pakistan, for instance, or when there is war or any threat to the nation, or when we travel abroad, that our sense of national identity comes to the fore. In such a context, and as we have witnessed the rising spate of fundamentalism in our country, even till recently, national integration becomes the all-important issue that needs to be addressed in a forum like this. It was the then Prime Minister, Shri Jawaharlal Nehru who convened the National Integration Conference on September - October 1961, to find ways and means of combating the evils of communalism, casteism, regionalism, linguism and narrow-mindedness, and to formulate certain policies and guidelines on which the country can move forward. The objective of this paper is to address the theme of this seminar by looking at the following sub-points: The reality of India as a composite society; threats to National Integration; the Foundation for National Integration; Christian contribution to National Integration; and the Christian Basis for National Integration.

India: A Composite Society

Along with Independence came the partition of India. The conflict which dominated Indian politics in pre-Independence period, was related to the communal issue and religious imbroglio. After Independence, conflicts based on caste and linguistic loyalties have come to the foreground. Demands for redrawing the boundaries of the member states of the union of India on a linguistic basis became very strong early in the nineteen-fifties, resulting in the formation of the National Re-organisation Commission. One example is Andhra Pradesh, the Telegu state created in 1953. However, political boundaries cannot really segregate people belonging to different languages, religions and castes. Living shoulder to shoulder with each other inevitably leads to confrontations, and differences are often highlighted resulting in group clashes and riots – language riots, religious riots, caste/tribe riots.

A society such as ours, is essentially composite in character—a composite of different cultures and distinct communities. Among these communities there is a constant interplay of both co-existence and competition. Co-existence, because no one community could completely eliminate the others even if it wanted to; and Competition because the total resources available for distribution is limited. If one community takes more, the other communities are left with less share. Moreover, these communities are not all of the same size or equal strength, and from time to time, they form different patterns of alliance. Under certain conditions, rivalry becomes pronounced.

A great society is essentially a composite one, holding within that whole, a diversity of tribes and castes, races and communities. No attempt at nation0al integration will be successful unless an attempt is simultaneously made to affirm the identities of each constituent to the integration. The real task of National Integration is to preserve the plurality of cultures and yet bind them together in a larger harmony. This, I believe, is the true meaning and significance of the ideal of unity in diversity

Threats to National Integration

In the Pre-independence era, the question of national independence was upper-most in the minds of the people. After independence, national integration has become the focus. If achieving independence was the major historic task in the earlier part of the 20th century, preserving national unity is the principal task today. Certain threats to that unity are not only visible but ominously recurrent. They come from different directions and take diverse forms.

Separatist tendencies prevalent in different parts of the country are a real threat to its unity. From almost every corner of the country, one hears clamorous demands for a separate nationhood, Kashmir, being a case in point. *Communal clashes* have become a regular feature. Every now and then, forces of disintegration raise their ugly head. India is a secular country where its citizens are free to follow any religion. But the reality of *religious fundamentalism,* more frenzied than ever before, seems to contradict this assertion; "nothing is more injurious to national integration than the assumption that Indian nationality is identical with the religion, culture or language of the majority communities."[2] Attempts at integration should not be aimed at homogenization – that is, to make everyone look alike. Some politicians actively exploit people in the name of religion. Secularism has become a mere lip-service. It is sometimes argued that the threat to India's national unity is grounded chiefly on economic causes. This is only partly true. Studies show that it is not always from the economically most deprived sections of the population that disruptive movements arise and receive support. Much more, the integration of the nation is being threatened by subversive political, ideological, and regional agendas.

When we look at the global scene, we find that various people and nations have, at different times, adopted varied methods and approaches to bring about national integration. Some countries have tried to foster national unity based on religion, for instance, Islam; others, on a particular ideology, such as Marxism-Leninism; and some countries try to achieve it by the use of naked force, or Dictatorship. These methods may not work in a country like India because ours is a pluralistic society. In such a society, for national integration to be realised, there is an urgent need to create and foster an atmosphere in which the different communities can freely cooperate and co-exist in a larger framework of harmony.

The Foundation for National Integration

If national integration is to become a reality in a country, any country, certain human values must be uphold. In his book *The Gandhian Way,* Amlan Dutta underlines the significance of shared human values as the cohesive factor that holds a society together – "a large society is not held together by economic and political interests alone, but a sense of shared values is equally important".[3] Recognising and upholding values such as honesty, morality, integrity and justice provide the foundation for a just and strong nation. Its pillars are human dignity and freedom, truth and knowledge, personal responsibility and stewardship, and the rule of the Law. To talk about Integration without these values is to talk of a nation where there is no true freedom and identity. Christianity as a whole, has contributed immensely in fostering and nurturing these said values.

The *Bible* teaches that all humans are created in the image of God, and as such, they are of worth, and are equal, one with the other. It is this understanding of the human worth and equality that is the basis on which Christianity rests. In seeking to practice and propagate this worldview, Christianity is in fact, adhering to, and promoting the very essence of integration.

Christian Contribution to National Integration

It has often been pointed out that the development of a nation is intrinsically related to the intellectual development of its members. Knowledge and intellectual development cannot be the monopoly of a few while the rest are denied their privileges. In this regard, it is worth to note Christianity's contribution in the field of education in the country, irrespective of caste, community and religion. It is education, the enlightenment and awareness that come with them that make people recognise not only their own rights and potential, but also to respect the rights and potential of others. The esteemed daily *The Hindu*, in its December 22nd, 2006 issue, reported: Thangam Thennarasu, Minister for School Education, said society is indebted to Christianity as it is instrumental in imparting education and providing health facilities to all irrespective of caste and community.

A free press is another dimension of the endeavour to disseminate the truth. Truth reforms, regenerates and liberates. A free press is absolutely indispensable for a just and democratic state. As a tool for reformation, it serves as a voice for the voiceless, a defender of the truth, a check on the abuse of power by the powerful—these and many other causes are served by a free press, and its role in the building up of a just and egalitarian nation can never be overemphasised. Keshab Chandra Sen, one of the greatest Indian reformers of the nineteenth century observes – "The Christian contribution to the nation-building of India is best appreciated when we note that it is with the Christian missions in India that the institution of the press and journalism began in this country".[4] It was at the Serampore mission in 1818 that we see the beginning of the modern Indian press, with the launching of *Friend of India* in English, *Samachar Darpan* in Bengali, and the short-lived *Dig Darshan* in Hindi. The three periodicals, under the general editorship of Joshua Marshman, a colleague of William Carey, was inspired exclusively by the Christian proposition that liberating power comes not from the barrel of a gun but from the Truth. The birth of the free press, was a non-official and non-commercial initiative [5]. *The Telegraph*, in an editorial by Sunanda K. Datta Ray, 4th October 2008 , Vol. XXVII, No.89 wrote – "William Ward, a Christian Missionary and two of his colleagues translated the *Bible* and hymns into Assamese, launched Assam's first news magazine, *Orunodoi*, published dictionaries and grammars, and established that Assamese is a distinct language and not a Bengali dialect... Christianity brought education to Adivasis and Dalits in Bihar, Orissa and Madhya Pradesh resulting in a greater awareness of the legal rights that caste-Hindu land owners, contractors, employers and official denied them.

It was also the gospel and Christian statesmen who introduced and gave momentum to the practice and rule of the law – justice and not power as the ultimate principle of Governance. Vishal Mangalwadi, a reputed scholar and writer notes in his book, *India: The Grand Experiment* – "As early as 1792, William Carey and Charles Grant had identified the law as one of India's greatest needs....the concepts of rule of law, human rights, equality of all citizens are not traditional Indian ideas. We inherited them from the British via Macaulay who is a committed Christian himself.

India cannot even remain one nation, let alone a just nation, if we give up the law".[6]

Cultural fascism and despotism or dictatorship have always rested on the will and power of mortals, who are always in the minority, but posed a serious threat to the majority, i.e. the rest of the community or nation. It is the rule of the law rather than the law of the ruler that ensures a just nation.

On looking at the North East Indian context, Dr. Bareh again notes: "It was Christianity which built bridges between clans and tribes and for tribal with the non-tribal world. They come to the level of sitting for peace talks. It was Christianity that brought head-hunters to peace talks".[7]

Thus, Christianity labours for a philosophical, moral and cultural regeneration of the worldview prevalent in the sub-continent and it is this commitment on the part of Christians and their missions that has played a vital role in building up the modern nation of India, constitutionally committed to the principles of secularism, individual freedom of conscience, equality of people and gender, and constitutional parliamentary democracy.

The Christian Basis

It is worthy to note that imbedded within the Christian doctrine itself is the basis for unity in diversity. When we talked about integration in a pluralistic country like ours, we understand it in terms of a unity existing in diversity. It is not in any one religion, ideology or person (dictatorship), but rather, about co-existence in a multicultural and multi-ethnic setting. Christianity believes in a God who is Three-in-one, a 'Triune' God (The Trinity), Three persons in One Being, (The Father, The Son and The Holy Spirit), distinct from one another but One in being – a perfect pattern of unity in diversity.

Secondly, the Christian faith is based on the *Bible*, and Christians are expected not only to believe, but also to obey what the *Bible* said. In the context of National Integration, the *Bible* is uncompromisingly clear in its stand. In his letter, the Prophet Jeremiah exhorts his people who are in exile in Babylon(593 B.C), to actively seek the peace and prosperity of the country of their exile, and to pray and work toward its well-being (Jer.29:4-13). In the book of Titus 3:1-2, Paul wrote to Titus his fellow worker to – "Remind the people (Christians) to be subject to rulers and authorities, to be obedient, to be ready to do whatever is good, to slander no one, to be peaceable and considerate, and to show true humility toward all men". Paul's letter to Timothy asked the Christians to pray for "Kings and all those in authority, that we may live peaceful and quiet lives in all godliness and holiness"(1st Tim 2:2). From these passages cited here, we can conclude that the *Bible* encourages and direct the followers of Jesus Christ to be people who promote peace and love in the country they live, and to respect and identify with all others who may belong to a culture and faith different from theirs.

Thus, the Christian perspective of National Integration, rooted in the Gospel values of Truth, Justice and Love, finds a parallel in the Democratic, Socialist and Secular India dreamt by social reformers and leaders - Mahatma Phule, Mahatma Gandhi, and the Constitution's Founding Fathers Jawaharlal Nehru and Dr B.R. Ambedkar.

Conclusion

In the history of our nation, Christians have always been viewed with suspicion, and at times, ignorantly labeled as 'foreigners' because Christianity has often been perceived as a foreign religion, and those who followed it as being anti-nationals. With all these negative views, however, Christianity has always been a force to reckon with when it comes to Nation-building and National Integration. May I conclude with the words of Dr. P.S.Jacob who wrote in his

Preface to the book written by M. T. Cherian – Hindutva Agenda and Minority Rights A Christian Response, "Since the vast majority of Hindus are not violent fundamentalists, there is scope for Christians in promoting better human relations and interfaith understanding while upholding Biblical faith with deeper understanding. It is hoped that the reverberating chants of Om Shanti (peace mantra) and the chiming bells of good news of Everlasting peace ushered by Jesus Christ, the Prince of Peace, will find peaceful co-existence in the spirit of religious liberty. May they meet each other amicably over the labyrinth of destructive forces of rising fundamentalism at a personal level and in a public domain ensuring religious freedom as well as contextually secular democracy for people of the Indian subcontinent!."[8]

NOTES AND REFERENCES

1. Quoted by Ebe Sunder Raj , *The Confusion Called Conversion*, (New Delhi:TRACI publications) p.44.
2. *Ibid*, p.45.
3. Dutta, Amlan, *The Gandhian Way*, (Shillong: North Eastern Hill University publication) 1986,p.58.
4. Quoted by Vishal Mangalwadi, *India: the Grand Experiment* (Surrey: Pippa Rann Books, 1997), p.266.
5. Matthew, C.V., "The Church's Role in Nation Building", *Missiology For the 21st Century – South Asian Perspectives*, Ed. Roger E. Hedlund, (Chennai: ISPCK/MIIS, 2004), p. 484.
6. Vishal Mangalwadi, *ibid*, p.260.
7. Ebe Sunder Raj, *ibid*, p.44.
8. Jacob P.S. "Preface" to M. T. Cherian – *Hindutva Agenda and Minority Rights: A Christian Response*. (Bangalore: Centre for Contemporary Christianity, 2007).

8

National Integration:
Role of Christian Educational Institution

—*Richard R.N. Bajpai*

Introduction

Rabindranath Tagore in his poem *"Bharattirtha"* expressed his noble feelings for the cause of integration. This encourages the people of any caste, any creed and any citizen to be embodied with the feelings of "Oneness" and ultimately the integrated Bharatbarsha. India is a home of diverse geographical environments, different religions, a score of languages, hundreds of dialects and profusion of culture. Each of these is recognized for its individual worth and significance. It can be said that the sense of National Integration has recently been under considerable strain because of diverse forces arising from castes, religions and regional considerations. Therefore, there is a widespread demand that effective counter-measuring must be taken to educate the Indian people about the freedom struggle and the value of national movements, the danger of communal and caste fragmentation and need to strength the composite customs and culture of India. It is felt that the present scenario is the failure of educational systems.

It is agreed that education plays a very vital role in "Nation-building". Every country plans and endeavors to implement its policies in education keeping in view its cherished political, social, economic and cultural objectives so that the integration and harmony in the nation may be achieved. We can justifiably be proud of the positive contributions and definite role that the Indian Christian Community has made in the development of education in India. We could have, however, done better in impacting the national outlook towards "National Integration."

Meaning of National Integration

On achieving Independence in 1947, the people of India at once become pledged to build up India into a secular and economic justice. This is the basis of National Integration. Another basis is individual's emotional integration. An individual is emotionally integrated, if he is a well balanced, completely satisfied personality, whose urges, aspirations and emotions are sufficiently submitted and directed towards wealth fruitful channels and who is sufficiently trained in the creed or temperature and tolerance. When we apply this term to nation, the National Integration means bringing about economics, social and cultural difference within tolerable range. It implies doing away on linguistic and cultural differences.

It aims at fostering increasing respect and affection for those belonging to other cultural and ethnic groups. It consists in serving people from emotional prejudices and prepossessions and creates and strengthens in them attributes of patriotism and national pride. Basic loyalties are liberalized and existing antagonism are minimized.

Role of Secular Education

It is agreed that education plays a very vital role in a Nation's Progress and progress is cumulative effect of the different culture, creed, caste and above all educations. Every country plans and endevours to implement its policies in education keeping in view its cherished political, social, economic and cultural objectives.

An ideal democracy to be worthy of its name, depends upon the training of its citizens in the most efficient matter through a planned educational system. A true citizen of a democracy must possess, among other qualities, a genuine love for his country and countrymen, irrespective of all castes, creeds, localities and language differences. He must be a patriot with keen sense of the value of National Integration. India is a land of variety and diversity not only in physical features and climate conditions, but also in respect of language, religion, manners, customs, traditions and folk ways, in the patterns of living prevalent among different sets and localities. Colonial bureaucracy (during the foreign rule) jeopardized Indian education. So the reconstruction of Indian national life in all its spheres, India needs trained man-power, efficient leaders and above all national unity. Education in India must be therefore, take into consideration to solve the problem of National Integration emerged keeping in view the following aims – i) Achievement of knowledge, ii) Retention and transmission of Indian culture, iii) Building of character, iv) Realization and practice of higher values of life, v) Development of personality, vi) Development of social efficiencies, vii) Maintenance of emotional balance, viii) Following of the concept of Integral view of man, ix) Formation of a cultivated society, x) Acceptance of the concept of secularization.

To foster the spirit of Indian National Integration, keeping in view to strengthen the unity and solidarity of Indian people, the first and foremost duty of the educational leaders, social thinkers as well as political personalities is to reorganize the Indian present education systems under the following dimensions: i) Removal of economic inequality, ii) Evaluation of Indian history and culture, iii) Acquaintance with different Indian languages, iv) Preparation of need-based text books, v) Simplification of grammatical construction of different Indian languages, vi) Arrangement for population education, vii) Observation of national days, viii) Proper use of mass media, ix) Maintenance of good public relations, x) Erasing out the religious orthodox, xi) Safeguard Indian constitution, xii) Strengthening the role of teachers and educator, engaged in respective areas of educational fields in shouldering the fostering of the sprit of National Integration among the coming generations of India as whole.

Approval of Value-based Education in National Integration

There was a time when India produced both spiritual and intellectual giants in various walks of life. Swami Vivekananda represents at least the best educated Indian and with his knowledge of western thought and experience of the Indian Spirituality. Even today after 100 years this personality draws homage from people of all walks, religions, culture and countries and must be taken seriously as we enter the age of globalization.

Swamiji personified two main principles – i) Divinity: man is divine spiritual being, and ii) Oneness of the universe (there is a unity running through this universe). The response he got on the world stage proves that we can ill afford to ignore these two principles in our educational systems. Essentially education at home, at schools and colleges has to make a concerted effort to raise from animal to human and eventually to divine level while allowing canalization of his psycho-physical energies. So first of all the whole education has to be *value based education* in the sense that it should make the person a purpose of life, individual and cosmic and of the process to realize the goal. The most scientific and the most educated twentieth century has succeeded in dehumanization of man. So the remedy that it has in education is for the humanization of man that elevates him free from his sensual life to spiritual life.

Value, based education starts from family. There is a proverb "Charity begins at home". Parents should give the children strength and habits to their mutual love. A house is not called home till it is taken care of by the mother. A good mother equals hundred teachers. The role of teacher in this value education can't be underestimated. A teacher practices what he preaches. He must lead an ideal life worth imitating, both inwardly and outwardly. The real thought of integration has been cropped up from the family disciplines.

Our day to day works are always influenced by childhood education. The values which we have adopted since our childhood are bases of mental soundness which keep in mind in order. Actually this helps a human being to keep the harmony in the society and utmostly helps on National Integration.

Evangelistic Engagement on National Integration

Through our institutions the wider society experiences our community and faith. The spiritual status of our institutions, therefore, influences the attitude of the society towards our community. It is imperative, therefore, to ensure that our schools and colleges do not bear false witness to our faith. The spiritual renewal of our institutions is crucial to our evangelistic engagement with the society.

We need to be 'good and faithful' custodians of the minority rights that we claim and exercise. Article 30(1) of the Indian Constitution is aimed at empowering minority communities to preserve their distinctive cultures and identities as well as to educate, develop and empower their members. A community that remains educationally backward is a burden on the land. Our calling, in contrast, is to be 'a blessing on the land' (Gen. 12: 1-2). Developing and empowering the members of one's own community is not communalism. It is true patriotism. It is, indeed, a national duty. Invoking minority rights, while disowning the responsibilities towards the community implicit in them, is dishonest and hypocritical.

Essentials of Christian Education

The one clear and overarching purpose that underlies the Christian mission in education is to evangelize the society. To 'evangelize' is to infuse the society with the gospel – the 'evangel'- values. Our model for this is God himself, who has been engaged in evangelizing the world since the fall of Adam and Eve. St. John lays bare the essence of this evangelization. "God so loved the world that he gave his only begotten son. . ." (Jn. 3: 16). Evangelization is an outworking of godly love. We seek to evangelize because we share God's love for the world and seek to express in context. Our enterprise in education becomes Christian when it is God's love for the world that we seek through it. This biblical insight is all the more crucial, given the epidemic of hatred sought to be spread by the agents of communalism, oppression and intimidation. This national epidemic needs to be seen in the light of our own failure to propagate a culture of love through education. We are being afflicted by our failure to evangelize the Indian society; as against 'converting' individuals here and there.

We are today carrying on with our mission to educate in the midst of large-scale collapse and as a matter-of-fact violation of basic values. The function of values is two-fold. First, values safeguard the value of life. He who violates values experiences an instantaneous cheapening of his own person. Second, values safeguard the cohesion and health of a society. Jesus did not ask us to establish institutions or to educate. We are to 'preach and heal' (Mt. 10: 7, 8). Education is not in itself the goal; it is only a tool. Our idea and practice of education must have a healing effect on the society. Our educational institutions must be to our society what our hospitals are to our institutions. They must cater to the health and wholeness of our society. Christian education, without due emphasis on value education is, therefore, woefully inadequate no matter how excellent the results we produce and how prestigious we become thereby.

Mission, whether it be in the domain of education, health care or social enlistment, is an outreach in love. To love is to give, as well as to bring out, the best from the object of love. We are to understand 'the best' that we are to give, or bring out, through education from a biblical, and not a worldly, perspective. In a commercial sense, serving the partisan interests of the privileged could seem 'the best'. 'The best,' as Jesus sees it, is set out in the Nazareth Manifesto (Lk. 4:18). Preaching the Good News to the poor, opening the eyes of the blind and leading people to freedom and empowerment comprise that missional or educational 'best'. This 'best' brings out 'the best' from the society as a whole; whereas commercialized education tends to aggravate inequalities and undermine the health and wholeness of the society. This is the prophetic element in the biblical vision for education.

Nurturing and propagating a caring culture is an important emphasis in evangelizing the society, especially in the present day context. Respect for the incalculable worth of every human being is the kernel of the caring culture. We care for what we value. Also, caring imparts value to what we care for. Education is an exercise in value-addition. Education affirms the intrinsic worth and activates the hidden potentials of a human being. This is a basic human need and a fundamental human right. A sustained focus on the intrinsic worth of every human being is the hallmark of Jesus' teaching. By teaching us, "Whatever you did for one of the least of these brothers of mine, you do to me," (Mt.

25:40). Jesus takes human worth beyond all man-made labels of caste, class or culture. It is not an accident, therefore, that the Christian mission of education endeavours to transcend the 'walls' of caste, class and creed and engages the challenge of social transformation.

Underlying Christian education is the recognition that God is the primary source of all worth. Whatever is oriented to God is of immeasurable worth. Conversely, whatever is alienated from God loses its worth. Hence it is that Christian education seeks to 'empower' human beings through godliness. Warehousing of information, as such, is not Christian education. Developing a personality oriented to life, rather than to death (Mtt.7: 13, 14) is the prime goal of Christian education.

A preferential option for the poor and the oppressed is basic to Christian education. The spread of the gospel has been, always and everywhere, accompanied by liberation and economic empowerment. Regrettably, this upliftment is often caricatured, by those who feel their vested interests threatened by it, as 'allurement'. As the victims of socio-economic degeneration embrace the faith and 'become the new creation' (2 Cor. 5: 17) and they give up their dark, senseless and superstitious ways and are empowered through education, the material circumstances of their lives improve dramatically. This is sought to be misrepresented as allurement. The Gospel of Jesus Christ is a catalyst for human liberation and empowerment. That is the 'Good News to the poor" that we are to proclaim.

The purpose of 'empowerment-through-education,' is to enable us to be good human beings. Arming and equipping a person to be a selfish predator or a social parasite is not 'empowerment,' but disempowerment, from a biblical angle. To be empowered is to be able to do justice to the uniqueness of one's creation: "in the image and likeness of God" (Gen. 1:

26, 27). It is this that we have traditionally referred to as 'character building'. In our desperate bid to make education more and more market-oriented, or to vocationalize it in the interests of livelihood, we are losing sight of this core Christian emphasis.

Church, Institution and Society

How we relate to our socio-political context is a matter of crucial importance to our mission to educate. St. Paul alerts us that there are two strategies. We can either conform to the dominant trends in the given context. Or we become agents of transformation. Every society coerces its members to conform. Conformation amounts to renunciation of freedom: freedom particularly to pursue a radical mission. The domination of the upper caste and economic elite is the hallmark of the Indian society. Corruption and commercialization are to the advantage of this tiny but all-important segment. There are material gains to be got by catering to them. This generates huge temptations to compromise our Christian vision and mission, both of which seem too idealistic and impractical. It makes sense that we behave like Romans while in Rome, but we cannot be Romans and Christians at the same time! When we behave like Romans and, at the same time, claim the privileges of being Christians (cf. Minority Rights) we are seen as hypocrites, which is a serious matter.

Bureaucratic hostility, legislative harassment and negative attitudes to the minorities, especially in view of the influence they wield in the society through education, are becoming noticeably hostile. Our institutions around the country face chronic bureaucratic harassment. They are put to enormous difficulties even in respect of routine matters. Many of them have to fight debilitating and wasteful legal battles to protect themselves from those very functionaries of the State who are meant to facilitate them. Institutions that try to be transparent and upright, and therefore do not dole out favours to *babudom* and the powerful elements in the society, come under even greater harassment. Often, our educational administrators suffer in silence. There is a need to stand by them, strengthen their hands and to mitigate their suffering.

Conclusion

Our Christian missions to upheaval the national integration through education and through evangelization have come to a point when India is facing a lot of problems in integration and harmony. Outreach is the hallmark of the Christian missionary response to the world. To reach out is to minister to those who cannot come to us on their own strength. Another key New Testament word is "koinonia". Its root meaning has to do with that which is common. It is used in the New Testament with no dichotomy between spiritual and material. It is used to desirable new life experience in the Church as common both with God and with each other, the koinonia, sharing the Holy Spirit. (2 Corinthians 13:13).

The following few lines should be a statement of Christian Institution as our principles of mission towards "National Integration:"

1. Telling the Good News of Jesus,
2. Calling people to faith in humanistic approaches,
3. Caring for individual people and communities,
4. Sharing the task of education for social and spiritual development and struggling for a just world,
5. Being alongside the poor: becoming friends with people of different cultures and faith,
6. Caring of earth,

7. Building partnership with Government for making contribution towards our Goal of Nation's peace and harmonization.

REFERENCES

Swami Vivekananda, *Call to the Nation* (Advaita Ashrama, 1976).

Swami Tattwa Jnanananda, *Value based Education* (Education Society and Environment, Academic Staff College, University of Burdwan, 17th July, 1996).

M.R. Banerjee, *National Integration in India* (Education Society and Environment, Academic Staff College, University of Burdwan, 17th July, 1996).

R.V. Siva Kumar, *Education-the Retrospect Graduate and Respect in Education* Vol. XXVII, No 4, October – December, 1997.

Church of North India; A proposed policy in three days Workshop at Nainital Policy on Education (draft) attended by the author.

9

The Contribution of Christianity to Nation-Building

H. Iangrai

A history of about 2000 years ago fulfills the eternal plan of God for peace and welfare. The birth of Christ is a sign of victory over the Devil and his works, which was defaced by sin and worldliness. Jesus Christ, sinless and blameless paid, redeemed and restores the right relationship with God the Creator and with fellow human beings. He is the answer to all humanity's problems and national crisis. It is he who is the example and provider of all human need and national development. He served as an ideal master builder.

Origin of Christianity in India

Christianity in India started in the first half of the first century AD when one of the disciples of Jesus, Thomas reached in India in around the year 52. Though there was an account that he was brought to India by King Gundaporus who was assigned to build a palace but Thomas built a spiritual foundation, but a story that he came to Kerala and started his mission there appeared to have popular support.

His death at the hands of angry local Priests at Mylapore, Chennai in c.72 earned him the first martyr in India. Therefore, Christianity in India is about 2000 years old.

Christian Missionaries and their Activities

The noble work of Christian missionaries in India is recorded in the year 1575 when the Portuguese established elementary schools, colleges, orphanages and printing press. They centered their activities in Goa and around Bombay, Daman and Diu.

The 16th century also marked the entry of Danes colonial traders that facilitated the arrival of the first Protestant mission in the early eighteenth Century. The pioneer Lutheran Tranqubar missionaries established several primary schools and Teachers training schools. Ziegenbalg also composed Tamil grammar and dictionary.

Women too got their first education centre in 1818 at Chinsura, and then followed at Serampore, Bombay and other places. Women received instruction in literacy, geography, needle works etc. Women can perform duties not only at home but also actively engaged in the social and economic life. No doubt, the Christian missionaries had their seeds sown in the Indian soil, though they passed through their services not without difficulties. The reasons had been due to the ignorance, prejudice, misunderstanding and resistance of the people. Yet, Christian missionaries laid the ideal and effective foundation of modern system of education in India.

Christian Activities in Meghalaya

In Meghalaya, the light of learning dawned in the first part of the 19th century. Thomas Jones presented to the Khasis the written script. He is called the Father of Khasi alphabet. He took a great pain to teach literacy among the Khasis. It took a long time and after a long struggle the script was introduced. Some of the problems faced by the Christian missionaries in the field of literacy and education are (i) the traditional belief that the learning of literacy would be a curse to the society, (ii) women would become barren if they go to school, (iii) the foreign belief would cause anger to the gods and so on. His initiative is the permanent victory that can never be erased in the literacy history. A great tribute also goes to David Scott (1816) and American Baptist missionaries that have introduced education, peace and stability in a trouble-torn region, health and general welfare in Garo hills besides the efforts of the Welsh Presbyterian mission among the Khasis; then followed by Roman Catholic and other Christian missions. It is to be noted here that the Education Commission (1964 – 66) has recommended development of language including mother tongue as the means towards national integration. Therefore, the role that Christian missionaries has done especially in the area of education of the natives has contributed to national integration.

Philosophical Background of Christianity

The question may be asked, why was Christianity involved in such many social works or activities? It may be answered that this is the example and commands of its leader, Jesus Christ. He did many good works, got the approval in the sight of God the Father and among men. The *Bible* says that Christian should be subjected to authorities. Authorities may be God's or human government. It says "Let every soul be subjected to higher powers" i.e. principalities, powers, magistrates as well as the ordinance of men for God's sake (Heb 13:1 – 2; Titus 3:1; I Pet 2:13). The reason is because they are not a terror to good works. Christ also acknowledged to pay tribute to Ceasar (Matthew 22:12). Paul also had to accept severe punishment in order to prevent anarchy and assure order (Acts 16:22 – 24, 37, 38). Jeremiah also called upon his peoples to pray for the peace of the land of their exile (Jer 29:7). St. Paul also urged all Christians to pray for kings and for all that are in authority (I Tim 2:1 – 2).

Principles of Christianity and Mahatma Gandhi

Mahatma Gandhi, the father of the nation, had similar views to that of Christianity. Some of the quotations below are examples.

(a) *Godly nature*: Gandhi said "His (God's) presence is proved not only by extraneous evidence but in the transformed conduct and character of those who have felt the real presence of God within". On the other hand the *Bible* says "Therefore, if any man be in Christ; he is a new creature; old things are passed away; behold all things are become new. (II Cor 5:17).

The above statements emphasize the need of the nature of God in the personal life. It is only this nature of God that can make the people think and do good. In other words, if God is present in the lives of the people the conduct and manners of the people would be no longer selfish or devilish. God always directs his people to do good. As the saying goes "a good tree brings not forth corrupt fruit; neither doth a corrupt tree bring forth good fruits".

(b) *To Bless others*: In the words of Mahatma Gandhi "what though we have different bodies? We have but one soul. The rays of the Sun are many through refraction, but they have the same source". On the other hand, the *Bible* says there are different kinds of gifts but the same spirit; there are different kinds of working but the same God works all of them and in all men. Now to each one the manifestation of the spirit is given for the common good (I Cor 12 : 4 – 7). It can be said that as the Sun gives life and energy, it rises on the evil and on the good and sends rain on the just and unjust, the service of God's people always is to bless others.

(c) *To love others*: Gandhiji stated "We love and serve God when we love and serve his creatures. Service of all therefore should be the first fundamental of every human being .... Man becomes great in the degree in which he works for the welfare of his fellowmen". On the other hand the *Bible* says "Any one, then who knows the good he ought to do and does not do it, sin (James 4:17). Further", no man hath seen God at any time. If we love one another, God dwelled in us and his love is perfected in us (I John 4), it is because of this love that Jesus gave himself to suffer and to die at the cross. Mahatma Gandhi too had his cruel death at the hand of the enemy. The nation needs love to sacrifice for others and to bind the people together. Killing and burning of human lives and property in some parts of the country show that love is lacking. It is the duty of the peace loving citizens to pray for the peace of the nation.

(d) *Value of the Soul*: In the statement of Gandhi "If it does not benefit man to lose his soul to gain the whole world, it does not likewise benefit a nation to gain the whole world and lose its soul". On the other hand the *Bible* says "For what is a man profited if he shall gain the whole world, and loses his own soul? Or what shall a man give in exchange for his soul" (Matt 16:28). Both statements lay emphasis on gain by right doing as an eternal value whereas gain by wrong doing will damn forever. It does not profit a man gaining honor, riches or power if it not by righteous means or the means that is not approved by God. It will be forever condemned and put to nothing. The nation needs righteous people; who think and do righteously and of high moral integrity.

Constitutional Principles

The Constitution of India has provided the right for all religions or religious denominations to establish and to develop. Art. 25 says 'Subject to public order, morality and health and to the other provisions of this part; all persons are equally entitled to freedom of conscience and the right freely to profess, practice and propagate religion'. Realizing the value of moral and spiritual character the Constitution encourages to develop and to spread religious principles. The restrictions imposed by some groups and their violent behaviour are not conducing to a healthy development of secularism in the country. It also shows lack of concern and value towards fellowmen and it is a crime against humanity. Religious fanatics in the form of killing and persecution should be condemned by all right thinking citizens. The Government should also ensure equality before law as enshrined in the Indian Constitution (Art. 14).

The Constitution also envisages in Art 30 (i) All minorities whether based on religion or language shall have the right to establish and administer educational institutions of their choice and Art. 30 (ii) state "The State shall not in granting aids to educational institutions discriminate against any educational institution on the ground that it is under the management of a minority whether based on religion or language."

About 50,000 educational institutions have been established by Christian communities in India and 80 % of them in rural India. These institutions have far national constructive and integrative implications.

Christianity Falsely Accused

Many sad events that had happened in the country have been blamed upon Christianity. It has been usually carried out by ulterior motives either to gain vote or to gain monetary benefits. Some instances are given in the following:

A. *The Poover Riot*

Poover is a place near Trivandrum. The riot took place in 1972. In this year there was a discontentment between the fishermen and middlemen. The issue was on increasing the profit share by the fishermen. The fishermen had been working very hard, day and night for the catch of fish but the major share of the profit went to the middlemen who worked as trawler, moneylender, and merchants and so on. Actually the target was against the middlemen but in order to involve the feeling and emotion it broke out in the form of religious issue. In reality, not only Christians but also Hindus and Muslims were in the same category. The conflict broke out between Christians and Muslims. There has been a great loss of lives and property. After a thorough investigation it was found that the cause was simply a conflict between the fishermen and the middlemen.

B. *Similar event took place in 1968*

The rumor spread that the Muslim had thrown a stone on a temple during their procession. Lot of Muslim assets had been destroyed. The target was mainly to those businessmen. Later, the cause was found to be false. There was no proof of stone throwing and no one came out to witness the event of stone throwing. It was later found out that the clash between the two groups was simply in regard to economic superiority.

Another rumor spread was that a pig was let loose in Moradabad mosque in 1982. The rumor adds fuel to the fire on the Hindu-Muslim conflict. Many bidi industries were destroyed. But actually no pig could substantiate in the proof. Similar thing happened during the time of Indira Gandhi assassination, the news went that the Sikhs distributed sweet on her death. There was no such event and it was simply a rumor and the motive was simply to satisfy the self- interested people who do not bother the value of lives of innocent beings.

C. The declaration by the RSS General Secretary on May 27, 1986 in Pune that the Hindus were losing their powers and the Government was playing at the hands of the minorities was a direct inflictment on other religious minority groups. The statement has generated the emotion and sentiment of the majority group to develop a prejudice against the minorities. It is ridiculous to consider that the 85 per cent of the population were losing their powers and the 15 per cent had gained supremacy. These inflammatory statements should be refuted at once. Majority are always on the advantage in a democratic setup.

Christians sometimes are treated at least as non-Indians. The third week of September 2008 was a memorable event in the history of India. Christians at Bangalore, Mangalore and other places were brutally injured, tortured, and mercilessly destroyed by certain fanatic groups. Conversion to another religion should and always be the will and decision of an individual; it can never be compelled or forced. Using of force is a violation to human right and against God himself. In this event 20 churches were burnt and 200 houses destroyed.

On 23rd January 1999 an Australian Baptist missionary, Graham Staines and his two sons were burnt alive in a jeep at Monoharpur, Orissa. As a missionary, Graham was involved in the care of the orphans and of other humanitarian services.

The killing of the religious leader of the Visva Hindu Parishad, Swami Laxmananda which was claimed by the underground outfit was led to the outrage against Christians. Christians in Orissa had been to be punished for the crime committed by unknown. About 50,000 people displaced, 4000 houses burnt and Christians has to flee for their lives; Christian houses and institutions were also ransacked and burnt. Though some may say that it is politically motivated as election is round the corner but Christians had to suffer for such political and economic reasons.

Studies in India

Some studies conducted in India would also reveal some

light on the nature and role of Christianity in the country. Forrest (1981) reported that the conversion of scheduled caste into Christianity during the 19th and 20th centuries was also a social movement aimed at the liberation from the stigma attached to the untouchables. The aim of the church is to integrate the marginalized sections so that they have a voice and just share in the decision-making process.

Fernandes (1988) pointed out that the church banned class distinction. He said just after Independence, Trichy and Pondicherry had already prohibited class distinction.

Neil (1964) also revealed that the fisher folk communities of Kerela and Tamil Nadu turned to Christianity in order to free themselves from the merchants who exploited them.

The Gujarat agitation which took place on the issue that Christianity was getting special advantage and the non Christian were deprived off is also another accusation against Christianity. The Chief Minister of Karnataka (2008) expressed suspicion on the aids by foreign agencies for Christianity. He accused Christianity on the ground that the motive behind foreign aid might be to woo people to join the religion. Similar allegation was made that Christianity promises material benefits, and method of forced conversions were used. Obviously Christian had never acted against people's conscience. It is unfortunate if inflammatory statements or remarks in India's vulnerable situations. Such should neither be encouraged nor entertained in the longer interest of peace and communal harmony.

Role of Christianity in National Development

Most Christian denominations appeal from time to time to its believers to exercise free and fair election. For instance, the Nagaland Baptist Church Council (1981 -82) resolved that election in the state should be in a better and fair manner. They appealed to citizens to faithfully carry out and on the valuable decision taken and to make election a successful one. It highlighted that churches and associations, public, students, government, officials and candidates themselves establish a unity, one spirit, one goal, one mind and one vision for the welfare of the people.

The Nagaland Baptist Church Council also expressed resentment against duplication of names in electoral list, house creeping, private canvassing, character assassination, inducement, or purchase, corruption, rivalries, enmity and so on. They also declared under age voting as a sin.

In Meghalaya, the Garo Baptist Convention (2008) has issued notices to voters to select candidates with integrity, honesty, and moral character. The General Secretary stated "We want to make the people aware that as Christians we are duty bound to fight against corruption. Second;ly, educated candidates who have a clear fvision for the people should be selected. Thirdly, it warned "Beware of those who thinks about personal gain, power and position. Do not cast votes for those who make empty promises. Fourthly, to avoid any negative comments and in verbal duels if you do not like the candidate. Fifthly, not to go to the candidate's residence to eat or to ask for money for by doing this, you will be forcing the candidate to recover the expenses for the money meant for the development. Sixthly, to refrain from asking the candidates for money for any religious purposes or enjoying feasts during Christmas and New Year.

Seventhly, it asked the voters to assess the performances of the sitting legislators who were seeking re-election. Another important advice was that Let God" fearing persons who would work for the development of the state and be people are elected. No Untouchability.

The Church is like a family. There is no discrimination on ground of religion. Christianity support Abolition of untouchability (Art. 17). Jesus touched the leper who was unclean (Mark 1:40 – 45) Jesus was bound by the law of compassion. Jesus also took the little children no matter from what background they came and blessed them. (Matt 19:13) He also commanded the believers to lay hands on the sick and they shall recover (Mark 16:16) In Christ there is no more difference whether Greek or gentiles (I Cor 12:13) Jesus also talked with the wicked woman, asked her for a cup of water.. He also gave her the answer of the living water. It is through the Samaritan woman that the villagers came and met him for peace and solution. In India many outcastes and lower castes received human face and dignity. For instance, the Dit of the Churha, an untouchable community in Punjab accepted the good news and helped 58,000 to live with respect and human value.

Deliverance

Jesus also delivered abnormal people. He released the demonized at Gadara, who had spent night and days in graveyard naked. After receiving sense of mind the proclaimed and spread the news that is Jesus who delivered him. Christians continue this humble serve to pray for the sick and heal different kinds of sickness, rebuke the power of darkness and bring deliverance. Concern for the abnormal and helpless is a noble service. It is through the contact and inner experience that people accepted the truth, the way and life.

Childbirth

Before the advent of Christianity in these hills, the method of delivering a child was traditional and unscientific, which may cause different kinds of complication? The women and the child were not properly treated and there was no guarantee for total health. The tools used were bamboo, basket, and leaves and so on. The traditional quack used to help in the delivering process. But with the introduction of new method by missionaries followed by training and education of local youth, appropriate methods are adopted. It is through these better methods that many unbelievers came and gets converted.

Feast for the Birth

The primitive people used to spend a huge amount of resources for the birth of a new child, but Christianity involved less money and the formality is also less. Modern feasts are followed according to the economic capacity of each family not by way or ordinance or compulsion. The Christian methods are more convenient and economically sound.

Communication

Before the coming of the Britishers in the hills the Khasis had frequent contact with Hindus and Muslims. But, not much change took place. The 18th and 19th centuries marked a sea change in the state. The adoption of Christian way of life has transformed the society from a savage to a well civilized society. The Christian missionaries have changed the static, traditional, rigid society into a moving, modernized dynamic and vibrant society. It enables the people to fearlessly interact and courageously express their opinion. It also widens the relationship not only with different part of the country but also all round the globe.

Marriage

Marriage is a sacred act of covenanted partners. The method for joining the two together in the past was through arguments. If the argument failed to arrive at a positive note there would be no marriage. Man among the Khasis was known as nine colors; that mean he could marry as many women as he wished. The practice was found among the Khasis. In Garo Hills, the method was done by catching the bridegroom while he was in the field. Due to these methods which were not out of real love it seemed has led to many families broken and the burden was added to the girl's family and to the clan. With the coming of Christianity, polygamous was stopped and monogamous is adopted. Fornication and adultery is a grievous sin, and he who does not keep his family well is more than an unbeliever. Early marriage also ceased. Christian's rules also prohibit marrying a near relative. Above all, the Christian way of life has brought peace and welfare in the family and the society as a whole.

Health

Christianity aimed not only for spiritual development but also for physical development (III John 1) Robert Gordon Hospital, Nazareth Hospital and others are example. At present there are many medical institutions like dispensaries, colleges, training institutions, nursing homes and so one established by Christian community all over India.

Prior to the coming of Christian missionaries the patients used to consult local herbal practitioners. They also used to break the egg in order to find out the cause of the disease. They also have to sacrifice to appease their gods who caused the sickness. Among the Garos, the more the sickness the more is the fury of the gods and goddesses. When the Christian distributed medicine they were wondering how the tablet could do wonders. Missionaries also taught the rules of health and hygiene. The old belief of ai bih, ai thlen, ai ksuid, ai sniew (Giving of evils) disappeared with the coming of Christianity.

Also, among the Garos the common practice to heal the disease was to apply the juice of a tree. They also had to sacrifice to appease their gods. But with the coming of David Scot and Bishop Heber, then Valentine William Hurley assistant apothecary who also served as a teacher and doctor the Garrow were much grateful and then cherished to Christian faith. The American Baptist missionaries realized from the beginning that as Christ preached the gospel and healed the sick so also they followed the same way in their ministry in Garo land.

Abortion

Christianity supports the laws against humanity like abortion or deprivation of the right to live. It is a sin against God and humanity. The *Bible* says that shedding of innocent blood is a sin (Proverb 6:16 – 17). It also say that God called people right from the mother's womb (Isaiah 49:1, 5) and it is God himself who formed babies in the belly. God designed people right from the mother's womb (Genesis 25:21-26). And God accordingly preserved John the Baptist, Jesus when they were in their mothers' wombs. It may be said that the church stands against abortion and support the Pre-conception and Pre-natal Diagnostic Techniques (Prohibition of Sex Selection) Act 1994.

Other Contributions

Christians all over are always involved in the reconstruction process. During the tsunami even in southern part of India, earthquake of Gujarat, various flood in Orissa, Bihar and others and other emergencies; the name and contribution of Christianity to have come forward to set up relief camp, distribute cloth, medicine, and other relief materials have been felt to those who have had the encounter and eyes to understand. Christians also show their sensitiveness, and prompt action in rescuing, restoring and bringing life to normalcy. The contribution in cash and kind are innumerable and indescribable.

Upward Mobility

It is a natural and social tendency to move higher on the social ladder in the society. The tendency is more when the eyes are opened and the understanding enlightened. The primitive people had experienced rigidity, closeness or narrowness. They were limited to a certain class or boundary. This belief and practice had hindered the growth and development of the personality and the society. But, with the coming of Christianity all people are made free. There is no class or race distinction in Christianity; all are one in Christ Jesus. It seems that the rigid and traditional condition of the past has propelled the people to move to Christianity for education and modernization.

I would like to present the resolution of the Reconstituted National Integration Council held at Vigyan Bhavan on 31st Aug 2005 in order to achieve a culture of integration.

By upholding the dignity of every citizen including his conscience.

Ensuring quality of life including basic education, concern for girl child and female foetus.

Development with a human face by empowering specially the marginalized and the twice discriminated such as women, dalit Christian, urban homeless.

Compassion towards rural India and its poverty. Poverty with its degradation is a national disaster.

In conclusion, Christianity stands through the test of time and forces in many countries they are born and brought up or are placed. The principles and the urges to serve others have been at time been in conflict with other communities/ groups. But from the above discussion it can be said that the patience and endurance and tirelessly striving effort and struggle for the betterment of mankind and of the particular nation owe a great deal towards nation-building and development. It is only eternity that can only value its reward.. Press on toward the mark and the high calling.

10

Christianity: Role in National Integration

—Dominic Jala

Introduction

Let me begin my reflections by quoting our Honourable Prime Minister, Shri Manmohan Singh's speech at the 14th National Integration Council meeting on 13th October, 2008.[1]

> "We are meeting at a time when our nation is facing many and simultaneous challenges. Responding to challenges, at best of times, is a very complex exercise. It gets even more complicated when the security calculus is a matrix of many imponderable factors.
>
> Throughout India's modern history, our country has seen many challenges, challenges that would have fragmented nations of lesser intrinsic strength or lesser will. I have, therefore, no fear of our ability to withstand the current challenges. I do believe, however, that it is important at times like this to look within ourselves, and draw upon our national genius to overcome problems that appear at times to overwhelm us."

The Challenges

This is the context also in which we are asked to understand how Christianity can act as a force to build communities of peace and harmony. But many challenges have arisen and these have to be taken into account by anyone who wants to engage in promoting integration.

The present day challenges have been succinctly presented by our Prime Minister himself: (1) to cultivate the consciousness that "in seeking short-term remedies the fundamental underpinnings of our inclusive society are not undermined;" (2) the need to maintain a strong sense of nationhood and to fight the "increasing fissiparous tendencies" that have made their appearances especially in North East, Jammu and Kashmir, in Orissa, Karnataka and elsewhere too; (3) The attempts that outside forces make to break the unity of the country especially by using ethnicity and religion as arguments (as in Orissa, Karnataka, Maharashtra...). We are therefore called to strive together to build a united and integral nation.

India has been known and admired for preserving its "composite culture." But, as the Prime Minister points out again, *"Perhaps, the most disturbing and dangerous aspect to-day is the assault on our composite culture."* Even within a historical narrative that focuses on wars, defeats and victories, we cannot fail to see the larger picture of a sub-continent in which people of all castes, communities, religions and languages lived together peacefully in the interaction among peoples cultures imbibe the best from each other. "Yet to-day, we see fault-lines developing between, and among, communities."

If in North, Central, East and South India the question of integration is an important challenge, it is more so for the diverse cultural groups that form North Eastern Indian society. This stems both from the stress given to ethnic identity and from the kind of alienation that especially hill tribes feel from the rest of the country.

While Christianity came to this subcontinent in the first century of the Christian Era, Northeast India received the Christian faith relatively in recent times only in the 19th century. This has made many false Indian integrationists tend to suspect the loyalty and the sense of identification of the tribal Christian people.

The Christian Response

Understanding and Accepting Diversity

"No other country in the world embraces the extraordinary mixture of ethnic groups, the profusion of mutually incomprehensible languages, the varieties of topography and climate, the diversity of religions and cultural practices, and the range of levels of economic development that India does."[2] "and yet India is more than the sum of its contradictions. It is a country held together, in the words of its first prime minister, Jawaharlal Nehru, "by strong but invisible threads.."[3] It is our task to get to these invisible threads and weave a society that is tolerant and constructive.

We acknowledge the variety that characterizes this rich tapestry of our Indian ethos. It "has been shaped by remarkably diverse forces: ancient Hindu tradition, myth, and scripture; the impact of Islam and Christianity; and two centuries of British colonial rule. The result is unique, not just because of the variety of contemporary influences available in India, but because of the diversity of its heritage."[4] We, with our various Christian traditions form an integral part of this heritage of the country.

We live in a global world but which has learned to accept diversity and the many possibilities that such diversity can offer to the cultures of the world.

Christian Churches in this country are placed in a very advantageous position to show that it is possible to live in unity with all the diversity that we experience. Christian communities are found in all the cross-sections of our Indian society today. The power of the Christian faith enables not only to live through this diversity but to be greatly enriched by it. There is a force to bind us that lies beyond one's ethnic and cultural identity.

Drawing Strength from Our Cultures and Religion

Our cultures, far from dividing us from others should help us to reach out and enrich others. "Every community falls back on its culture (its belief and value-systems, traditions, practices, guiding norms, priorities) as an abiding resource to build on."[5] People who are rooted in their cultures are able to get to their cultural heritage to resolve problems. "Tribal values like a communitarian sense, honesty, industriousness, resolution of problems through dialogue, respect for traditions are great assets in a community."[6] Christian leaders can strengthen such positive resources but also challenge their own communities by "opening out new visions and possibilities to their people...That is what Jesus did when he affirmed, 'You have heard it said—do not kill—but I tell you...'. In fact, the period of rapid transition is a time for the re-evaluation of existing traditions and prevailing concepts; it is a time for their rejection or re-acceptance, an occasion for further deepening of ideas, widening of horizons, and redefining of roles. That is why fresh, relevant, insightful re-interpretations of cultural elements in context are necessary from time to time."[7] We can use cultural symbols effectively not to drive people against each other but to bring about peace and understanding.

Religion is often invoked as motive for divisive and violent action. No religion in its true essence should lead to intolerant violence. Rather religion contains within it enough power to make us strive for true human and social development. "Religion and religious sensitivity are the factories that manufacture morality that society and business both need to function. Faith is authoritative, unconditionally normative. Religion, which is called the depth memory of humankind, gives depth, meaning, unconditional values, norms, motivations, ideals. It is the spiritual home of security, trust and hope."[8]

In the worst of times for Christians who are persecuted what wins is not retaliatory action but positive and assertive presence not only of those who suffer but of the whole Christian community. The assertion by Christians of what they believe fundamentally and the rightful claim to their constitutional rights comes from the moral position that the Gospels enjoin on every follower of Christ. (Cf. *Mt.* 5:38-48: the law of forgiveness).

Balancing Ethnicity

Among the factors that are blamed for a disintegration of society is the insistence on identity, especially ethnic, cultural or religious identity. In its neutral form we can understand ethnic identity as "the subjective and symbolic use of certain elements of culture by a group of people to differentiate themselves from other groups."[9]

Ethnic differences can give rise to conflicts when there is competition for resources, or contention for power, especially where power controls resources. When there is a perception that a group is marginalized or denied its fair share of what is available, the differences can even be invoked as motive for conflicts that could lead to violence.[10]

Over insistence on ethnic difference can lend itself to forces who want to artificially generate an atmosphere of hatred and violence. Or even, as the Prime Minister Manmohan Singh rightly points out, "short-term narrow political ends are driving some of us to encourage forces of divisiveness that are today threatening the unity of our people."

Christianity does not destroy any ethnic identity. Rather through various means, as is apparent in North Eastern India, it has contributed to an enrichment of the various ethnic cultural groups.

The Christian message draws from our commitment to the person of Christ who became a man in a specific cultural environment but transcended the narrow boundaries of such an environment. The apostle Paul, was the clearest exponent of this universality of the power of Jesus Christ. When narrow minded groups tried to demand that followers of Christ had to submit to the religious and cultural traditions of the Jews first, Paul stood for the open world in which Christ is to be received age after age. In Christ all barriers are broken. But we see that the message of Christ does not do away with the differences between communities. Rather these differences do not impede the Christians from reaching out to each other and to everyone else. Christ heals us of ethnocentrism (Cf. *Gal* 3:28).

The Diginity of the Human Person

To speak of a tolerant and open society is to focus on some very basic beliefs that the Christian Gospel insists upon. Among these, one of the central elements is our firm belief in the dignity of the human person.

When there is violence in any form of conflict, the natural outcome is blindness to the sacredness of life and of God's gifts in nature. Driven by hate and blinded by prejudices, people lose sight of this fundamental fact of creation.

The Christian message calls us to work "diligently for fundamental decisions to be taken in economic and political affairs, both on the national and international level which will everywhere recognize and satisfy the right of all to a human and social culture in conformity with the dignity of the human person without any discrimination of race, sex, nation, religion or social condition.[11] This flows from our biblical faith first of all in the fundamental unity of all human beings for we all have been created by the one and the same God, no matter what our differences. (*Gen* 1:26-31) Every human person, no matter how degraded he may seem in our eyes, is precious in the eyes of the Lord for he cares for each one of us with great love. (Cf. *Psalm 8; Mt* 6:25-34). This applies universally. Every person is precious because he/she has been redeemed by Christ.

Building up Every Person

National integration is not just the absence of strife among people. Real integration can be realized when all have equal opportunities and when all have the possibility to live decent human lives. We can speak of a national unity only when there is no oppression by one group over the other. When the stronger ones extend a helping hand to the weaker ones, when the minorities do not have to suffer indignities or have to go begging all their life.

The Christian faith impels the believer to work for the integral development of the whole person and thus to address the positive aspects of true national integration. This is the heart of the message that Jesus preached at the synagogue at Nazareth.

> The Spirit of the Lord is upon me,
> Because he has anointed me
> To bring good news to the poor.
> He has sent me to proclaim release to the captives
> And recovery of sight to the blind,
> To let the oppressed go free,
> To proclaim the year of the Lord's favour. (*Lk* 4:18-19).

This is what Jesus did and this becomes the mission statement of all those who claim to follow him. To be redeemed is not just to be counted among those whose souls are saved. To be a believer in Christ is to commit oneself to the very same mission that he undertook.

It is for this reason that Christians cannot cease to work for the marginalized and the oppressed, for the ignorant and the abandoned. Perhaps this is the very cause for opposition shown to the many activities that the Churches undertake especially among the dalits and the tribals. The opposition should not make the Christian communities shirk from their mission which flows from the person of Jesus Christ himself. Rather, the opposition itself shows the meaningfulness of what has been undertaken. The works of social upliftment, of empowerment of the poor, of conscientization, and especially of education have to contribute towards building up a society in which everyone can stand upright and claim one's rightful place in the country.

Promoting the Capacity of People to Think

One of the causes of violent fissures in our society is the incapacity of people to think rationally and act accordingly. When clashes take place rumours are spread, interpretations are given to incidents both by the rumours and even by the media. This reduces the capacity of people to judge sensibly. Usually when violent incidents take place, the first expected action is that the violence is denounced. This is needed because it shows where people stand in such situations but it is not enough.

It is a much more arduous task to get people to think and make right decisions and not to further aggravate the situation. Writing on the role of religious leaders in such situations, Archbishop Thomas Menamparampil advises us to undertake this demanding path which certainly bears much more lasting fruit.

> "Eliciting thought, guiding reflection, being involved in taking the analysis forward, being prepared to revise one's understanding of a situation as it keeps changing, watching out for opportunities for goal-oriented action, strengthening the religious, cultural and human resources for intelligent reflection and purposeful action, bringing together beneficent forces in the community, linking up scattered energies, helping people to put together scattered resources, leading persons and movements to realistic solutions....with a human touch and a human heart....this, in my view, is the central task of religious leaders when they are engaged in public issues. Any public stand they take can only be an external expression of this service." [12]

We deal with people as adults and draw upon our own religious and cultural principles in order to act constructively. In such a way, a Christian leader "becomes adept at dealing with meanings, insights, purposes, motivations, commitments, and not develop merely into a political mobilizer or a manipulator of a community. He/she persuades. It is only when a person has personalized his own message that he/she is going to change his/her life and the life and value-systems of others. Change of heart, change of life, transformation of society, that is his/her real goal."[13]

I believe that this is God's way of dealing with us too. He kept sending prophets and teachers to show his people the right way to life. He sent us Jesus who by his life, his death and resurrection and by the living Word he gives us, sheds light on our own situations and leads us to fullness of life in communion with every one.

The many forms that Christian mission takes in our country can be powerful instruments in instilling into people this capacity to judge rationally. The educational institutions, the various associations in the Churches, the prayer meetings, the faith education of the members are ambiences where this can be nurtured. In particular, the educational institutions serve as a fertile environment for promoting real integration and harmony that comes from right judgement, right attitudes and cooperative action. We need to emphasize in the present world of technology that Christians can make use of the electronic media in order to disseminate ideas for constructing a nation of peace and harmony. The scope for creative enterprise here is unlimited.

Promoting a Civil Society

In his thought-and-action provoking research, *Ethnic Conflict and Civic Life,* Ashutosh Varshney[14] gives us an insight that should serve us Christians in promoting a violence free society in which people feel at one with each other.

Varshney admits the fact that ethnic groups will never be able to live in this world free of conflicts and tensions. The more crucial fact is how to we cope with such conflicts and tensions that tear apart the fabric of a nation. A pointer in this direction comes from the observation of a fact: "Sooner or later, scholars of ethnic conflict are struck by a puzzling empirical regularity in their field. Despite ethnic diversity, some places – regions, nations, towns, or villages – manage to remain peaceful, whereeas others experience enduring patterns of violence. Similarly, some societies, after maintaining a veritable record of ethnic peace, explode in ways that surprise the observer and very often the scholar as well."[15]

If we accept basically that to work for national integration is to attempt to identify and describe the processes that bind people together in a shared identity thus reduce or, better, block the destructive path of conflicts among groups, we can see the value of the suggestion made by Varshney. He proposes that the explanation for variations in patterns of conflict between the peaceful and the violent manifestations lies in the existence or absence of a *civil society*. This was drawn from observations of the Hindu-Muslim riots that shook India between 1990 and 1995.

Civil society refers to the 'space in a given society that (a) exists between the family level and the state level, (b) makes interconnections between individuals or families possible, and (c) is independent of the state'.[16] Civil society expresses itself in various forms like trade unions, associations of businessmen, traders, teachers, doctors, lawyers and others that are communally integrated.

Two mechanisms usually connect civil society and ethnic conflict. (1) The first promotes communication between members of different religious communities or civic networks and thus makes it possible to foster peace in the neighbourhood in which they normally interact informally. People are able to come together especially in times of tension and form peace committees which can stem rumours and create confidence among conflicting groups. (2) The second mechanism refers to "associational forms of engagement" which are sturdier and can deal with tensions more effectively. This is especially so in urban settings. "Organized civic networks, when intercommunal, not only withstand the exogenous communal shocks – partitions, civil wars, desecration of holy places – but they also constrain local politicians in their strategic behaviour."[17] Civil society organizations will prevent violence from erupting because of their own interests in having peace and harmony. But on the positive side, such organizations express very well the true meaning of integration at the micro level. The macro level can exist if at the micro levels there is resistance to violent conflicts of any kind.

Why cannot Christian Churches play a proactive role in promoting such a civil society? I believe that this is one fundamental task that Christians have to be engaged in, even in taking leadership for such ventures. The Christian disciple is in this world though not of this world and this makes it imperative for him/her to be positively involved in this world in such a way that the power from above flows into it.

Christian Witness and Christian Prophetic Engagement

As in every generation, the most power instrument that Christians have for transforming the world is that of Christian witness. The way Christians acted especially in the face of persecution manifested the inner power about which Paul the apostle wrote, "therefore I am content with weaknesses, insults, hardships, persecutions, and calamities for the sake of Christ; for whenever I am weak, then I am strong" (2 *Cor* 12, 10). "I can do all things through him who strengthens me" (*Phil* 4:13).

The Christian call to live a life of love and harmony extends beyond the boundaries of the Church community. The invitation "Put away from you all bitterness and wrath and anger and wrangling and slander; together with all malice; and be kind to one another, tender-hearted, forgiving one another"(*Eph* 4:31-32) should be re-echoed by every Christian. If Christians are able to live in love, they can be also effective agents of reconciliation.

Christians have the duty to show by the way they exercise their civic duties that they are honest and loyal citizens who are committed to the progress of every one irrespective of social status or religious affiliation. This demands especially from Christians the commitment to fight against all that is evil in public life. In concrete, concerted efforts to fight corruption in all it forms in public life is an urgent call for all Christians for they profess to stand by the values of Christ.

The Christian communities have also the important obligation to be prophets in a world that is so easily divided by narrow prejudices and hate. We have the possibility of drawing the attention of the public as well as of leaders to the fundamental values that make for peaceful and constructive co-existence such as justice, honesty, and love. We need to keep reminding everyone of the need for cooperation among all, beyond the limited boundaries of tribe, caste or religion.

Finally we should emphasize the duty of Christians to pray for the country and its leaders. Paul the apostle instructed his disciple Timothy, "First of all, then, I urge that supplications, prayers, intercessions and thanksgiving should be made for everyone, for kings and all who are in high positions, so that we may lead a quiet and peaceable life in all godliness and dignity." (1 *Tim* 2:1-2).

Conclusion

If there is one important virtue that Christianity keeps offering to the world that despairs of peace, it is hope. It is easy to slide into cynicism in the face of an apparently hopeless situation. But the faith that Christians have in God and in the potential for good in every human heart makes room for hope even against all signs of hopelessness. The nation that appears at present torn apart by divisive forces can still find a different way for co-existence. We walk on, trusting in the power that is not our own but which is from above.

NOTES AND REFERENCES

1. http://www.thaindian.com/newsportal/tag/prime-minister-manmohan-singh
2. Shashi Tharoor: *India: From Midnight to the Millennium*, p. 7.
3. *Ibid.*

4. *Ibid.*
5. Archbishop Thomas Menamparampil, SDB., "The Role of Religious Leaders in Peace Initiatives" in website, http://www.cbcisite.com/cbcinews2464.htm.
6. *Ibid.*
7. *Ibid.*
8. *Ibid.*
9. M.N. Karna, "Ethnic Identity and Socio-economic Processes in North-Eastern India" , in Kailash S. Aggarwal, ed., *Dynamics of Identity and Intergroup Relations in North-East India,* Indian Institute of Advanced Study, Shimla, 1999, pp. 29.
10. Cf. Shashi Tharoor, p. 332.
11. Vatican II, *The Church in the Modern World,* n. 60.
12. Archbishop Thomas Menamparampil, "The Role of Religious Leaders."
13. *Ibid.*
14. Ashutosh Varshney, *Ethnic Conflict and Civic Life: Hindus and Muslims in India,* Oxford University Press, 2002.
15. *Ibid.* pp.5-6.
16. Cf. *Ibid.,* p. 40.
17. Cf. Ashutosh Varshney, p. 10.

11

Harmony and National Integration Through Culture and Development[1]

—*Sebastian Karotemprel, SDB*

Introduction

People in general look for peace and harmony. Harmony and national integration are sine qua non factor and condition for a multi-religious, multi-ethnic and pluri-cultural society such as India. In order to have peace and harmony it is not sufficient to have material development only. It is here that Christianity can make a contribution. The Christian vision of God, universe and man is capable of promoting harmony, integration and development of people. When we look at the situation of India we can see that Christianity has played this role and continues to play a vital role in promoting culture and development of the people of India. In this paper I concentrate *my attention* only on the North East India (NEI) context.

The Tribal World of NEI

Both numerically and qualitatively, Christianity is an

established fact in Northeast India. In the course of its 175 year-old presence among the tribal peoples of NEI, Christianity has accompanied them from an isolated and in some ways illiterate and primitive living conditions to modern living conditions. No one will deny that Christianity, for better or worse, has shaped, along with other sociological factors, the lives of the people of NEI, directly and indirectly.

An evaluation of the role played by Christianity in NEI is, by its very nature, a difficult and complex task. An absolutely neutral and objective evaluation is impossible. Some do it on the basis of ideologically vitiated pre-suppositions. The recently published *Religious Demography of India*[2] is an example of such biased evaluations. The book carries a Foreword by L.K. Advani.[3] Following the divisive Hindutva ideology it categorizes, a priori, the people of India according to their religious affiliation into Indian Religionists (Hindus, Sikhs, Buddhists, Jains, and the Traditional or Tribal Religionists) and all others as non-Indian Religionists.[4] Muslims and Christians are gratuitously called non-Indian Religionists. Curiously enough, the tribal population of NEI is put among Indian Religionists. All through the book, the authors assume that Christianization of NEI is a grave danger to national unity and integration. The Hindutva ideology of hatred, divisiveness and opposition to Christianization reeks from every page of the book. Unfortunately, all this is done by the authors and their promoters, without consulting the tribal people themselves. They write from the ivory tower of pre-conceived ideologies and paradigms. With one contemptuous word "dkhar" (outsider) and its equivalents in most tribal languages, the tribal people dismiss the Hindutva assumption of the book, namely, of categorizing them as *Indian Religionists.*

Secondly, an analysis of the role of Christianity in promoting harmony and integration in NEI[5] can only indicate the dominant trends. It cannot ignore the weaknesses and failures of Christians and their Churches collectively. Christianity is not a purely spiritual movement, but also a human enterprise and a sociological phenomenon. As such, there will always be shadows and lights in such a large canvas as Christianity in NEI. The following analysis, therefore, can only indicate the major thrust of Christianity in NEI, keeping always in mind that something contrary may be said against its overwhelmingly positive role.

A Brief Historical Survey of Christianity in NEI

The two major forms of Christianity that have been operative in NEI are the Protestant Christianity and the Catholic Christianity. A brief historical survey of Christianity in NEI will be in order to understand its role in nation-building.

(a) Protestant Christianity in NEI

American Baptists and Welsh Presbyterians were the first to introduce Christianity to the tribal peoples of NEI. The Protestant missionary work started around 1830.[6] Protestant Christianity spread rapidly in Mizoram. By 1930, most Mizos belonged to the Baptist or Presbyterian Churches. Similarly, the Baptist Church made headway into Nagaland by the middle of the 20th century. A large part of the tribal population of Meghalaya is Protestant. Another area into which Protestant Christianity spread is Manipur, especially among the various hill tribals while the Mitheis of the Imphal plateau, though originally tribal, have been mostly hinduized. During the last 25 years it has spread into Arunachal Pradesh.

(b) Catholic Christianity in NEI

Catholic missionaries had several sporadic contacts with NEI from the XVII century onwards. They used Assam as a passageway to Tibet and China. NEI became a mission sui juris (an independent mission) only in 1890 when it was entrusted to the Society of the Divine Saviour (SDS), the

Salvatorians. Thus, systematic missionary work among the native people of NEI began in 1890.[7] By 1914, the Salvatorians managed to establish the Catholic Church in NEI on very sound foundations. With the expulsion of the German Salvatorians from India by the British government during World War I, the Catholic mission was entrusted to the Jesuit Fathers from 1914 to 1921.

In 1922 Salesians of Don Bosco were entrusted with the "Assam Mission." From 1945 onwards, Indian Salesians joined the ranks of the foreign missionaries. Again, Indian diocesan priests from Kerala started missionary work in NEI in 1954.[8] The Catholic community today stands around 1.3 million.[9]

Role of Christianity in Promoting Harmony and Integration

(a) Defense of Tribal Identity

Harmony and integration imply peaceful co-existence and mutual adjustments inrecognizing the identity of each one. The merit of Christianity in general is that it was quick to recognize the identity of the tribal people, support, defend and promote it by various means, especially by the promotion of tribal languages, cultures and customs.

(b) Integration

Christianity has succeeded in bringing people together on inter-tribal and on supra-tribal platforms. The fact of becoming Christians brought them into contact with all the Churches of India and abroad in conferences, in all India associations and international meetings. Such contacts and exposure were an integrating factor between tribal peoples and the larger Indian society. Writing on this topic, Downs says: "As already suggested, not only has Christianity been a vehicle for bringing together different tribes and also the peoples of both hills and plains, but it has also been one of the main agencies of positive association between the people of the region and those in other parts of the country."[10] Both within NEI and in the rest of India, Christian and non-Christian tribals have come into religious, social and administrative contacts with the people of India. Although such contacts have had unavoidable limitations, they served as an integrative force.

(c) An Added Worldview

A worldview embraces one's vision of the universe, of mankind and of oneself. Our responses to and relationship with the universe and with other human beings are conditioned by our worldview. The horizons of the tribal worldview were mostly limited to one's family, village, clan and tribe. This limited worldview was not shattered by Christianity but enlarged to include the whole family of man and nature.

Not all Christians may have fully assimilated the new worldview supplied by Christianity or made it an operative principle of conduct. But there is no doubt that the process has been set in motion. Through various Church organizations, exchange of personnel, studies abroad and service and leadership functions in India and abroad, exposure to a world different from the tribal world was made possible. Exposure to a new world with its culture or cultures, with its economic systems and structures, its political philosophies and forms of government, its educational and social infrastructure, in general totally different from those of tribal peoples living in isolated geographical and cultural pockets, was bound to alter the worldview of the tribal people. And this could be considered one of the major areas of impact of Christianity on the tribal people.[11]

Christianity has, in fact, been one of the most powerful integrating agencies within and among the tribes, as well as between the peoples of the hills and those of the plains. It has also played a significant role, popular notions to the contrary notwithstanding, in the process of integrating the hill people of NEI with the rest of the country.[12]

(d) Literacy and Education

When the Christian missionaries came into NEI about 175 years ago, they found a tribal society that practically non-literate. Often even before places of worship were built, primary schools were built. Even today in many parts of Arunachal Pradesh, in remote and inaccessible villages in mountains and valleys, the only educational presence is that of the Christian missionary. If literacy rate in NEI stands around 70%, much of the credit for it must go to all the Christian Churches that have made literacy their main goal.

Education in schools, boarding schools and colleges has brought together thousands of students of tribal and non-tribal origins into close interaction. They have promoted religious harmony and national integration. There is no better way of integration and harmonization of cultures than bringing young minds and hearts to live together, study and play together and strike life-long relationships. Education has helped to introduce the tribal people many new avenues in life and opened the doors to many new possibilities. They acquired the capacity to assert themselves, question powers that would dominate and exploit them.

(e) Tribal Languages and Literature

Most tribal languages were only spoken languages without a script, grammars, printed books and literature till the arrival of the Christian missions. Even a non-tribal language such as Assamese was saved from extinction by Christian missionaries: "They provided the Assamese with a modern literature and literary style, both through their own compositions and the publications of the Baptist Mission Press at Sibsagar and by stimulating a literary renaissance."[13]

Speaking of the contribution of the American Baptist Missionaries in Assam, B.K. Barua says: "The missionaries definitely achieved one thing. Up till now Assamese literature was more or less an oral literature confined to the villages and the Ahom court. Now it takes a definitely urban complexion, and at Gawahati, Sibsagar, Nowgong and such other headquarter towns literary circles sprang up."[14]

The process of saving tribal languages from extinction by giving them a script, grammars and building up a body of literature is still continuing in many areas of NEI such as Arunachal Pradesh, Mizoram. Once the script and grammar of the language are established the next step is the translation of the *Bible* or at least of New Testament into the given language.[15] Once a tribal language is established, the growth of literature is assured if the tribe concerned has a sufficient number of people to justify publication of magazines, newspapers, scholastic books, hymn books, books for worship and literary works. The Khasi language is an example of such progress.[16]

Translations and original works in tribal languages continue to grow. One significant example is the projected 80-volume commentary on the *Bible* by Fr. Sylvanus Sngi Lyngdoh. He has already published 24 volumes during the past 15 years.[17]

(f) Transition from Tribal Society to an Integrated Society

One of the major contributions of the Churches in NEI towards national integration during the last 175 years is to have helped the tribal society to move from isolation into an integrated part of the mainstream national life. The Churches have been mainly responsible for the more or less smooth transition from "tribal" social organizations towards "modernity".

Today the tribals form part, though not fully, of the national democratic form of government. Their "tribal" economy has absorbed the modern national and international economic structures. The tribal society has more or less come under the purview of the national administrative services. Thus the tribal people form part of the Indian administrative services. They are part of the Indian police forces, the defense establishment, Indian Foreign Service, the Indian legal system, the Indian industrial complex, and the Indian educational system.

It must be admitted that the participation of the tribal population of NEI in national life is slow, is not uniform for all tribal groups and not without resistance to full integration.[18] This is partly due to the neglect of the region in general. On the other hand, there is no doubt that the process of integration has been set in motion.

The Churches in NEI have made some outstanding contribution towards national life, harmony and integration. They have produced a speaker of the Indian parliament,[19] a chief election commissioner,[20] several governors,[21] several ambassadors,[22] a central minister,[23] several vice-chancellors of universities,[24] a chairperson of the Union Public Service Commission.[25] The Churches have also produced outstanding professors in universities such as R.R. Thomas, a Khasi, who occupied the distinguished Chair of Philosophy in Calcutta University. This is an impressive performance by the tribals of NEI by any standards and an example of national integration both for the tribals and the mainstream Indian society.

We may, therefore, conclude that Christianity, by design or by chance, did help the tribal society towards transition to modernity. Downs is not far from the truth when he says: "Whichever way one views it, the fact remains that the Christian faith has served an important social function in the North East, and that this at least in part accounts for the large numbers that embraced the new faith in certain areas."[26]

Integration and Harmony Through Development of Persons

(a) Empowerment of Women

Christian Churches in NEI have set in motion a vast movement towards the empowerment of women. The education of women and girl-children is a typical area where the Christian Churches have played a key role in introducing the concept, initiating a movement and providing the necessary infrastructure, and material and human resources for the empowerment of women.

The education of women and girl-children in Assam was initiated by Christian missionaries.[27] Similarly the education of the Adivasis of the Tea Gardens of Assam was undertaken by missionaries through a large network of primary and secondary schools in most tea gardens of Assam.[28]

The problem of development among the Adivasi women in the Tea Garden of Assam is another huge agenda for all social workers. Through school and college education, vocational training, grihini schools, and self-employment schemes the Churches are a major agent of change among them.[29] Women's education, emancipation and empowerment in the tribal societies may be considered a major contribution towards the development of the tribal societies of NEI. This is acknowledged by the tribal themselves and by historians: "Time and time again both missionaries and indigenous Christians refer to the positive changes in the status of women brought about by Christianity."[30]

Missionaries have recruited women from abroad and from among the tribals to speed up the work of development among women. Speaking of their work, Downs says:

> These in their turn encouraged the development of women workers among the local Christians – variously called Bible women, women evangelists

or women pastors among the Protestants, and indigenous women religious among the Catholics. The indigenous congregation of sisters founded in 1942, Missionary Sisters of Mary Help of Christians, has been the most successful recruiter of local religious.[31]

(b) A Network of Developmental Works

From the very beginning of the Christian mission in NEI, development of peoples was an essential dimension. J.B. Bhattacharjee says: "To be more precise Christianity involves the missionaries in two types of work (i) spiritual and (ii) temporal. These two types of activities are not only interdependent but also inseparable."[32] Development always starts with persons. By helping young people to qualify themselves as doctors, nurses, teachers, social workers, engineers, technicians, etc., the Churches have multiplied the agents of development. Thus Bhattacharjee speaks of every Christian as an agent of social change: "Christianity has made an impact on the people of North-Eastern region particularly in Nagaland, Mizoram, Manipur and Meghalaya as regards development and change are concerned."[33]

Apart from the vast network of educational institutions at all levels,[34] hundreds of developmental projects have been initiated by the Churches in NEI. What is said about Don Bosco Technical School is representative of many other areas of development in NEI: "(This) could happen because of the role played by the Don Bosco Technical School which has been over the years imparting new types of skill and those acquiring the skills found good opportunities in the construction and other sectors of the economy and succeeded in having a good footing for advancing economically and educationally."[35]

We need only enumerate some of the developmental projects in NEI established by the Churches. There are several formal and non-formal technical schools, agricultural training centres, shelter homes for youth at risk, printing schools, training centres for competitive examinations, teachers, B. Ed. colleges, self-help projects, computer training centres, night schools for drop-outs, employment training centres, leadership training centres, etc.

Thus as a result of Christian presence and efforts, many tribals received vocational, medical and legal education and large numbers of teachers, lawyers, doctors, public servants, writers, modern farmers, landowners, traders, industrial and business pioneers, salaried preachers, and evangelists formed part of the tribal middle class.[36]

(c) Healthcare Works

Healthcare is one of the main foundations of any form of development. The concept of modern healthcare was almost non-existent in vast areas of NEI till the arrival of the missionaries. True, country medicine, now called alternative medicine did play a role in the life of the people, but it was inadequate. In fact, any system of medicine, whether allopathic, homeopathic, ayurvedic or naturopathic, is inadequate for all health problems.

With Christian mission, preventive, curative, surgical healthcare became a powerful movement. Major hospitals such as Khasi Presbyterian Hospital in Shillong, Nazareth Hospital in Shillong, other hospitals in Guwahati, Kohima, Imphal, Chabua, Dibrugarh, Tura, Haflong, etc., and dispensaries in remote villages form part of a large network of healthcare in the whole of NEI.[37] Healthcare also introduced the concept of healing ministry and the training of nurses as a religious vocation and mission. Today the Churches conduct a number of nursing schools in NEI.

The Churches conduct several other humanitarian and health-related works in favour of the mentally retarded, physically handicapped, those impaired in speech and sight, rickets-affected children, dyslexic children and those caught up in drug-addiction.

(d) Leadership

The Churches have, through education and development, been instrumental in preparing the political leadership of NEI. Mavis Dunne Lyngdoh, a Khasi was a cabinet minister in the then Assam government already in the 1930s. Especially after Independence, many political and government leaders came from the ranks of professors in Christian colleges and from Church leadership.

The Christian Churches have played a key role in the peace-negotiations and peace-process in Mizoram. In Nagaland it is even now an on-going process. A similar role is being played in the peace-process between the Bodos and the Adivasi-Santal population of the Assam plains.

The leadership of the Churches, over the years has passed on to local people in most Churches. By the very nature of the Church and historical models of functioning, the transition of Church leadership took place within a short time in the Protestant Churches. In the Catholic Church it has taken place rather gradually. Both processes have merits and demerits.[38]

(e) Promotion of Culture

The Churches of NEI have been promoting culture through a vast array of activities. We need only mention some of them here to show what has been and what is being done in the area of promotion of culture, thus promoting harmony and integration among peoples.

The first printing presses and publications in several states and languages of NEI were Church inspired and sponsored. Christian printing presses in Guwahati and Shillong were among the earliest ones. They were instrumental in spreading educational books, books in tribal languages, periodicals, and reviews. Christian Literature bookshops are found all over NEI. They have contributed immensely to the spread of *Bibles*, hymn books, books for worship, and good reading material.

The Library movement started in most states of NEI with Church libraries. They make books on various topics such as ecclesiastical, spiritual, literary, scientific and other themes from all over the world available to the people of the region most of whom otherwise would remain ignorant even of their existence. Church libraries must be considered among the most powerful instruments in the promotion of culture in NEI.

Over the years, the Churches in NEI have given attention to the preservation, promotion of and research into tribal cultures by setting up anthropological and historical museums. The most important and the most comprehensive anthropological museum in NEI is the Don Bosco Centre for Indigenous Cultures, Shillong. Smaller, but significant cultural museums are found in Shillong, Dibrugarh, Dimapur and Imphal.

The Churches in NEI run a number of Bible Colleges, Clergy-Pastor Training Centres, Theological Colleges and Philosophical Colleges for the preparation of high level clergy and pastors. We may mention some of the most important among them such as Jorhat Theological College, Shillong Theological College, Oriens Theological College, Sacred Heart Theological College, etc. They are important centres for the promotion of ecclesiastical and secular culture in the region.

Forces of Disintegration: Insurgency, Militancy, Resistance, Separatism

No one can deny that there are negative and debilitating forces at work in NEI.

Often vested interests, anti-minority groups within and without the government blame Christianity for them. This is a serious charge and must be answered.

In the first place the accusers must explain the existence of similar forces such as the Naxalite movement in West Bengal and other states, Peoples' War Groups in Andhra Pradesh, Khalistan movement in Punjab, Shiv Sena in Maharashtra, Pro-LTTE movement in Tamil Nadu, etc.

Secondly, separatist movements in NEI take on a fresh significance because of the region's geo-political situation, surrounded as it is by Bhutan, China, Myanmar, and Bangladesh. The geo-political factor, no doubt, has favoured the growth and continuance of insurgency and militancy.

Thirdly, corrupt administrators and politicians at the Centre in collusion with their local counterparts in NEI have siphoned off thousands of crores of developmental resources from developmental works. By the government's own admission, only 15% of developmental money finally reaches the people.[39] All the rest is looted and continues to be looted with immunity because the administrators who have also charge of the control mechanisms which could make individuals, groups and departments of the government accountable are themselves corrupt.

During the last 60 years or so sections of the police force, the income tax department, the judiciary, the auditing agencies, the electoral process, the party systems, the legislative bodies and similar agencies have all been vitiated and emasculated to suit and favour the political-administrative-contractual complex in India.

Peoples' patience has a limit. The Soviet system of repression, command economy and military control collapsed under its own historical weight after about 70 years. Either we reform or will see more peoples' war groups! Christianity has nothing to do with it. Obviously, Christians being better educated better informed and better organized than their counterparts elsewhere, we will be in a position to see through the political and economic fraud perpetrated on people better than the illiterate masses of Uttar Pradesh, Bihar and Madhya Pradesh, reduced to silence through 3000 years of cast oppression.

To speak of *Christian insurgency* is an insult not only to the intelligence of Christians but of all educated Indians. This has been done recently by Dr. Togadia and Mr. Venkaiah Naidu who have coined this new phrase *Christian insurgency* in NEI.[40]

Successive administrations, the military and irresponsible and too frequent use of the CRPF and other arms of the government have alienated many groups of people such as the tribals, the Kashmiris and the Dalits. Discrimination, intimidation and harassment of innocent civilians have alienated the people and their goodwill. Government-supported Hindu groups and agencies are favoured while tribal Christians are discriminated against. Their freedom of movement is limited or even denied. *Inner line pass* and check points are only a mockery or at best a joke. They are meant to harass the *bona fide* citizens. No wonder, then, that over decades, people become militants and insurgents.[41]

Speaking of the problom of insurgency, Patricia Mukhim, a reputed journalist, says:

> As a body, it (the Church) was responsible for brokering peace in many conflict-torn areas. The Church has been a pioneer in education and health initiatives in the region. Education is a great eye-opener. The educated person has a liberated mind that can understand and discern injustice when it is perpetrated on an unsuspecting people....The

> Northeast, too, may be a conflict-torn area because of historical wrongs. This has nothing to do with Christianity.[42]

Weaknesses and Failures

(a) Divisions, Hostilities, Rivalries

The role played by the Christian Churches in NEI is not all lights. There have been and there still are serious shadows and dark holes. The first among them is the transference of bitter denominational rivalries and hostilities of Europe and the United States into a historically innocent tribal population. The hostilities were more pronounced between the Protestant Churches and the Catholic Church.

One reason for the hostilities is the historical background of the Post-Reformation Churches and the Catholic Church. Inter-Church conflicts from the home countries were transferred to the tribal areas of NEI.[43] Secondly, many Protestant Churches went along tribal lines in Christianization. As a result, inter-tribal rivalries became inter-Church rivalries.

Inter-Church tension was particularly bitter between Catholics and Protestants. Historically, the British policy was "*cujus region, ejus ecclesia*". That meant an area was given exclusively to a Protestant Church to evangelize. Hence they considered the Catholics as intruders. Thus Horam wrote: "Religion is at the same time both a unifying and dividing factor. The age-old rivals of Christendom, Roman Catholics and Protestants have brought their rivalry into Naga society as well. The schisms which rend the Church affect the harmony in the Naga world."[44]

(b) Superficial Christianity

For theological and historical reasons, the preaching and communication of the Christian message by some Churches tended to be superficial. Theologically, Luther's famous dictum *pecca fortiter, crede fortius* (sin as you want, only believe even more forcefully) seems to have been followed if not *ex professo*, at least *de facto* by some Christians. At times, some missionary efforts were directed to numerical strength rather than true conversion of heart. Thus some forms of Christianity that was communicated to the tribal people tended to be shallow and left them in a "liminal" situation, allowing them to swing between "tribalism" in its negative connotation and Christian conduct of life. This has happened also within the same Church with some sections of the converts.

(c) All Pervasive Corruption

In a number of States, Christians are holding the reins of government and in control of political parties. One would expect Christian administrators to have a heart for social justice, honesty in administration, social responsibility and accountability to the public. On the contrary, several Christian politicians and administrators have amassed huge amounts of wealth. The criminal nexus of politician-bureaucrat-contractor in looting the tax payers' money, budgetary allotments, developmental money funneled through various regional bodies, central and state universities[45] and other channels is visible all through NEI, among Christians as any others.

In some cases, Christian legislators have shown little social and civic sense in introducing reforms in land-holdings, taxation and preventing concentration of wealth in the hands of a few tribals. In a number of States urban land, capital, political power and government machinery are in the hands of a few tribals. Christian principles of social justice do not seem to have an impact upon the social conscience of some of them. As a result, tremendous disparities have been introduced into a relatively egalitarian tribal society. To this extent, Christianity has failed to set in motion social harmony, integration of peoples and their development.

(d) Anti-Outsider Phobia

During the last 25 years or so the tribal society in NEI has been in the grip of anti outsider phobia. All will admit that some degree of protection of tribal economic and cultural interests is necessary to prevent large-scale "invasion" of non-tribals into tribal areas, leading to disruptive demographic changes and elimination of tribal cultures. Yet an exaggerated anti-outsider phobia can be damaging to tribal economic and cultural interests. It can lead to the flight of capital, professional expertise and professional services. No society today can avoid being interdependent. Anti-outsider phobia does hinder the process of social harmony, economic development and transition into modernity. In concrete situations, some Christians and Churches have failed to give enlightened leadership in the matter.

Conclusion

The role of Christianity in NEI in promoting integration social harmony through development and culture may be discussed and evaluated from two different angles and with two different criteria. We may evaluate it objectively or relatively.

Viewed objectively, no one can deny that, like any other human enterprise, the Christian movement in NEI has lights and shadows. We can admit of some serious black holes too. Even granting the shadows and even using the objective criterion, it cannot be denied that the light outshines the shadows. Darkness cannot overpower the lights. If we could wish away, by some magical power, the entire Christian phenomenon in NEI, what remains of NEI would be a poor caricature of the region.

If a relative and comparative criterion is used, it will be clear that the presence of Christianity has been a strong integrative and developmental force in NEI. Let us use the criterion of religious demography. The Hindu-Muslim divide has grown in the past years especially after the wanton Gujarat programs under BJP government supported by the dependent on RSS and VHP extremism. The Hindu-Sikh divide after the 1984 massacre of the Sikhs is still an open wound that needs to be healed.

The millennia-old caste-divide within the Indian society, especially the Hindu society, itself is still crying for a solution. The economic divide between the rich and the poor has grown in recent years despite the deceptive façade of "India Shining" campaign at the cost of taxpayers' money. All this means that measured by the relative and comparative socio-economic criterion, the tribal society in NEI is far better integrated than some other societies elsewhere in India.

We may compare the tribal society in NEI with the society in Bihar, Uttar Pradesh or Madhya Pradesh or in large tracts of rural population in other States, using a cultural-educational criterion. Literacy rate in NEI stands around 70% today in stark contrast to the illiteracy level of 60% to 70% in several parts of India. The educational scenario at high school, college and university levels shows relatively faster growth in NEI due to Christian contribution to education at all levels.

Sociologists could use several other criteria to measure the levels of integration, harmony and development achieved by a given society under the impact of various historical forces, such as per capita income, access to education, social mobility, human development parameters (HDP), living standards, habitat, access to medical and healthcare facilities, etc. On any count the tribal society in NEI will be seen to be better off than several other societies.

Finally, the tribal people themselves must evaluate the contribution of Christianity to NEI and not the vested, communal and divisive groups such as the VHP-RSS combine. Let them visualize a tribal society that retained its pristine social, cultural and economic infrastructure, but sans Christianity. Let them visualize a tribal society that had become a Hindu society with all its attendant caste-system and other social and dietary shackles. The alternatives will be found to be no better than the present Christian demographic reality of NEI.

In conclusion, I have no doubt that if history were to draw up a balance sheet of Christianity in NEI today purely as a sociological phenomenon, it will score higher marks than other imaginary but possible social phenomena in the area of social harmony and integration.

NOTES AND REFERENCES

1. This article was prepared for *Christian Contribution to Nation-Building: A Third Millennium Enquiry*, edited by Selvister Ponjumuthan, 2004, Documentary Committee of CBCI-KCBC, pp.49-64.
2. A.P. Joshi, M.D. Srinivas, J.K. Bajaj, *Religious Demography of India*, Chennai, Centre for Policy Studies, Chennai, 2003.
3. *Ibidem*, see L.K. Advani's "Foreword" pp. xv-xvi.
4. Cf. *Ibidem*, p. xviii.
5. Cf. F.S.Downs, "India, Churches of North East India," in *A Dictionary of Asian Christianity*, ed. Scott Sunquist et al. Grand Rapids, Eerdmans, 2001, p. 363-65. .Cf. also F.S. Downs, *Christianity in India*, Vol. V, Part 5, *North East India in the Nineteenth and Twentieth Centuries*, Bangalore, The Church History Association of India, 1992, pp. 65-89. Hereafter Downs, *History*.
6. Cf. Downs, *History*, p. 92.
7. Cf. S.Karotemprel, *Evangelizing Methods in NEI*, Shillong, 2003, pp. 17-18 (for private circulation only). Hereafter, Karotemprel, *Impact*.

8. Cf. *Ibidem*, pp. 17-18.
9. Downs, *History*, p. 135.
10. Cf. Karotemprel, *Impact*, p. 10.
11. Downs, *History*, p.131.
12. Downs, *History*, p.187.
13. B.K. Barua, *History of Assamese Literature*, pp. 106-7, Delhi, 1964, pp. 106-7.
14. The latest example is *The New Testament in Maram*, Catholic Association, Maram, 2004.
15. Cf. Downs, *History*, p.190; "Contributions of the Catholic Church to the Cultures of NEI," *Indian Missiological Review*, 12(1990), p.180. Cf. also Mrinal Miri, ed., *Linguistic Situation in North East India* (1982), pp.38-43.
16. So far 24 volumes have been published and run into nearly 12,000 pages.
17. Cf. *The Telegraph*, 17.2.2004, p. 1, on the neglect of NEI. The region's history does not figure in national history books.
18. Purna Sangma, a Garo.
19. James Lyngdoh, a Khasi.
20. Ripple Kyndiah (Governor of Mizoram).
21. R. Wallang (Seychells), Rudolf Warjri (Chile), R. Major Khathing (Burma), F. Manners (Indonesia), G.G. Swell (Switzerland).
22. Ripple Kyndiah (Minister for Tribal Welfare).
23. B. Pakem (NEHU), Milton Sangma, Pro-Vice-Chancellor (NEHU, Tura), Lalthang Thuanaga (Pro Vice Chancellor, Aizwal).
24. Rose Mathew (UPS, Chairperson, N. Delhi).
25. Downs, *History*, p.209.
26. Cf. Downs, *History*, pp.159-160.
27. Cf. S.Karotemprel and B. Dutta Roy, ed., *Tea Garden Labourers of Northeast India*, Shillong, VIP, p. 364; Walter Fernandes, *et al.* (ed.) *Primary Education of Plantation Labourers' Children in Assam: Draft Report*, North Eastern Social Research Centre, Guwahati (no date).

28. Cf. Elizabeth Kaniampady, *Status of Women Working in the Tea Plantations (A Case Study)*, Akansha Publishing House, New Delhi, 2003.
29. F.S. Downs, *History*, p.159.
30. Downs, *History*, p.162; Cf. (I M R), 12 (1990).
31. J.B. Bhattacharjee, ed., *Sequences of Development in North East India*, N. Delhi, Omsons Publications, 1989, p.19. Hereafter, Bhattacharjee, *Sequence*.
32. *Ibidem*, p.20.
33. Cf. P.N. Dutta Ray, "The Emergence and Role of the Middle Class in the Khasi-Jaintia Hills 1824-1950", in B. Dutta Ray, *The Emergence and Role of Middle Class in North-East India*, New Delhi, Uppal, 1983, p.132, Hereafter Dutta Ray, *Emergence*.
34. B.B. Dutta, "Emergence and Role of Middle Class in Meghalaya", in Dutta Ray, *Emergence*, p.174.
35. Cf. P.N. Dutta Ray, in Dutta Ray, *Emergence*, pp. 131-133; H. Bareh, *The History and Culture of the Khasi People*, p.445.
36. Karotemprel, *Impact*, pp. 20-21.
37. Downs, *History*, pp. 90-93.
38. Cf. K.N. Phukan, "Education, Corruption, Waste: Wretched Interactions," in *Man and Society: A Journal of North East Studies*, 1(2004), pp. 25-48. Hereafter Phukan, *Man and Society*.
39. Karotemprel, *Evangelizing Methods*, p. 38.
40. *Ibidem*, p. 128.
41. Patricia Mukhim, "Church and Politics," in *The Telegraph*, Tuesday 28 January 2003, p. 18.
42. *Ibidem*, p. 128.
43. M. Horam, *Naga Insurgency: The Last Thirty Years*, New Delhi, 1986, p.29. Cf. Downs, *History*, p.131.
44. Cf. Phukan, in *Man and Society*, pp. 25-48.

12

Christianity and National Integration with Special Reference to the Role of the Christians of South Kanara

—*Kranti Kiran Farias*

Introduction

The Presupposition

The assumption that Christians have a separate history from that of other communities of India, namely 'Indian Church History' or 'Indian Christian History' as it were, is distortion of historical facts as well as a play on communalism in historiography. The history of the Christian community in India has to be viewed as a participatory movement in the composite history of the national community or national history.

India is, as it has been for so many centuries, a country with different religious, ethnic and linguistic groups. Today, our politicians and political parties indulge in communal politics. Those who are concerned about the future of our country in the light of the beautiful homogeneity in spite of its diversity, are called upon to weigh the seriousness of the situation and take appropriate steps to maintain and continue to build the national community it became in order to achieve the country's independence. Independence was gained at a cost that was very heavy. It must be sustained and ensured to all, not merely against external aggrandizement but also against internal factions and discrimination.

Economic backwardness was one of the serious challenges that India faced at independence but with three successive five-year plans, inaugurated between 1951 and 1964 under Nehru's leadership, India produced increasing amounts of food.

Linguistic regionalism eventually reached a crisis stage and undermined the Congress' attempts at nation-building. Whereas in the early 1920s, the Congress had deemed that the use of regional vernaculars in education and administration would facilitate the governance of the country, Partition made the leaders, especially Nehru, realize how quickly such provincial or sub-national interests would dismantle India's fragile unity.

However, in the face of widespread agitation for linguistic separation of states, beginning with the Telangana Movement in 1953, in 1956 Nehru reluctantly accepted the recommendations of the States Re-organisation Commission, and the number of states grew by reorganization along linguistic lines. The states became the loci for democratization of political processes at district levels, for expression of regional culture and popular demands against a national culture and unity, for economic development at strategic localities in the rural areas, and for proliferation of opposition parties that ended the possibility of a pan-Indian two-party system.

So we find that National Integration remains a crucial issue in India, notwithstanding the fact that we boast of a civilization, which is nearly 5000 years old. While, some of the divisive factors may be inherent in the history, geography and culture of our country, there are also forces, which accentuate these factors. Religious fundamentalism is one such force while linguistic diversities constitute another. There are people in this country who hold an exclusive view of religion which drives them into a sectarian frenzy that does not admit of tolerance of other faiths. Despite a shared culture of so many years, linguistic diversities have often generated tensions and conflicts amongst different communities threatening the fabric of national unity. The same holds good for regionalism exacerbated no doubt by inequitable development amongst different regions of the country. The age – old caste system has also contributed in no small measure to weaken the bond of unity among different sections of the society. All the above forces and factors pose a serious challenge to India's unity and integrity and, therefore, conscious efforts will have to be made by all her citizens, and buy those in authority or governance to preserve the same.

The history of the Christian community when it unravels may appear to be mere 'Mission history' and be dismissed as such by some, but this is indeed regional history, also subaltern history for the greatest contribution to the district and the region came in during this time when the two Missions worked at upliftment of the subaltern, for his enlightonment and that was indeed a great outreach even if the core thrust remained evangelization and mission work.

Therefore, this Paper showcases the role and participation of the Christian community in Indian nationalism, fight for independence and contribution to national integration, showing how deeply conscious and committed the Indian Christian community was just as other communities in India in fostering unity and national integration. The Christian community is as sincere as those of other religious persuasions in the promotion of dialogic involvement of their followers in the historical tasks common to them as Indians.

Sources

The source material used is from Primary Sources such as Government Reports and Orders and other documents; Records of the various Missions and Churches; letters and diaries of persons interviewed or acquired from; Published works which are both primary and secondary records; Personal interviews.

Terms or Concepts

Terms or concepts like nation, patriotism, nationalism, communalism, nation building are linked as they refer to or revolve round people and are therefore significant.

Nation

A nation is a 'human, cultural and social community'. Members of a 'nation' share a common identity, and usually a common origin, in the sense of history, ancestry parentage or descent. A nation extends across generations, and includes the dead as full members!.

Patriotism

Patriotism denotes positive and supportive attitudes to 'fatherland' or 'motherland' by individuals and groups. Patriotism covers such attitudes as: pride in its achievements and culture, the desire to preserve its character and the basis of the culture, and identification with other members of the nation. Patriotism is closely associated with *nationalism*, and the terms are often used *synonymously*. Patriotism also implies that the individual should place the interests of the nation above personal or group interests.

Nationalism

Nationalism is a term referring to a 'doctrine' or 'political movement' that holds a nation, usually defined in terms of 'ethnicity' or 'culture'; has the right to constitute an independent or autonomous political community based on a shared history and common destiny.

Nationalism may manifest itself as part of official state ideology or as a popular movement and may be expressed along civic, ethnic, cultural, religious or ideological lines. In all forms of nationalism, the populations believe that they share some kind of common culture.

With the rise of 'Third World Nationalisms', which occurs in those nations that have been colonized and exploited, the nationalisms of these nations were forged in a furnace that required resistance to Colonial domination in order to survive. As such, resistance is part and parcel of such nationalisms and their very existence is a form of resistance to imperialist intrusions. India is such a nation.

'Indian nationalism' refers to the consciousness and expression of political, social, religious and ethnic influences that help mould Indian national consciousness. Indian nationalism describes the many underlying forces that moulded the Indian independence movement, and strongly continue to influence the politics of India. The Indian Christian is as much a nationalist as his fellow Indians.

Communalism

This concept is the negative aspect whereby the enemy of nationalism in India within Indian society is "communalism' . Communalism is the social, political and economic functioning of mutually isolated , self-seeking and self-protecting groups.

In communalism the ultimate loyalty of the group is to its own narrow solidarity based on caste, religion or language or a combination of these. Communalism is a contradiction of nationalism which seeks to open isolated traditional groups such as Christians, Hindus, Muslims to one another and to build a national community on the basis of their common humanity and common participation in a social, economic and political nationhood.[1]

Freedom Movement

The term 'freedom movement' is the political aspect of nationalism, externally, an organised activity against the British Raj and internally, a struggle within India against communalism.

Integration

The essence of integration is specified in the definition of integration by two processes: (i) social homogenization of the society based on knowledge of a common language and local, regional or national identity on one hand and (ii) by preserving communal differences through recognizing the minorities' cultural rights on the other hand.

What is the Role of the Indian Christian Community to Unity and Integrity?

Striving for identity within religious pluralism

India has striven to maintain its spirit of religious freedom for it acknowledges that it is a pluralistic society. Religious pluralism is not a bad thing as along as we do not allow it to disrupt national life. We already have divisions based on class and caste. There is also division based on creed; based on sex; based on locality (North and the South) with its varied cultures, traditions and customs; based on language; about script etc.

Therefore to have a homogeneity and that which is the best is the need to have a people who can discern impartially and dispassionately. There has to be the awakening of mutual respect and trust between the various religious groups we have in this vast land of ours!

There is a need for opening up of our cultures. It does not mean loss of one's identity, rather the enrichment of it stated

T.V. Philip[2] Only then can India become a dynamic national community.

The Christian community in India was born out of a people of different faiths and religious communities of India which had accepted the Christian faith and with it the practices brought by the missionaries from the West. The first such community was in the when St. Thomas, Apostle of Jesus came to India, to the Kerala and the Tamil Nadu areas in the First Century A.D. Christianity in the other parts of the West Coast was introduced with the coming of the Portuguese in the Sixteenth Century. Involved in colonial aggression India in the nineteenth century was under the shadow of the Cross and Western culture. While at first these Christians found difficulty in having an Indian identity being compelled to conform to Western cultural forms of life and worship during the period 16th to the 19th Centuries they did get one in the next century.' We can see that there were self-revealing, revitalizing and transforming elements within the process that brought out the Indian renaissance and Indian nationalism.

This background however does not diminish the fact that the Christian in India is first and foremost an Indian. Religion has to be separated from secular and political life. Who can dare say that the Christian in India is "only" a Christian and not an Indian? Who gives the right to any other to classify or label 'who an Indian is, He has as much strain of Indian blood flowing in his veins as any other, born in the same holy precincts of this great Motherland of ours?

We do admit with some regret, that the stand taken by the Church had a lot to do with the passive and submissive stance of the average Christian Indian. Therefore he may have appeared to be more Christian than Indian, such was the influence of the Church! However, in the Twentieth Century the Christian community sought not just an identity for itself but sought the identity of being an 'Indian' community as other communities, and it did find a niche in the social milieu.

Since it is clear that our cultural unity is a unity in diversity and our religions and cultures encountered each other, in the process of encounter a unity emerged. Indian culture is not the product exclusively of any one religion or group. Aryan, Buddhist, Islamic and Christian influences have gone into it. We are reminded of this fact from an article by Badr-ud-Din Tyabji in '*The Statesman*'[3] on the role of minorities in which he pointed out that very often, unconsciously, the Hindu norms of life, because of their numerical predominance over the others, are regarded as the only authentic Indian way of life and all others as deviations. This is the principal reason; he said why the insistent call to the minorities by the majority community "to merge in the mainstream of the Indian way of life" rouses mixed feelings in the minds of the minorities. The minorities want to know what the contents of "the mainstream" are.[4]

Mutual understanding and contribution to the common life have to be evident only then will our culture grow and become dynamic. It is necessary for people of different communities and Faiths to meet and enter into dialogue not only on religious issues but also on social and national issues.

Manifestation of the Spirit of Nationalism

Some historians think that a national consciousness began to develop in the second half of the Nineteenth Century, but it was only in the last quarter of the Nineteenth Century that the course of the Freedom Movement began. The intellectual elite in all communities was roused to reform in religion and society and who conceived the idea of common national community with common national goals. They were becoming aware that '*we are Indians first, and Hindus, Mohammedans, Parsis or Christians afterwards*'.

The Indian National Movement

Tarachand in his "*History of the Freedom Movement in India*" refers to organisations formed before 1857 as reaction to social reforms carried out by the British and the Western missionaries. These associations were meant to guard Hinduism and certain other interests. With the development of Indian nationalism towards the end of the Nineteenth Century, many National leaders perceived Christianity as a tool in the hands of the foreigners to make Indians subservient to Colonial rule.

In the Uprising of 1857, it could be seen that the Indian Christians were unfortunately wholly on the side of the Government. It kept the Indian Churches away from the mainstream of Indian cultural and social life as a community apart, enjoying the patronage of the Colonial power. Both in British India and Portuguese India, we find Colonial protection and missionary paternalism prevented the Indian Church (the Christians) from understanding their own identity and seeing their proper role in Indian society.

So now, the Church would have to find a place that was legitimate in society at large. The Christian could not afford to lag behind others in responding to the spirit of nationalism. From an attitude seemingly imperious, as '*a civilizing mission to save souls*' the Church would have to work at being '*at service to the nation*'.

The Indian National Congress founded in 1885 became the main instrument of political nationalism and it committed itself to maintain the geographical unity of India and affirm the common aspirations of all groups in the Indian community. With the rise of the *Swadeshi* Movement in 1905-1906 and the agitation against the partition of Bengal in 1905 we see the beginning of the 'Indian Revolution'. Christ's teaching on non-violence was the principle on which Mahatma Gandhi based his non-violent, non-cooperation movement. He wanted to fight for truth or *satyagraha*. So *satyagraha*, non-violence, non-cooperation and civil resistance to British authority were intertwined and only through these means could the movements towards nationalism and freedom succeed.[5] The Movement took the form of a multi-faced boycott-of everything British and a struggle to establish national independence in economic, political and cultural areas. The *charkha* and *khadi* became the symbol of emancipation and Indianness.

Regional language found a new place in the country, and soon, the Movement from being an exclusive one in the hands of the educated English lawyers and public men, turned to be a mass movement. Protestants in Maharashtra like Baba Padmanji, Pandita Ramabai and Narayan Vaman Tilak called for the promotion and use of the vernacular language to reach out to the masses on religious or social issues. In South Kanara, the study of Konkani, the mother tongue of the Catholics, and Kanarese and Tulu, the language of the other Christians was encouraged as a bond to be fostered with people of the region such as the Hindus, Jains and the Muslims.

Influence of Growing Nationalism on the Church in India

Christianity is a benchmark for initiation, progression, expansion and consolidation. Christianity played a major role in the "building of a community", not just an endogamous but a homogenous " community of love and concern" within pluralistic India. The Indian Church had to give the "Good News" the mandate given by Jesus to His Apostles. But the mistake made by the early European missionaries was in trying to impose their own personal religious experiences or their own Christian sub-culture on the converts though the zeal for conversion was the foremost of their objectives. There seemed to be a 'foreignness' of the Church in India, taking on foreign patterns of institution, liturgy and theology, incorporating only in very small degree indigeneous cultural values.

Indian Nationalism presented by Hindu leaders as a 'religion of nationalism' led to a fear complex in Christians along with other minorities. In addition, the Christians were also confronted with the negative reactions of Western Christian missionaries towards Indian nationalism. In the wake of the rise of the National Movement, changes began to take place within the Church. Religious, cultural and political awakening took place in the nation challenging the Indian Christians to reconsider their position in Indian society.

We soon see that Indian Christian scholars sought to interpret Indian thought and other Indian religions, in its relation with Christianity. This helped to bring Christians into sympathy with non-Christian thought and aspiration and in presenting Christianity to India in terms that India is able to understand '*so as to plant the universal message of Christ deep in the deep soil of the Indian soul*' says Pandita Ramabai in her Testimony.[6] Indian Christians were awakened to the fact that they were now members of the "Church", not of the "Mission". There was a need to have an 'Indian' expression of Christianity without clinging to the Western garb or traits any more.

Where would this lead? It meant that Indian Christians were aware that they were part of a common Community with common destiny. It meant that they were aware that they were and are an integral part of India. It meant that they had to integrate with the rest in India.

In the Nineteenth and Twentieth centuries, there was an awakening to pluralistic consciousness due to political movements unifying people, and the consequent awareness of a common moral responsibility and the need to help in inter-faith dialogue and reforms. The crucified Jesus, the symbol of suffering love attracted religious-reform leaders and secular thinkers and the artistic world in India. Leaders such as Raja Ram Mohan Roy, Keshub Chandra Sen, Swami Vivekananda and Mahatma Gandhi recognised the human suffering and expounded on how to come to grips with it. Gandhiji, on seeing the image of the crucified Christ in the Vatican, wrote in the *Young India*:"[7]

> The image of Jesus Christ which I saw in the Vatican at Rome, is before my eyes at all times. The body was covered only by a small piece of cloth such as is worn by poor men in our villages. And what a wonderful look of compassion He had!

At the beginning of the Twentieth Century, some Indian Christian leaders felt that the National Movement and political independence would bring about a new awareness of the identity of the "Indian Church" and as V. Chakkarai in 1917 wrote,

> " The awakening of the national consciousness in India has touched the thinking Indian Christian more deeply because it has revealed to him the present condition of the Indian Church .... From indifference to the national ideal, the Indian Christian is now passing into joyous recognition of the claims of nationality in his mind and heart. The country has entered upon its manhood much more quickly under the uplifting influence of the national spirit.[8]

The Response to the Call to National Integration by Indian Christians

The Constitution of India has guaranteed that our country is a secular state and Christianity has certainly entered into the warp and woof of Indian thinking and has been regarded both critically and cordially by non-Christians. The Church grows in society. The society in which the Christian lives in largely forms him, gives him the language he speaks, the value system he holds and the customs which feel good to him. It is good if the Christian thinks of himself with those of other communities as part of the same society, with its culture and its ethnic linkage.

There are two angles from which we can study the Christian community and its role in nationalism. One is the role of individuals and the other of institutions, associations and groups in the Church. While it may be accepted that the usual charge against Christians is that only a miniscule section of the Community took part in India's Freedom Struggle, it cannot be said that Christians did not contribute to nation building. It was this contribution which helped prepare the ground for a nationalistic spirit among all the people of India. It also is an indication that Christians generously contributed to national integration!

There was both a progressive and a reactionary reaction to Mission work Vishnushastri Chiplunkar and later Bal Gangadhar Tilak in Maharashtra. But missionary efforts to propagate Christianity by criticising Hinduism, was responsible for stimulating Hindu revivalism as it did with Ram Mohan Roy of Bengal and other revivalist leaders of Hinduism as M.G. Ranade, R.G. Bhandarkar, Justice N.G. Chandavarkar and Justice K.T. Telang of Maharashtra who saw the progressive and positive benefits of Western education. The outcome was that Reform movements like the Brahmo Samaj and the Arya Samaj shook both Christians and Hindus. Christianity led to social reform and progress, started an attack on poverty and suffering, and glorified work. It led to the liberation of the oppressed which included the low caste people and women, helped them to find a new identity. Christianity was both a challenge and an inspiration to many Hindu intellectuals.

Justice Chandavarkar , President of the National Social Conference in Maharashtra paid a tribute to the missionaries thus, " It is now the fashion in some quarters to cry down the Mission.... if today there is an awakening among us on the subject of religion and society, that is a great deal due to the light brought to him.... by the Christian missionary...is due to a great extent the credit of the religious and social awakening of which the school of Hindoo Protestantism of the present day is the fruit.'[9] Similarly S. Natarajan in his book *History of Social Reform* has said that the tradition of social service has come to India chiefly through the example of Christian Mission.

John Newton said,

> The services of the Christian missionaries may be labelled as 'social service', removing prejudice against Christianity and positively winning sympathy and respect for Christians.[10]

This is contrary to the general criticism levied at Christian missionaries is that the missions and missionaries shared the cultural pride of the West: that they are principal representatives of the Western culture, asserting its innate superiority in the lands which came under the dominion of the Western nations.

The Role of the Christian and the Institutional Church in Integration

(a) *Religio-political integration*

Response to the call for *swadeshism*: transition to indigenous Church *"Swadeshi"* also gave a new direction to the Indian Christians to move into the mainstream of national life. An Indian Pastor (D.L. Joshi) in Bombay called upon the Christian community just as Rev.Babu Kali Charan Banerjee of Bengal had, saying: *"Awake Indian Christians, Swadeshism is in the air. Is it without lesson for us?"*[11].

It was the protest of Indian Protestant Christians against Western domination and Western missionary paternalism that had led to Church unity discussion in some of the missionary conferences in India.[12] There was a growing agitation for self-government, against the control of foreign missions and missionaries in their socio-religious institutions. In the Twentieth Century missionaries and national leaders worked steadily to purge the younger Churches of lingering Westernism and make them thoroughly indigenous. The way in which the Churches began to be governed and supported was indigenous too. Foreign Missionary leaders were replaced by national leaders and thus we have an indigenous Church with regard to Protestant Churches in India.

As Rev. W.E. Tomlinson of Mysore instrumental in handing over of power by the Basel Evangelical Mission to the Kanarese Evangelical Mission (Protestant) in South India expressed , " we wish to give the Indians a far fuller share in the conduct of the affairs of the Mission.... that in this country the Church should be Indian in thought and feeling".

Out of the impulses given by the *Students' Volunteer Movement,* and the *Young Men's Christian Association*, the *Home Missionary Society Movement* and rising nationalism, grew the *National Missionary Society* (Protestant) formed in December 1904 at Serampore . It seemed to be in the context of the Swadeshi Movement. Raja Harnam Singh, (father of Rajkumari Amrit Kaur), one of the founding leaders and President of *The National Missionary Society of India* (hereafter, *N. M. S.),* desired an expression of nationalism by Christians in the religious sphere, even if it meant matters of communal interest and communal association.[13]

So emerged the *Christian Ashram Movement* with 'Indian men, Indian financial resources, Indian management and Indian methods in spiritual and temporal spheres. The characteristic of the *N. M. S.* was that it laid stress on the indigenous expression of worship[14]. The *N. M. S.* gave Christians the opportunity to evangelise without becoming agents of foreign missions for as Abraham Mar Thoma, the Metropolitan of the Mar Thomas Syrian Church had declared, " If India's millions are to be reached and won for Christ, it will be by India's sons."[15]

The stress that the new Church must be an Indian, a National Church, the National Missionary Council at its meeting in 1919 wanted that all Missions review the whole policy and organisation with a view to transfer the responsibilities from the Mission to the Church. The Report noted with satisfaction that "the Missions are beginning to understand that the success of a Mission is to be gauged not by the amount of burden that it carries on its unaided shoulders, but by the amount of responsibilities it has transferred to the Indian Church."[16]

Soon Protestant Missions like the Church Missionary Society and the Friends Mission transferred their educational institutions to the Indian Council. The transformation of the National Missionary Council (N.M.C) into the National Christian Council when the new Constitution was adopted in January 1923 epitomized the principle that the Church in the nation is the chief factor in the Christian movement in India and the natural leaders of the Indian Church ought to have a substantial voice in its affairs. The Church in India had come into its own with the recognition of indigenous leadership.[17] The Council was renamed "The National Christian Council of India, Burma and Ceylon".

It thus may be argued that the hopes and aspirations voiced by Indian Christians for unity and for transcending denominational barriers, for equality and even freedom from Foreign Mission control came closer to 'national awakening' as understood now than the objectives adopted by groups representing other religious communities during the 19th Century.

Unfortunately, the Catholic Church in India with its allegiance to the Vatican, faced the problem of *Double Jurisdiction*, leading to much controversy and even schisms. The abolition of *Double Jurisdiction* in 1884 , and further to it, the steps to introduce Indian personnel (clergy) in the Church by Pope Benedict XV by his Apostolic letter, 'Maximuni Illud', of 30th March 1919 led to indigenization in the Catholic Church.

The Catholic Bishop, Paul Perini voluntarily accepted the scheme informing the Vatican of his support and co-operation in establishing the *Indian Catholic Hierarchy* and entrusted the Diocese of Mangalore to native priests in 1923. Local Church leaders took over, with the 'Agreement of 3rd May 1928' signed between the Holy See and Portugal whereby Indian clergy gradually replaced the Western clergy and the Foreign missionary societies finally when the 'Hierarchy of India' was established after the 'Agreement of July 18, 1950'.

Likewise for the Protestant community was a movement towards unification of Churches in South India, the formation of native pastoral and lay leaders culminating in the active participation of the ordained and laity in all Church matters through the *Synod*. The United Basel Mission Church joined the Church of South India in 1947 while the South Kanara and Coorg Unit and Bombay Karnataka took its time and finally joined the Church of South India only in 1958. This act of handing over in itself is an indicator that the Church did not just talk about unity, but initiated unity and integration. It was almost like having an Indian National Church.

(b) *Socio- cultural integration*

(1) *Through Indianization and Inculturation*

Nationalism in its narrowest sense is patriotism and the path trodden to achieve freedom. This includes the participation of the people in the building of the nation. It also indicates a step toward 'national integration'. In India it involved Indianization and inculturation by Indian Christians and the communication of Faith was to be complemented by active service.

Oriental scholars such as William Jones had appreciated greatly the Indian civilisation and religion. William Carey the great Protestant missionary and visionary said,

> It is not to impose one culture upon another.... We must show practical sympathy with whatever is noble in the ideas and ideals of the rising school of Nationalism... Catholic education must endeavour to inculcate in the Catholic youth a sympathy with the essential aspirations of his nationalistic friends[18].

Indigenisation in practice means acceptance of our cultural heritage with a creative effort to adapt it in the light of modern cultural development. Indian art, drama, song, music etc. were gradually introduced as these influence, inform and convert the minds of men. Christian feasts and customs such as at births and marriages, and Church feasts or on cultural themes such as the harvest festival were kept up in Indian style.

The Protestants made an earlier start working at Indian nationalist spirit as Hogg and N. Minz did, in trying to apply the principle of Gandhian non-violence to Christian thought. The Catholics attempted cultural revival when in 1921 the Catholic Bishops discussed the need for teaching more Indian philosophy in their seminaries[19] and at the 'Catholic Bishops' Conference of India' in 1944, when Indian independence seemed inevitable, efforts were being made to understand the Gandhian idea of what the Christian missions should be for, not for evangelising, but for service which he had expressed in *Young India* dated 7th May 1931.

(2) *Through literary works*

Lay individuals and missionaries showed the way A Protestant leader like Narayan Vaman Tilak of Maharashtra (1862-1919) when converted insisted that the ceremony of baptism be conducted by an Indian Pastor. It was the that he composed the hymn *Priyakar Hindustan (Beloved Hindustan)*.[20] He expressed his great love for Jesus as well as for his Motherland through poetry in Marathi seen in his poem "My Motherland".[21] Tilak felt that patriotism could transcend the differences of religion or sect, and be a powerful bond for uniting a divided India".

It will be a blessed day for India," he used to say, "when every Indian, of whatever school, sect, or religion he be, unites with others in the common service of the Motherland, under the inspiration of patriotism. There is only one thing that will unite Christians, Mussalmans, Parsees, and Hindus, with their thousand and one castes, and that is the love of country."

Narayan Vaman Tilak believed that Christianity in India should interact with India's rich spiritual heritage. He introduced a unique movement called the '*Darbar of the Lord Jesus Christ' in 1917 to form a meeting point with other religions , to form a brotherhood of baptised and unbaptised disciples.*[22] He expected it to develop into a Church independent of foreign personnel and foreign support and which would bring together people on the basis of their loyalty to Christ. One of the ways he helped his fellow Christians become more truly Indian was by teaching them to study and love the older Marathi literature specially devotional poetry of Hindu saints like Nāmdev, Tukārām and Dnyāneshwar. He had declared that "over the bridge of Tukārām' s verse" he had come to Christ. He stated that poetry and music gave insight into peoples' hearts. His poems appeared in the monthly Marathi magazine, *Manoraòjan.*

Tilak conscious of India's spiritual wealth was convinced that Indian Christianity should express itself in forms congenial to the Indian spirit and free herself from all alien rites and customs from the West![23] This came across more strongly towards the end of his life when he felt that the Indian Church was fast reaching a point at which it could work out its own salvation and think out its own expression of Christian doctrine and Christian life and wished that the Western missionaries would leave and go. He said to them, "How long are you going to spoon-feed us? Let us stand on our own feet. Do not interfere; let us try. Let us battle with the waves, let us die, but let us learn to swim."[24]

South Kanara and Mission Work

In South Kanara when the two Missionary societies worked here, the Society of Jesus (the Jesuits) during the years 1878 to 1923 and the German Evangelical Mission of Basel (Switzerland), from 1834 to 1935 they did not remain as mere evangelical missions but were builders of the Nation. It is owing to these Missions that a real integration came about.

Both the Catholic and Protestant missionaries in South Kanara had the same objectives for they pursued a similar path for helping the Christians. The only difference lay in the fact that while the Basel Missionaries had to work for the upliftment of their neo converts, mostly the *Billavas*, the Catholics worked with the already established Christian society as well as for the neo converts. Their efforts were for the conversion and upliftment of the *pariah* and the *koragars*, the untouchables of South Kanara.

Social integration in South Kanara

The Basel Missionaries as did their counterpart, the Jesuits through numerous initiatives made work productive, and using education as leaven, brought dynamics into the social, economic and cultural areas. The contribution of the missionaries towards amelioration of the depressed classes was so great that it impacted society not a little. The neo converts grew in stature, as, from despised, unprivileged low caste people (the koragar and the pariah) they came to find a beacon of light and hope, a status of dignity and experienced well being too. With their refusal to endorse the widely practiced 'caste distinctions', the Christian missionaries initiated the way to integration of people, especially as the employment place and their schools were places where any such caste and class distinctions were not tolerated. As for the old Christians, they led the community to greater heights of success, achievements and thereby recognition within and outside the region.

Through Missionary Institutions and Education

The great contribution of the Church was to education. With the passing of the Charter Act of 1813 the door to Mission work was opened to all foreign Missionaries. We could call the Christian Missions "Educational Mission" as this seemed to be the primary aim of the Protestant missionaries to get their converts, though at this time it was the secondary aim of the Catholic missions. Christian action was heightened by the great impact their educational institutions had, making education relevant to life by opening vernacular schools, technical and teachers' training schools, and even schools for girls.

St. Aloysius School and College served as a beacon of light to all boys and young men, regardless of being a Catholic institution. So did the St. Agnes High School and College for girls.

The Basel missionaries generally ran three types of schools. (1) a boys' school teaching basic curriculum of English, Indian languages, Arithmetic, History, Geography, the Bible and the Catechism, generally in the heart of the town or near village bazaars; (2) the orphanage and boarding school with an industrial branch attached; (3) the girls' school which might at the start be for day scholars or serve as orphanages and later cater even to Hindu and Muslim girls. The opening of the Anglo -Vernacular Schools in Mangalore and Kanarese schools for boys and girls by the Basel Mission was a contributory factor of their success in the mission field.

Through their schools the eradication of the baneful caste system was sought and achieved as the aste distinction was not tolerated.

Amelioration of the low caste and the outcaste

Christianity had become the religion of the outcastes in Mission. Both the Basel Mission and the Jesuit Mission worked for the upliftment of theses marginalized people. While great workers among the Jesuit fathers like Fr. Faustine Corti, called the "Mansere Guru" by the pariah (outcaste) and Angelo Gaviraghi worked for the pariahs, Fr. Alexander Camisa worked for the Koragar, the tribals and called himself a 'White Koragar'. The Bael Mission worked for the billavas (the toddy tappers) and other shudra who were poor and wantonly wasting their little earnings on drinks..

Through their other works of mercy

There was upliftment of the people through 'their works of mercy' and charity .The opening of orphanages and charitable asylums opened by both the Missions such as the St. Joseph's Asylum for the Sick, the Anthony's Charitable Homes and a Leper's home by the Jesuit Fr. Augustus Muller S.J. in Mangalore and a Leper's home also by the Basel Mission in 1906.

The Medical Mission initiative e were the opening of the Kankanady Hospital (and renamed after his death) by Fr. Muller and the Basel Mission Hospital by Dr. Eva Lombard of the Basel Mission hospital in Udipi in 1923 show their concern for the medical health of the people.

Through Christian Movements

Movements and associations formed both by the Protestant Church and the Catholic helped to bridge the gap between the people particularly the youth such as The Young Men's Christian Association (Y.M.C.A.) a movement started in 1844 in London and in India in 1891. It was meant to serve all youth, irrespective of religion and to be true witness for Christ by crossing religious and other barriers.

Associations like the 'League of Catholic Action' were formed for the laity by the Holy Father, Pope Pius II so that there was ' cooperation of the laity with the hierarchical Apostolate of the Catholic Church....[25] Catholic Action was to be essentially detached from politics, but it had to be thoroughly formed and had to equip the members to be the best, the most enlightened, the most honest public men for the business of the State.[26]

Cultural Integration

The main content of any State program is to promote the integration of individuals around a strong common ground. Language plays such a role, in fostering and cementing bonds. Thus, in a territorially defined area cultural integration rests upon a common language – here Tulu is the language spoken by all in South Kanara, by Hindus, Muslims and Christians. The Tulu language, binds the people together, whereas the other two languages of the District, Kannada is the basis for the functioning of the institutions of the public sphere and the language of administration, and Konkani the third language is the mother tongue of the Catholics and is very much one of the languages of India.

The larger society in South Kanara that Christians belonged to was guaranteed the preservation of its languages, Kannada, Tulu and Konkani, as also cultural peculiarities as customs and traditions and the promotion of the activities of various cultural societies. The Society of Jesus (Catholic), and the Basel Mission (Protestant) in South Kanara made a great contribution to this cultural renaissance. Inspired by the example of their missionaries, the old and the new Christians began to take greater interest and pride in their native language and its heritage and soon they followed suit in producing beautiful works or studies in the language that interested or touched them.

We find that both the Protestant and the Catholic missionaries of South Kanara showed keen interest and the highest respect for the study of the local languages and also culture and by writing about these. The Basel Missionaries like Rev. August Manner compiled the two Tulu-English dictionaries, Rev. Dr. Ferdinand Kittel the Kannada-English Dictionaries, and Rev. Fr. Angelo F.X. Maffei a Jesuit complied the two Konkani Dictionaries and the Konkani Grammar, "*Konkani Rananthlo Sobit Sundhar talao.*" Rev. Herman Möegling started two Kannada papers, the *Mangalure Samachara* (1843-44) which was not evangelical at all and the *Kannada Varthika* in 1857 to inform and create awareness about the 1857 uprising."

A Konkani periodical was published , the *Konkani Dirven* by Alex Paes, an advocate of of the Mahars in Bombay who after retirement settled in Mangalore and continued its publication. Later others also started writing Konkani. Petry and novels.

Economic Integration

The standard of living was improved by providing the means of livelihood as also care taken to make them self-sufficient and ban their wasteful habits of consuming liquor and toddy.The Basel Mission opened establishments like the weaving establishment, the tile factories, the printing press and the mechanical establishment. The Catholic Church started a printing press at Codialbail also a smithy and a foundry shop, a carpentry and shoemakers'shop and a statutory shop.

Political Integration

The Indian Christian and his response to the Freedom Struggle The Church was still not rising to the call for the freedom struggle. Did the Christians respond to the call for nationalistic aspirations? There was uneasiness among nationalist Christians that the Church had kept too much out of political questions. While the Christian stood for the freedom of his country, there could be no possibility of his participation in civil disobedience because of the warning of their Church leaders. Indian Christians therefore with the exception of a few were opposed to rising against the British. Later we find a change in the attitude though by and large as leading Indian Christians lamented the fact that Christians were apolitical and were not in the mainstream of the Movement.

Second Phase of the Freedom Struggle

Joseph (Kaka) Baptista the doyen of the East Indian community Kin Bombay, patriot and leader was a staunch loyalist of B.G. Tliak who entered the second phase of the Nationalist struggle. As early as 1900 the idea of '*Home Rule*' emanated from him, long before Mahatma Gandhi took it up as a war cry and was the author of the memorable but elusive phrase of Indian politics, *"Responsive cooperation"*, long before Dr Annie Besant took up the war cry for '*Home Rule*'. He was the first President when the *Home Rule League* was inaugurated at the Belgaum Conference on 28th April 1916. This was the first Indian Home Rule League to be established.

He did not subscribe to Gandhi's civil disobedience. With the death of Tilak, an irreparable loss to him and the *Home Rule League* losing its importance, Baptista's political career started declining. He was a strong advocate of Dominion

Status and the British Council and would have nothing to do with unconstitutional methods. In 1924 Baptista was elected from North Bombay to the Bombay Legislative Council and in 1926 was elected uncontested to the Bombay Legislative Assembly.[27]

Later other Christian leaders demanded Christian involvement. Prof. C.J. Varkey a Keralite settled in Mangalore admonished, "Let the Indian Christian community try to advance politically and nationally. Let them be not only Christians but also Indians....[28] We have to join hands with members of other communities for common civic and political purposes.[29]

The Protestants had already begun to respond when at the All-India Conference of Indian Christians of 1917, they had opposed Home Rule. But Christians got elected on seats reserved for the depressed classes and tribes. The Catholic Church waited and watched. It only watched the interests of Catholics — specially regarding conversion and education. Hardly any reference was made to the Freedom Movement; not even to the Jalianwala Baug tragedy in the Catholic periodicals and other works till the late 1920s.

There was a division of opinion among the Catholic laity where the educated among them seemed to be in disagreement when the Round Table Conference of 1920 was to take place. There was an awakening of national consciousness, that Catholics could not afford to sit back and remain in the background. It was necessary to keep abreast with the rest. Prof. C. J. Varkey in his address at Trivandrum said: "*Let the Indian Christian community try to advance politically and nationally. Let them be not only Christians but also Indians....*[30] *We have to join hands with members of other communities for common civic and political purposes.*"[31]

The All India Conference of Indian Christians (A.I.C.I.C.) conveyed to the Statutory Commission (in 1927) that the

Christian Indians were willing to renounce special electorates for Christians. But there was a difference in opinion among Christians. The Catholics were not in favour of joint electorates.

While the majority of the Protestants had begun to accept the demand for independence, the Catholics asked only for Dominion Status.[32] *The Examiner,* a Catholic Weekly in Bombay, took a stand on this issue as when in 1929, it informed the Catholics that the Freedom Movement was confined to Hindus and therefore, was a communal movement and declared its definite opposition to it.[33] Even *The Anglo-Lusitano,* another Catholic Weekly, warned that boycott of Legislature, withdrawals etc., were *impracticable and dangerous.*[34]

The question of separate electorates had come up at the second session of the Round Table Conference of 1930 when Protestant leaders as S. K. Datta and K.T. Paul took an uncompromising stand against it as also Bishop V. S. Azariah. But the delegates representing the Muslims, the Depressed Class, Europeans and Roman Catholics proposed that separate electorates be granted. Rao Bahadur T. Paneerselvam a representative of the Catholic community took a very narrow and communal view, pleading for separate electorates in order that "*the Indian Christian community might attain its rightful place in the legislative bodies in India.*"[35]

There was no solution to the communal problem. British Prime Minister Ramsay MacDonald in his well known *Communal Award,* offered representation in the new Council on the basis of communal electorates. This led to Gandhi's fast for twenty one days against separate electorates for the depressed classes which made Christian leaders to awaken to the fact that they should change their stand for separate electorates.[36]

But Jerome A. Saldanha of Mangalore (ex-judge of Bombay) recommended joint electorates as in the rest of India "in order to secure communal representation for Indian Christians, dependent on the joint electorate system as recommended by the Simon Commission, with due regard to our comparatively greater advancement in education."[37]

But by the 1930s liberal minded Europoean missionaries openly supported the Indian cause. Fr. Elwin Verrier (Swami Satyanand), Leonard Schiff (Brother Sachidanand) and Fr. J.C. Winslow (all British) identified themselves with Indian nationalism and openly advocated Indian Christian involvement in the Freedom Struggle. Fr. Elvin was the strongest advocate for Gandhi and his call of *swadeshi and swaraj*'. The two books written by Fr. Elvin and Fr.Winslow urged the Indian Christians to get involved in the Freedom Struggle and thereby assist in building a new and free India. Wilson College run by the Scottish Mission in Bombay produced some of the outstanding Indian nationalists and Indian Christians.

In July 1930, the All India Christian Council, the All India Christian Conference of Indian Christians met and adopted resolutions which though did not subscribe to the Civil Disobedience Movement, declared its solidarity with the thrust of the Nationalist Movement. The Conference called upon the Government to give up the policy of violence and repression, to release political prisoners and to show faithfulness to the award of Dominion Status. K.T. Paul (Protestant) and Rao Bahadur Paneer Selvam (Catholic) represented the Christian community at the Round Table Conference. But since the very problem was communal representation which they wanted and which Congress was opposed to the Conference was adjourned in total deadlock.

At a Catholic Conference which met in Mangalore in August 1930 chaired by Dr. Francis Xavier de Souza, I.C.S.

Retd., he expressed that since political matters were outside the scope of the Constitution of the Catholic Federation, there was a need for forming an All India political organisation to give expression and effect to the political opinion of Catholics and to arouse them from their present lethargy. He said:

> Citizenship and Catholicism are not synonymous and we should identify ourselves with political parties as citizens and not as Catholics. We have to have political branches to elect representatives to the All -India organisation to get political opinion of all Catholics and not as Government and semi-Government servants. Our supine attitude towards public life and continuous indifference to political advancement will in the end be detrimental to our interest. When after the present struggle, Government and the Congress come to a rapproachment, a disuniting minority like ours which had sought safety in silence will be ignored and our belated support spurned...[38]

The Mangalorean Review, published in Bombay reported that Dr. F.X.de Souza lamented that the Indian Christian Community was devoid of organisation and wanting in internal cohesion[39] J. A. Saldanha had strongly opposed the separate electorates, saying in his letter of 12th August 1930 to the Konkani Dirven, a Konkani cum English periodical: *"Division by creeds and classes means the creation of political camps organised against each other by teaching more to think as partisans and not as citizens..*[40]

The Irwin-Gandhi Truce of 4th February 1931 was welcomed by all classes in India. The outcome of the Round Table Conference was a fairly amicable and acceptable settlement to both the Indians and the British. Boycott and picketing was to be stopped while repressive measures against those who had participated in the Civil Disobedience were withdrawn.[41] Hoisting and salutation of the (National) Flag was indicative of the intense national consciousness finding expression in India, seeking to control its own Government and its economic development.[42]

Dr. F. X. de Souza as President of the All India Catholic Union in 1934, felt since the Roman Catholics were classed with Protestants under one political unit as Indian Christians by the Constitution, it was imperative to join hands with the Protestants in political affairs in order to project their political views as an Indian Christian community.[43]

Kaka Baptista's reaction when Indian Christians were to be granted separate electorates by the Communal Award was expressed thus:

> *"The moment you separate Indian Christians in water-tight constituencies, they cannot have any influence at the polls and on other communities. No Hindu or Moslem or European or Anglo-Indian would care for the views or grievances of Indian Christians. If they were included in a general constituency they would have some influence by their votes. I believe votes are more powerful than mere seats of a limited number. . .Time will no doubt come when* measures *will be dealt with on merits alone, without reference to communal interests. But for the present, it is better for the small communities not to alienate the sympathy of the major community by clamouring for separate representation.*[44]

Rev. Fr. Jerome D Souza, S.J., a South Kanarite, who was member of the Constituent Assembly, representing the Madras Legislature vehemently opposed communal electorates was. He agreed with Dr. H. C. Mukherjee that Christians should give up both separate electorates and the reservation of seats on the grounds that Justiciable Fundamental Rights were sufficient guarantee for all minorities.[45]

The editorial of '*The Mangalorean Review*' issued a warning to the Catholics:

> *"Let our efforts embrace not only the Catholic community but the whole country with its millions of variegated people and let us merge ourselves into the full life of the country ... We have to broaden our outlook, rise higher for more expansive prospects ... So long as constitutionalism prevails, there is no danger to our religion and when the safety of our religion is assured, there is no need for a distinctly Catholic party or policy. Only let us guard the Constitution. ..."*[46.]

In Bombay when the Nationalist Christian Party was founded by Joachim Alva and Jos Benny in 1930 it was lauded by F.L. Silva as "*a landmark in the evolution of the Catholic community in India!*" This Party had not only Catholics but also Protestants and it voted for support of the Congress. We see how a strong nationalist sentiment was beginning to be seen.

Many Christians were involved at the all India level in the Freedom Movement. Within the Indian National Congress were Rajkumari Amrit Kaur, S. K. George, George Joseph, J.C. Kumarappa and H.C. Mookherjee. Raja Harnam Singh, (father of Rajkumari Amrit Kaur), one of the founding leaders and President of the National Missionary Society of India, desired Christian expression of nationalism even in the religious sphere. So emerged the Christian Ashram Movement with "Indian men, Indian financial resources, Indian management and Indian methods" both in the spiritual and temporal spheres. This was the protest of Indian Christians against Western domination and Western missionary paternalism. It also gave the new direction that Indian Christians had to be part of and move in the mainstream of national life.

The 'Quit India' Call

It was in the 1940s when the National Christian Council came under the leadership of Christian Indians it changed its attitude towards the nationalist struggle. The Council openly declared its solidarity with the 'Quit India' Movement. The All India Conference of Indian Christians and other associations expressed their disapproval to view Christians and other minorities as separate from the total nation.

Gandhi's 'Quit India' call of 1942 called for concerted action viz: non co-operation with Government in every sphere of activity; non payment of taxes; strikes, peasant uprisings and such things which meant the setting up of a parallel "National Government" in order to paralyse the existing administrative machinery and compel the British to withdraw from the land.

The reaction of Christians to the August Resolution (1942) at a conference of Christians in Bombay was that it declared its complete sympathy with the nationalist aspirations. It called upon the Government to make a clear declaration as soon as possible that India would attain freedom immediately after the War. Most people joined the People's Voluntary Brigade though the Church did not favour the 'Civil Disobedience Movement'. Many students responded even though they were discouraged or forbidden to do so. Catholic parishioners in Bombay were warned not to indulge in anti-British activities and the nationalists were dubbed as *Communists* and *Fascists*[47]. Protestant Christian leaders including Raja Harnam Singh and Bishop V.S. Azariah also publicly disapproved a civil disobedience movement in the situation prevailing in 1942 .

The great Movement gathered such momentum that freedom for India seemed imminent. Yet it took five more years as the World War II rubbed its effects on India also.

Role of Some Outstanding South Kanarite Patriots in Bombay during the Freedom Struggle

The general apathy of Christians all over the country we have observed, has been due to its trickling down to them through their clergy which resulted in passivity and obedience in more than 98% of their flock - which was *to render unto Caesar that which was Caesar's and to God that which was God's*: that *the ruler is a Minister of God*, in this case, the Caesar being the British authority. Nationalism was looked upon with suspicion and misgiving. The Protestants of South Kanara had been long under the Basel Mission pastors with their German background and therefore, had to be careful, and subservient to British authority. Life in the mission areas including the large town of Mangalore, was of a *mission compound* and *ghetto* type, allowing no room for much individual thinking or action. It seemed that livelihood and spiritual life were the only two things that mattered to this section of Christians.

The conclusion for the apathy of the Protestant Christian community of South Kanara as per his study on them by Godwin Shiri is (i) the Protestant Christian community of the whole of Karnataka is politically inactive, which included their participation in the whole of the Freedom Movement. (ii) The theological orientation and low socio-economic conditions were the major reasons for this inactivity.[48]

On the other hand, the Catholics had already started playing a vital role in public life besides Church life. Their contribution went beyond their Church, to the larger interests of Society. There were many who were actively involved in Municipal local bodies and Provincial Government, and they felt as the Church did, that His Majesty's Government was for the good of the Indian People. Even when the question of the *Communal Award* arose, the immediate reaction was to seek separate electorates and even desire *Dominion Status*.

But we have seen in the previous sections, how slowly their attitude changed. Owing to the impact of the Catholic secular bodies and the All-India Catholic Congresses, with the passage of time it was felt essential, in fact imperative that the Catholics entered the mainstream of national life, and not remain in isolation as this spelt danger to their own future identity as Christians who were already a minority community.

One sincere Gandhian in Mangalore, and openly so, was the School-master Marcel A. M. D'Souza. He was the Headmaster of St. Xavier's Kadri School. He obeyed the dictum of Justice Ranade that on the revival of industries depends the reconstruction of the Nation, and launched Higher Education in 1911 for the poor, leading them to industrial education after their Middle School Course. He continued to help the poor always espousing the cause of education. He started the South Kanara District Famine Relief Fund, and also helped P. Machado, Cloth Merchant at Kadri to organise a Missionary Work Help Fund, then later, the District Central House for the Incurables. He was a Gandhian, boldly donning *khaddar* clothes and advocated temperance and *swadeshism*. He popularised cotton spinning and *charkha* weaving among the Mangalore Catholics, and was the first Catholic to wear the Gandhi cap.[49]

One man involved in the early phase of the Indian National Movement in the 1920s was Cyril P. Paisley. Born and educated in Mangalore, he left and started a business in Hyderabad which he closed down to join the National Movement. He became Secretary of the Home Rule League under Annie Besant from 1914 to 1920. He joined the Non-cooperation Movement in 1921 and was responsible for the activities of the Freedom Movement in Hyderabad State and was therefore externed by the Nizam from where he came to Madras. He was also very closely associated with Sarojini Naidu, and took part in the *satyagraha* along with Sarvashri.

S. Sathyamurthy, Kasturi Ranga Iyengar, C.R. Das, Ramaswamy Iyengar, Yakub Hussan Sait and others. However, he escaped imprisonment by the British Government by going underground. The Muslim Convention of South India later awarded him the *Bahadur-e-Watan Medal* along with Shri Kamaraj, Bakthavatsalam and Basheer Ahmed Sayeed at the hands of Jayaprakash Narayan.[50]

In the 1930s Jerome Anthony Saldanha, formerly a judge became a strong advocate for nationalism asking Indian Christians to agitate for the repeal of the Salt Tax, wear Indian made cloth, preferably khaddar and foster Indian industry which would give the Indian Christians a common platform with the Gandhi satyagrahis.

South Kanarites in Bombay

Joseph (Jos) Bennie a Catholic in Bombay was one of the founding members of the Nationalist Christian Party. He was one of the first Christians to go to jail during the Civil Disobedience Movement (C.D.M.) of 1930.[51]

Charles Mascarenhas, was a close associate of M. N. Roy of the Radical Democrats. He was arrested with Roy and twelve others in 1931 for conspiracy to overthrow the British Government.[52] He spoke for the oppressed labourer and the necessity of bringing about unity between their ranks and by increasing their strength by establishing an *Anjuman*, He was the editor of *Independent India*, the organ of the (M.N.) Royist Group during which time, he propagated his revolutionary ideas.

Frederick Michael Pinto joined the *Indian National Congress* in 1930 and participated in the freedom struggle and served sentence after his arrest in 1932 when he was sent to the Yeravada Central Prison. In 1934, along with Jayaprakash Narayan and others, he was one of the founder members of the Congress Socialist Party. He also took part in the 'Quit India' Movement.

John Francis Pinto called by those who knew him *Gandhi Pinto* joined the freedom struggle in the C.D.M. of 1930. Joachim Aranha also responded to the C.D.M. call of 1930 and 1932. He went to jail three times.[53]

Violet Alva was a Protestant Christian. She was an active member of the National Christian Council of India and was Vice President of the All India Christian Conference in 1946. She was also Vice-President of the Nationalist Christian party in Bombay.[54]

Joachim Alva, her husband, a Catholic and she were immersed in the Freedom Struggle for many years. He was the co-founder of the *Nationalist Christian Party* with Jos Benny. The Alva couple founded the *'Forum'*, a periodical which was used fearlessly to express views against the British Raj. They both served jail sentences.

Alva motivated Ida Dickinson, the first Christian woman M.L.C. of Bombay, an Englishwoman to join the *Nationalist Christian Party*. She threw away the *Kaiser-i-Hind Medal* awarded to her for social work at the behest of J. Alva!

A. P. Serrao had migrated from Mangalore to Bombay in 1932. The repressive policy of the British made him desire to fight for his motherland and soon he came in contact with Subhas Chandra Bose, Veer Nariman and B. G. Kher and joined the *Forward Bloc* which Subhas Chandra Bose founded.

Alice and Cyprian Alvares a Mangalorean couple in Bombay responded to the call of the C.D.M. of 1942 — the 'Quit India' Movement and carried on subversive activities by operating a wireless system from their own Muslim Children's School premises at Masjid a highly volatile locality. They were arrested on 18th November 1942. Cyprian was sentenced to imprisonment at the Worli Jail and Alice was sent to the Yeravada Central Prison, Poona for more than two years , with Ushaben Mehta as her jail companion.[55]

Of Other Christian Communities

Peter Alvares, closely associated with the Socialist Movement in India participated in the Freedom Struggle from his youth and joined the Quit India Movement of 1942. Leela, a Hindu lady whom he married and Peter worked for the Freedom Movement together. She was a political and social worker and also actively involved like Peter, in the Trade Union Movement.[56]

Professor Aloysius Soares who was a great educationist in Bombay and the pride of the Goan Christian community was another nationalist but who was of a moderate bent of mind. He was a contemporary of Kaka Joseph Baptista and later became the Principal of Dr. Antonio School.

Dr. Joseph Alban D'Souza is to be remembered for his role as one of the architects of the Indian Constitution. When he entered the Bombay Legislative Council in 1927 he was Professor at the Grant Medical College and, therefore a part-time Government servant.

When the Constituent Assembly of India commenced functioning as the Constitution making body for pre-Partition India, in December 1946 of the seven Christians nominated to the Minorities' sub-committee, Dr. Joseph Alban D'Souza was one. The others were Raja Sir Harnam Singh, M.V.H. Colins, Roche Victoria, Dr. H.C. Mookherjee, Frank Antony and Rajkumari Amrit Kaur. The Chairperson was Sardar Vallabhbhai Patel. They were entrusted with the task of safe-guarding issues on Minorities' Rights. One of those who was invited to the drafting of the Constitution was Fr. Jerome D'Souza S.J. a Principal of the Loyola College Madras, a close friend of Rajaji.

From records in the Bombay Archives and Police Records, some names of Christians who were imprisoned for shorter spells can be cited. A Christian lady who attended the All India Congress Committee meeting of 1942 referred to in the records is Miss Anil DeSilva.[57] Other Christians who are mentioned in the C.D.M. 1942 files are: Marian Salvadore Lobo, Louis Manuel Dias, Maurice Rebello, Alfred Joseph, Maurice Hilal and Cathleen Chapman.

Attitude regarding Representation of Indian Christians in Government: Christians and the Electorates

In the 1930s and the 1940s, there had been increasing fear among Christians as tensions increased between Hindus and Muslims, so much so that C. Rajagopalachari in 1944 asked the Christians to discard their apprehensions that majority would rule tyrannically on the minorities, assuring them that the rights and privileges of the Christian Community and the freedom to preach would be safeguarded.[58]

The All India Conference of Indian Christians in its session in 1945 not only reaffirmed its faith in joint electorates but also gave up claims to reservation of seats.[59] This was the voice of members like Benjamin Balraj, Mrs. Violet Alva, R. L. Rallia Ram and D. S. Ramachandra Rao when they passed the Resolution giving up communal electorates and reservations.[60] This decision would no doubt have far reaching results in the future politics of India.

Jawaharlal Nehru also assured the Christians in 1946 saying: *"Why is the cry of 'religion in danger' used when everybody knows that the fundamental creed of the Congress is freedom of religion and all that goes with it. Christians form the third largest religious group of the country and it is absurd for anyone to imagine that their religious or other rights can be suppressed or ignored."*[61]

We can sum up the attitude and sentiments of the Indian Christian community to the attainment of freedom of India, echoing the words of M. Ruthnaswamy, President of the *All India Joint Committee of the Catholic Union of India* and the *All India Conference of Indian Christians* on the occassion of the first Independence Day thus:

> "The Joint Committee rejoices at the attainment of complete freedom by the country without a violent upheaval, and expresses its full appreciation of British and Indian statesmanship on bringing about a peaceful solution of India's contribution problem... The Committee pledges the whole hearted allegiance of Christians of India to the Indian Union and that the country enjoy peace and prosperity and attain its due status in the assembly of Nations."

Role of the Christian Press

Christian papers and journals such as *The Christian Patriot*, in Madras, *The Examiner* , and *The Anglo-Lusitano* in Bombay; *The Harvest Field* in Bangalore and *The Guardian* in Calcutta had editorials or articles on political issues and some were opposed to Christians joining the Freedom Struggle.

The Harvest Field in 1909 supported the Government's suppression of the Extremists who had already demanded complete independence for India declaring that: *it holds strongly that the British Raj is necessary and will continue to be necessary for many years to come, for the maintenance of peaceful progress.*[62]

Again, downright against the Extremists' demand for complete independence in its issue of 1910 the Journal stated:

> The Christian should love his country and people as no Hindu or Muhammadan can, for he ought to

> look at it through the eyes of Jesus Christ.... But, his Scriptures also teach him to be loyal to the Powers that be. The Christian Church must then be loyal to British Rule, for that undoubtedly is supreme.[63]

As the Protestant attitude so the Catholic. *The Examiner* of 5th January 1929 stated that 'the Freedom Movement was confined to Hindus' and therefore it was a communal movement and declared its definite opposition to it.[64] *The Anglo-Lusitano*, a Goan Catholic weekly, warned that boycott of Legislature, withdrawals etc., were *impracticable and dangerous.*[65]

Kaka Baptista used his Paper "*The East Indian*" to establish an Indian identity for the community he belonged to. He also used the Paper to project his views on the Nationalist Movement and its partisans and also to justify his support of the *'Home Rule'* which he advocated along with B.G. Tilak when they founded the *"Home Rule League"*.

Similarly, Joachim and Violet Alva used their periodical "*The Forum*" to whip up the nationalist spirit and to boldy criticize the Government.

'The Mangalorean Review', a periodical published by the Mangalorean Association in Bombay in an article by Francis L. Silva, declared, *"It is time to march shoulder to shoulder with those of set purpose, break the laws and refuse to acknowledge their allegiance to the Government of the country, no matter how dire the consequences may be.*" The *Konkani Dirven,* a Konkani-cum-English periodical published in Mangalore but whose editor was Alex Pais, an advocate in Bombay was similarly supportive of the cause of the struggle.

Charles Mascarenhas of Bombay was the editor of "*Independent India*", the organ of the (M.N.) Royist Group using which he propagated his revolutionary ideas. In

Calcutta, he formed the Congress Socialist Group and then started the paper *Congress Socialist* with Dr. Ram Manohar Lohia as editor.

The *Times of India*, quoting Sir Veerandra Heggade's speech under the headlines *India's Secular Spirit stressed* writes:

> It was the Christian missionaries who had the peoples in India that God was not worshipped merely by extolling Him and observing religious ritual and customs, but also through service to humanity."[66]

Therefore, the Indian Christian Community has to be acknowledged as being one with the other communities of India in exhibiting its "Indianness", its patriotism and dedication to the Nation.

NOTES AND REFERENCES

1. George Thomas.........p.15
2. T.V.Philip, *Indian Journal of Theology,* Calcutta, January - March, 1981, p.7
3. *The Statesman,* Calcutta, 12th August 1977.
4. *"Christianity and the National Movement"* (Editorial), *The Harvest Field,* Mysore, January 1910, pp.3,4.
5. A. Appadorai, p.40; The Satyagraha Vow, *The Bombay Chronicle,* 2nd March 1919, p.153; *Advocate of India* 3rd March 1919, p. 154, *Abstracts of Report of Intelligence,* Maharashtra State Archives, Bombay.
6. Ramabai, Pandita, *A Testimony of Our Inexhaustible Treasure,* Pandita Ramabai Mukti Mission, Khedgaon, India, 1977, p.47.
7. *Young India,* 14thJanuary 1932.
8. T.V.Philip, Theological Tradition in India, *Indian Church History Review,* Bangalore, Vol.21,No. 1, June 1987, p.37; *The Harvest.Field* July 1917, p. 247.

9. Chandravarkar, N.G., *Speeches and Writings*, Bombay, 1911, p. 331.
10. *ibid* , p. 133.
11. George Thomas, p. 153 cf D. L. Joshi, A Call to Indian Christians, *Church Missionary Intelligencer,* March 1906, p. 195.
12. T. V. Philip, *op. cit.,* p. 33.
13. N. M. S. was founded on Christmas Day, 1905 at Serampore (West Bengal); H. F. 33, No. 9, September 1913, pp. 338,339.
14. Sundkler, p. 35.
15. George Thomas, *op. cit.,* p. 149.
16. Proceedings, M.M.C. p.16. G. Tom, p.184.
17. George Thomas, p.185.
18. *Kanara,* 28th July 1918, No.31, p.674; Abstract when the sub-inspector of the District reported that *those there are not many who take an interest in politics do not approve of the Montagu -Chelmsford Reforms,* No.13 of 29-3-1919 (MSS) Bombay - March 25th - announcement that Churches observe Sunday as day of fasting and prayer annually as declared by Gandhiji, p.203 (MSS).
19. Walter Fernandes, p. 264, M. M. Thomas, pp. 19 - 21; N. Minz, *Mahatma Gandhi and Hindu Christian Dialogue, I. R. D. Series 3,* Bangalore, 1970, pp. 116 - 120.
20. Lakshmibai Tilak, *From Brahma to Christ, The Story of Narayan Vasman Tilak and Lakshmibai his Wife*, London, 1056, p.39.
21. *Narayan Vaman Tilak,* p. 50.
22. *Indian Christians*, Natesan & Co., 1st ed., Madras, 1928, p.309.
23. No. 168 in Abhanganjali expresses this thought.cf. p.59 of NV Tilak.
24. *Lakshmibai Tilak,* op.cit, p.82.
25. *Catholic Action Defined*, The Mangalore Catholic Women's Conference 1935, Part IV pp. 110-113 (hereafter. M.C.W.C.), Mangalore, 1936.
26. Victor Rosario Fernandes, Bishop of Mangalore, *Pastoral Letter,* M. C. W. C. App. I, pp 110-115, 199.

27. *The Examiner*, Bombay, Vol. 77, 6th February 1926, p.62.
28. *Indian Christians and Politics,* K. D. 25, No. 16, 16th August 1936, p.ii.
29. A Catholic Leader's Advice, *The Guardian*, X, No. 17, 2nd June 1932, p. 198.
30. *Indian Christians and Politics,* K. D. 25, No. 16, 16th August 1936, p.ii.
31. A Catholic Leader's Advice, *The Guardian*, X, No. 17, 2nd June 1932, p. 198.
32. Walter Fernandes, p.252; cf. J. H.; J. H. Beagle Hole, *The Indian Christian, Study of a Minority,* (Modern Asian Studies), 1st January 1965, p.6533 Jos Bennie, *Indian Christian Nationalise,* M. R. 12, X'mas 1931, pp. 22 - 25.
33. *The Examiner*, 5th January 1929, p.2.
34. *The Anglo Lusitano*, 18th September 1920, p.5.
35. Editorial Report on *All India Catholic Conference held at Mangalore from 15th to 17th August 1930 with Rao Bahadur Pannirselvam, Bar-at-Law, as President,* K. D., 2nd September 1930, p.17; *Indian Christians and Round Table Conference,* The Guardian, 4th June 1931, p. 253; *The Examiner*, 10th January 1931, front page editorial.
36. G. S. Devdhar, *The Provincial Conference of Indian Christians,* held at Poona on 26th November 1932, (Box No. 2, 1929-33), K. T. C. Archives, Mangalore.
37. J. A. Saldanha's letter dated 8th September 1932, K. D. 2, No. 18, 16th September 1932.
38. *Catholic Conference held in Mangalore,* M.R. 1931 , pp 2-3
39. Jos Bennie, *Indian Christian Nationalise,* M. R. 12, X'mas 1931, pp. 22 - 25.
40. K. D. August 1930, suppl. p.1.
41. K. D., 16th July 1931.
42. K. D., 16th April 1931, pp. ii, iii.
43. Catholic and Protestant Cooperation, *The Guardian*, 12, No. 15, 1934, p. 732.
44. *Ibid.*

45. V. L. Sundaram, *Speeches and Writings of Rev.* Fr. Jerome D'Souza S. J. (1897 - 1977), published on the occasion of the Golden Jubilee in the Society of Jesus (1921 - 71), Madras, 1972, p. x; V. L. Sundaram, *A great Indian Jesuit,* Fr. Jerome D'Souza, S. J. (1897 - 1977), Anand, 1986.
46. M. R. 8, 1927, pp. 4, 5.
47. Interview with Messrs. C. J. Alvares and F. M. Pinto at Bombay.
48. Godwin Shiri, Karnataka Christians and Politics, Bangalore, 1978 passim. V. S. Dornakal (V. S. Azariah) *The Bishop's letter,* The Dornakal Magazine, September 1942, p. 2.
49. Marcel A. M. D'Souza, *An Appeal for help,* K. D. 14, No.37, 13th November 1925, pp.i,ii; Correspondence of William X. D. Sequeira, Retired Tehsildar, Karkala, dated 23rd November 1978.
50. Interview with C. P. Paisley at Madras in May 1978; *Freedom-Fighter, C. P. Paisley, 90 years, The Mangalorean,* 25th December 1978, p.15.
51. Letter from J. Alva, dated 23rd May 1979, *op. cit.*
52. *Bolshevism, Prosecution under Section 124 A and 153 A,* File No. 543(28) Box No. 47, Home Dept Sp. Branch, 'A' Class Translation of Urdu Speech by Charles Mascarenhas at Dongri Maidan on May Day 1932, p 53, Maharashtra Archives, Bombay; *Gazetteer of India, Maharashtra State, History of Bombay, Modern Period,* K.R. Chaudhari, Bombay Gazette Depaertment,Government of Maharashtra,1987, pp.239, 243, 244.
53. *Papers of Joachim Aranha with his Family.*
54. Mourning Card of Violet Alva(1970); Joaquim Alva, Letter to the present author dated 23rd May 1979; C. E. R. Easter 1935, pp.21-23; *Dictionary of National Bibliography,* p.44; Joachim Alva, *Men and Supermen of Hindustan,* Bombay 1943, publisher's note.
55. *The Times of India,* 23rd November 1942; , The Bombay Chronicle, 21st April 1943 and 12th October 1943, *The Bombay Sentinel,* 5th June 1945;; papers in connection with the arrest of Alice Alvares, Home Department (Pol), Bombay Castle, 19th

May 1944; Home Department, Pune, 16th August 1944, Letter no. 12611 of 1944, Yeravada Central Prison Office dated 22nd September 1944;Order No. SDV/S-14(1)-63, Bombay Castle 23rd November 1944 regarding release of Alice Alvares; Letter no. SD IV/S-XIV (1) 63, Home Department (Pol), Bombay 12th February 1945; No. SD III/-S XIV File No.1110(61)-X 1943-44, Box 283, Home Dept (Poll) Special Branch(5) Maharashtra State Archives, Bombay and correspondence between Alice and Cyprian Alvares with Government on the above subject; A Vanguarda, 25th October 1992, Goa (Freedom Fighters newspaper); Interview with Dr. Usha Mehta, Freedom fighter, social worker, awardee of Padma Vibhushan at Mani Bhuvan, Bombay on 6th March 1998; also entries in the jail diary of Alice Alvares issued to her on 13-10-1943 by the jailer at Yeravada Prison, p. 3.

56. Life sketch of Peter and Leela Alvares, Acquired from their family at Worli, Mumbai.
57. File No. 1110(1) Home Dept.(Sp) Branch (5) Bombay City SB I. Maharashtra Archives.
58. C. R.'s assurance to Indian Christian's, The Guardian, 30th November 1944, p.428.
59. Bhaskar Yesupriya, The All India Christian Conference Second Day's Proceedings & impressions, *The Guardian*, 5th April 1941. p.iii.
60. George Thomas, pp.212, 213, Joachim Alva's letter to the author dated 23rd May, 1979 at New Delhi.
61. Mr. Walter Fernandes, op. cit., p.252;*Christianity and the National Movement* (Editorial), *The Harvest Field*, Mysore, January 1910, pp.3,4.
62. *The Congress of 1908*, (Editorial), *The Harvest Field*,Mysore, January 1909, p.2.
63. *Christianity and the National Movement* (Editorial), sH. F.January,1910,pp.3,4.
64. *The Examiner*, 5th January 1929.
65. *The Anglo Lusitano*, 18th September 1920, p.5.
66. K.J.C.S., p.42.

13

Wesleyan Methodist Missionaries in Bankura – A Case Study

—*Pranab Puitandi*

It was towards the end of the 18th century that a good number of people of Great Britain began to feel the moral responsibility of preaching the Gospel as well as of forming an empire. It led to the foundation of a number of missionary societies.

At the very same time the British parliament after a long debate, abolished the monopoly of the East India Company in trade (Royal Charter of 1813) and also allowed the missionary societies to come down to India to preach the gospel. Being encouraged towards administration and preaching of gospel, a number of societies born, the Wesleyan Methodist Missionary Society being one of them (1913).

The main objective of the Methodist Mission is obviously telling the good news of Jesus. But what attracts most is that the mission cares for the individual people as well as the communities, sharing in the task of education and social and spiritual development, becoming friends with people of different cultures and faiths.

With such an aim and obviously Proselytisation as the prime aim the Wesleyan Methodist Missionary Society began to work in Bankura, southernmost part of Bengal in the 2nd half of 19th century. The district Bankura was officially formed in 1807, earlier known as Jungle Mahal.

Rev. J. Mitchell and Rev. J. R. Broadhood, two pioneering figures in Wesleyan Methodist Mission, worked hard in Bankura to get a solid foundation. The Methodists working in this stage, were centering around the Bankura town only. Gradually the Methodists entered the southern part of the district and in 1888 reached Sarenga where the Santal Mission was established.

Now to reach the goal the Wesleyan Methodist Missionaries like all other missionaries, undertook the policy of social welfare, spread of literacy and modern medical facilities among the aboriginal people of this backward area. They have concentrated in two main areas–Medical and Education.

Medical

The Wesleyan Methodist Missionaries found that there was no medical facility in the remote villages of Bankura and the people were at the mercy of the quacks and superstition. The aboriginal people even did not hear of modern treatment. Another important thing to note here is that Bankura, at one time, contained the largest number of leper population compared to other leprosy prone districts of India. The census of 1901 recorded that 3.67 per mille among the males and 1.68 per mille among the females were lepers in the district.

To make the tribal people health conscious and to provide them with much more modern treatment, Dr. Cabell Davis reached 'Sarenga' and subsequently Santal Mission Hospital was established (now Khristiya Seba Niketan). It is a complete rural hospital nowadays and providing modern medical treatment to people of a backward region like "Sarenga'.

Another outstanding contribution of the Missionaries in the field of medical services is opening up a Leper Hospital in the northern part of the town in 1903. Mrs. Bryan, a lady resident of Brighten in England extended financial assistance for the construction of the Hospital. The Hospital not only provides medical treatment but the wards of the affected families are also provided with general education and training in handicrafts.

Education

In the field of education, the contribution of the Christian Missionaries of Bankua was remarkable and is still working a lot. Rev. Jon Richards founded a School in 1870 at the Bankura town. In 1880, Rev. J. R. Broadhood established the Wesleyan Middle School at Bishnupur. The *District Gazetteer* (1908) also referred to a Santal Boarding School which was shifted to Sarenga in 1900. The School founded by Rev. John Richards was promoted to Secondary level in 1889. It was under the purview of Calcutta University and produced a number of scholars. The Missionaries established village school at several places of Bankura and Raipur thana area. A middle vernacular school was established at Sarenga and became successful in bringing the aboriginals within the modern education framework. A Santal girls' boarding school was also founded in Sarenga.

The McAlpine Report of 1909 reveals a vivid report of the contribution of the missionaries in the field of education, particularly among the Santals of the Sarenga area. Rev. G.E. Woodfords, endeavours deserve special mention in this regard.

Another outstanding contribution of the Methodists was the opening up of Wesleyan College in Bankura town in 1903, currently known as Bankura Christian College. Still it is one of the best Colleges in the University of Burdwan and the college ha been honoured by the University as Constituent College.

However, despite the efforts of a century of social activities, Christianity as a religion made a little progress in Bankura. A clear picture of the number of the Christians living in the district can be had from various census reports. The last census report of 2001 records the following figures.

Religions	*1997 Census*		*2001 Census*	
	Total Population	*% of total Population*	*Total Population*	*% of total Population*
Hindus	2444545	83.15 %	2693022	84.35 %
Muslims	186021	06.63 %	239722	07.50 %
Christianity	2824	00.10 %	3018	00.09 %
Jains	1953	00.07 %	3487	00.11 %

The numbers of Christians living in rural and urban areas are as follows:

	Rural	
Male	Female	Total
1007	1053	2060
	Urban	
Male	Female	Total
468	490	958

This date reflects that the people in the rural areas of Bankura, mainly in the Sarenga area, which is mostly inhabited by the Santal accepted Christianity as their religion, and in the urban areas the people who embraced Christianity mainly those who were from the rural areas and settled in the town for getting jobs or other facilities extended to them by the Christian missionaries.

Now in case of the Santals, only 0.42% of the total number of the Santals in the District accepted Christianity as their religion as reported in 1931 census. In the above context if we examine the conversion process from the Baptism register, we will find that the first conversion took place in February 13, 1884, when Mukundalal and his family became Christian.

As far the record goes is between 1884 to 1900 the total number of conversion was 45 and ¾ our of this total of 45 high castes. Majorities were outsiders coming from Bilashpur region to work in the railways and were influenced by G. Stoaling, a Railway Inspector to be Christians.

However, on one occasions, anti-missionary riot occurred– when Kudaprasad Pande embraced Christianity in 1890. It wounded the honour and prestige of conservative Brahmins. In between 1900 to 1920 as many as 400 Hindus embraced Christianity but 360 out of this were lepers and socially neglected people. All this happened in or around Bankura town.

In the village area, as census report of 1891 records, there were 56 Christians and it reached the number of 828 in 1911. Out of this total, 300 people were from Sarenga region where the Santals live.

Noticeable thing is that

(1) The coverts somehow became close to the missionaries and were highly pleased. Rev. C. C. Pandey's father was an orthodox Brahmin but was struck by the service rendered by the Methodist Missionaries during an epidemic of cholera in the region.

(2) In spite of such philanthropic works Proselytisation did not achieve any spectacular success. The reasons

for the relatively lesser impact of Christianity as religion in the district of Bankura are as follows –

i) The southern parts of the district where the Missionaries concentrated were basically Santal dominated areas. The social and religious bondage of the Santals are relatively rigid. Again the Santal living in Bankura had undergone immense changes in their religious behaviours since 1855. A new religious movement developed in Bankura, known as 'Sridharma' in this period, which had its base among the tribal population and encouraged tendencies of acculturation with Bengali Hindu peasant culture while trying at the same time for the preservation of tribal identity. The result is that orthodox Hinduism never gained absolute ground in the district. This factor did not help the missionaries to win over the hearts of the Santals or aboriginals of the districts.

ii) The Santal usually take any king of decision as a community, not as an individual. They are very much obliged to their traditions and beliefs and never take a bold decision like embracing Christianity unless they have no other way out.

iii) Christianity appeared to be in conflict with some of the socio-religious behaviours of the Santals. As for example drinking Hardia (Rice beer) has been a sign of hospitality and in worship it is used as libation. Even while in an interview, Rev. Amiya Das, In-Charge of Bankura Central Church, admits that in some cases the Christain Santals remain loyal to this habit even now.

Conclusion

The missionaries in Bankura, particularly the Wesleyan Methodist, are still working relentlessly in the field of education, health and other social services. Shyamdi a small tribal village bordering Purulia and Medinipore Districts is an example of it. Even in Bankura town, Bankura Central Church runs Inter-Faith Community Study Centre where boys and girls of slums are taught regularly. In this Centre I have come across 60 students, out of which 47 are Muslims, 12 Hindus and only 1 Christian. They are being supplied tiffin, dress, books, etc. The fact helps me to conclude that the Wesleyan Methodist are no longer concerned about proselytisation, but engaged themselves in the process of making a healthy society. The Missionaries have Indianised themselves. Through health and education they are strengthening the backbone of a nation.

REFERENCES

1. T. Hembram, *The Santals*, Puthipustak, Calcutta, 1996.
2. M. C. McAlpin, *Report on the condition of the Santals in the District of Birbhum,* Bankura, Mednipore and North Balasore, Calcutta, 1981.
3. *District Census Handbook.*
4. Dr. Pradip Chattopadhyay, *Santals and the Neighboring Religious Faith–A Process of Acculturation in Bankura District – Bengal Past and Present,* Vol. 124, 2005.
5. *Methodists in Bengal,* Shantigriha, Diocese of Durgapur, 2007.

14

Christianity and National Integration in Northeast India: A Study of the Role and Contribution of Rev. J. J. M. Nichols-Roy

—*Merostar Rani*

Introduction

The term "Christianity – National Integration in India" is vast and complex and I am in no way able to bring out an adequate explanation. However I feel it would be appropriate and it is related to this theme to write a brief paper on the role and contribution of the (Late) Rev. James Joy Mohon Nichols-Roy (1884 – 1959). This paper will touch upon his life, political developments from 1919 and Nichols-Roy's response and a summary of his national integrative role.

Rev. J.J.M. Nichols-Roy's Life

U Tirot Sing the great of Nongkhlaw Syiemship was the grand uncle of Rev. J. J. M. Nichols-Roy. Ka Rimai Syiemlieh had left Nongkhlaw area in the hills for Shella in the south of the region probably because of economic hardships following the British conquest on the Anglo-Khasi War in the 1820s. Ka Rimai Syiemlieh then married to U Khah Than Roy Umsong and gave birth to U Joy Mohon Roy on the 12th of June, 1844. By the time of his birth the entire Khasi-Jaintia hill area was already placed under the British administration.

He had his early education at Lba Shella. However, following the great devasting earthquake on 12th June, 1897 that razed the School to the ground, Mr. J.M. Roy could continue his studies at Shillong Government High School in 1898 and completed his Entrance Examination or Matriculation in 1899. After that he pursued his college education at Duff College (today Scottish Church College) Kolkata and completed his B.A. degree in 1904. His study in Kolkata could have provided him the opportunity to come into contact with the Bengal renaissance and nationalism.

Rev. Nichols-Roy did not join any teaching or government job but after graduation; he worked full time with the indigenous Church of God. He and Rev. Wolley Mohon Roy were founding members of this Church in 1902. This Church was indigenous because it did not have any connection with foreign mission societies. Though the connection that was made later through Rev. John A.D. Khan of Kolkata with the Anderson Church of God in the US had gone out well but it was discontinued in 1927 following Rev. Nichols-Roy's active involvement in state politics. He married an American missionary Miss Nora Evalyn Nichols in 1907. This union led to the creation of a new clan Nichols-Roy.

In about fourteen years of his ministry in the Church of God, Rev. Nichols-Roy started a joint stock company known as the United Fruit Company Limited in 1918. Its main works were in the production and sale of orange squash, motor transport, distribution of skim milk and plantation.

Besides that he joined politics as early as 1920 and was instrumental in the formation of the Khasi National Durbar in 1923. He was elected member of the Governor's Council in 1920 and was made Cabinet Minister in February 1927. Again, he was successful in the election to the Assam Legislative Assembly in 1937 and became Cabinet minister until late 1942. The then Assam Government elected him to represent at the Constituent Assembly – an Assembly that framed the constitution for an independent India. He was the author of the Sixth Schedule to the Constitution.

He was again elected a member of the Assam Legislative Assembly in 1952 and in 1957. He died on 1st November 1959.

Rev. Nichols-Roy's Response to Political Changes from 1919 to 1947

The short biographical sketch given above is just a background but serves as an indication for his role not just in shaping the destiny of the hill people but in national integration. His response to political changes might well be described as follows:

First, Opposition to the Division of Khasi and Jaintia People: The British colonialists were responsible for annexing the hill areas with the larger India union in the early 19th century. Their political annexation was dominating because of their divide and rule policy. The Khasi Jaintia hills were once ruled by independent chiefs but after the British annexation, the entire area was divided into state and non-state. While state status retained traditional rule through its elected chief, durbar and ownership of land but non-state means a conversion to British area. That is, the traditional political system was removed and also the land holding system. For instance, the new imperial power terminated the Jaintia chief and converted the Jaintia state to British area in 1835.

The interference was such that its subsequent impact on the unity and integrity of the hill people was in most cases disastrous. Two examples are in order.

One, division of people's ethnicity: British action of changing traditional Jaintia state had the effect of developing a new sense of separate ethnic difference and identity. Though this development did not become apparent there and then but appeared to have grown on a gradual slow pace over a period of time.

Two, changing territorial integrity: What had the Khasi-Jaintia people lost much of their land and people were mainly in the border areas with both Bangladesh on the south and Assam on the north and the east. The British made up decision single handedly without considering the territorial integrity of the Khasi-Jaintia people and took away paddy fields and plain areas in southern part and annexed to Sylhet district and also on and east to Assam, i.e. Kamrup, United Mikir and Cachar Hills.

In this manner the Khasi-Jaintias who lived on the other side of the border though continued to remain as Khasi-Jaintias and inherited their cultivable lands are however by this unmindful bifurcation, living in another country or land. More importantly in this divide and rule policy was the loss of Jaintiapur to Bangladesh; Nongwah and Blocks one and two to Assam. Rambrai chief who was lured and trapped by the British appeared to have sold off some plain areas to the British.

Secondly, Rejection of Brahminical Alienation of the Hill people: The legislative process introduced after the promulgation of the Government of India Act, 1919 was experimented and in 1927 the Government appointed the Simon Commission. Its objective was among other reasons, to further reconsider, modify and to make changes for larger people's representation in legislature. During that period, certain British native leaders planned to exclude the Khasi-Jaintia people and other hill tribes from active participation in the modern legislative system. There were at least two reasons behind this planned exclusion.

1) Some political leaders did not have a good attitude towards the tribes. They still regarded them low and outclass or as "untouchables". There was therefore a sense of incompatibility to sit together in the legislature for nation building process. At the same time, tribes were regarded unfit to make laws not just for themselves but specially for the advanced of high class plain people.

2) The other plan was to keep the tribes under a "caretaker" parental administration. This was a British policy to design a political rule for their own interests. The intended plan was to exclude the hill people so that their distinctive identity was preserved. In this respect, Rev. Nichols-Roy came up highly against this policy of exclusion and explained that preservation of the distinctive identity of the people should go side by side with the progressive idea. That is while the tribes participate in the modern legislative process, they too should take initiative for development and growth.

The intended plan was also in reality a design under the "divide and rule" policy. As the Khasi-Jaintia hills area had been divided into British area and Khasi States, the concept of exclusion would further aggravate the people as well as the area.

Thirdly, Fighting against the British crown colony: Side by side with the intended plan of excluding the tribes from the modern legislative political process, the British masters brought out another political design and that was to place the hill areas under the "newly planned Protectorate" or the British crown colony. While this plan could have been idealistically good for the hill areas in the region but insofar as it did not apply to the entire Khasi-Jaintia people and area, the implementation of the crown colony would result in political disaster. That is, its application could become effective only in British areas but not on the Khasi states and so the damage on the people and territory would be difficult to rectify later.

The crown colony concept was also connected with the attitude. Those who were instrumental for designing it had a highhanded thinking that hill tribes in general and Khasi-Jaintia in particular were still backward, primitive and so needed to be kept apart. Hence, the kind of government to be introduced was what had been termed as "Parental". While such attitude could have been ideal from the side of the British masters, it was in Rev. Nichols-Roy's in-depth perusal very humiliating.

His protest was successful and the idea of a crown colony was removed. This success resulted in keeping the people and territory in unity. Though the Khasi-Jaintia were politically divided, their ethnic unity remained mostly unaffected. More importantly both British areas and Khasi States were brought with India and under its constitution.

Fourthly, Against Greater Eastern Bengal: When one attempt was jeopardized, do not think that the war was over. The British and other political designers who were not successful with the crown colony plan had tried another and that was to place the Khasi States with Assam and British areas (Khasi and Jaintia Hills District) with Eastern Bengal. The plan was first of all to create a new province to be known as Eastern Bengal. Sylhet district would be the main part of this proposed province and thus would include the Khasi and Jaintia Hills district or only the British areas.

The protest that Rev. Nichols-Roy put up was that, tagging of British areas with Greater Eastern Bengal would mean losing of the entire Jaintia hills area and other British villages in Khasi hills. The loss of unified ethnic community and territorial integrity would be permanent. This was nothing but a policy of disintegration. He also foresaw discrimination and exploitation of the Khasis and their system of land ownership under the newly proposed Eastern Bengal-Sylhet province.

Fifthly, Wrote against Grouping of Assam and Bengal: The threat to the integrity of the entire region was not to the hill areas but to Assam in general. Certain British officials and native leaders under the name of the "Cabinet Mission Declaration" were planning to group Bengal and Assam together in representing to the Constituent Assembly. Rev. Nichols-Roy sent a strong written memorandum raising opposition to the plan on the grounds that Assam with 10 Congress representatives only as against 60 Muslim League members from Bengal would make Assam on the most disadvantageous position. The other fear was that the grouping policy would bolster Pakistan's claim of Assam.

It appeared that the leader of Pakistan continued to put up his demand of Assam and specially the hill areas for their inclusion with Pakistan. Rev. Nichols-Roy opposed Pakistan's claim in the Constituent Assembly and even after the general election in 1952.

Sixthly, Integration of hill areas with India: As a member of the Constituent Assembly, Rev. Nichols-Roy's main role was with the hill people and areas of Northeast India. That assertion was by no means discrediting his contribution to democracy, secularism and freedom of one's faith. In one of his memoranda to the Constituent Assembly, Rev. Nichols-Roy submitted a description of all hill areas in Northeast India arguing their integration with India.

In his national integrative plan, he was instrumental for introducing the Autonomous District Council plan that was incorporated under the Sixth Schedule of the Constitution of India.

Conclusion

Rev. J.J.M. Nichols-Roy who was a prominent church leader, played a constructive and integrative role for the nation through his active political participation in nationalism and nation-building.

REFERENCES

1. P. R. Kyndiah, *Rev. J. J. M. Nichols-Roy: Architect of District Council Autonomy* (1993).
2. O. L. Snaitang, *U Rev. J. J. M. Nichols-Roy: Ka Balang U Blei bad ka Jingiatylli Khristan* (1983).
3. O. L. Snaitang, *Ka Biography* (1993).
4. O. L. Snaitang, ed., *Memoirs of Life and Political writings of the Hon'ble Rev. J. J. M. Nichols-Roy Vol-I* (1997).

15

Understanding Culture and the Christian Interface: A Sociological Perspective

—*M.W. Lyngdoh Nongbri*

People ache to believe that we human beings are vastly different from all other species—and they are right! We are different. We are the only species that has an extra medium of design preservation and design communication: "culture". Some would say that is an overstatement! Other species have rudiments of culture as well, and their capacity to transmit information "behaviourally" in addition to genetically is itself an important biological phenomenon. But these other species have not developed culture to the takeoff point the way our species has. We have for instance 'language', the primary medium of culture, and language has opened up new regions of Design Space that only we are privy to. In a few short millennia—a mere instant in biological time—we have already used our new exploration vehicles to transform not only our planet but also the very process of design development that created us.

Hoggart says that Culture is 'the wider life people live'. It represents human life and portrays human achievements, i.e., as a great social heritage of entire mankind. It refers to the whole way of life of the members of a society which includes how they dress, their marriage, customs and family life, their pattern of work, religious ceremonies and leisure pursuits. No part of culture is inborn. It is conceived on two basic critics, i.e., as a 'continuous' and 'cumulative' reservoir containing both material and non-material elements that are socially transmitted from one generation to another generation. It is 'continuous' because cultural patterns transcend years, reappearing in successive generations and 'cumulative' because each generation contributes to the reservoir.

The British Anthropologist Edward Burnett Tylor first explicitly defined the concept of 'Culture' in 1871. He used the term to refer to "that complex whole which includes knowledge, belief, art, morals, law, custom, and any other capabilities and habits acquired by man as a member of society". Through Tylor's definition we understand that culture on one hand is an outcome of society and interactions among various groups and people, and on the other hand, society is able to survive, perpetuate itself because of the existence of culture.

A living and vital culture is rooted in authentic and healthy traditions, has the capacity of continuous renewal and adaptation, and is developed by new aspirations and bold innovations; in this way the 'past;' the 'present' and the 'future' are reflected together in that life of the mind and the spirit that is the indefinable complex of culture. (Kirpal, Prem, *Culture and Development*, Har Anand Publications, New Delhi-110017, p.63). Like 'love', culture will always elude definition and remain an awareness beyond words and concepts, a precious belonging that is within us and also around, linking us to a whole expanse of life, retaining its own uniqueness in time and space. For each of us, it will have a special meaning and significance. Without culture, man would not be human at all.

Culture is a unique possession of man. *Spencer* states that Culture refers to the super-organic environment, which is peculiar to man alone. Russian sociologist *E.V. Roberty* regards culture as the body of thought and knowledge both theoretical and practical which only man can possess. The dictum *'Man is a social being'* can be redefine as *"Man is a Cultural Being"*. *Bronislaw Malinowski* has rightly defined Culture as *'a cumulative creation of Man'*.

The Sociology of Culture contains two basic traditions, one deriving from *Max Weber* and the other from *Emile Durkheim*. Weber focus on meaningful action, and for him the fundamental unit of analysis was always the individual actor. Idea developed and promoted by self-interested actors (rulers seeking to legitimate the rule, elites attempting to justify the privilege, religious entrepreneurs seeking followers), come to have an independent influence on social action. The second crucial strand in the Sociology of Culture comes from *Durkheim*. For Durkheim, Culture is constituted by *'collective representations'*. This may range from vivid totemic symbol to moral beliefs to modern society's commitment to reason an individual autonomy. Durkheim writes not of' ideas' and 'world image' but of representations, rituals and symbols. Symbols concretize ' *collective consciousness'*, making the animating power of group life palpable for its members. Symbols do not reflect group life: they constitute it.

'What we are' is very much a matter of what culture has made us. (Dennett Daniel C., *Darwin's Dangerous Idea, Evolution and the Meanings of Life*. Simon and Schuster, New York, 1995, p.340). Thus MacIver declared, "Our Culture is what we are". How we live, behave and interact with each other, how we think and feel, all falls under cultural concerns.

Often today we are reminded that almost the entire grave threats confronting human and planetary survival originate in human actions. While developing cultural values that also requires the support of the people-to-people relationships, *Religion,* as one important characteristic of Culture has been a major influence in the world. Edward Burnett Tylor views that religion originated in speculation about dreams, trances and death. To Tylor, the belief in souls i.e., 'Animism' was the earliest form of religion. *Sigmund Freud* who believed that early humans lived in groups each of which was dominated by a tyrannical man who kept all the women for himself. Freud believed that these early beliefs gradually became transformed into the worship of deities or gods modelled after the father. Bronislaw Malinowski saw that religion is born from the universal need to find comfort in inevitable times of stress. For Durkheim, it is society that is really the object of worship in religion. Citing the example of *'Totemism'*, he thought that nothing inherent in a lizard, rat or frog inherent in some Australian aboriginal groups would be sufficient to make them sacred. The totem animal present in each clan must therefore be a *'symbol'*.

Religious beliefs have a strong influence on the culture of a community. Even where people in the contemporary world believe that the traditional beliefs of their parents and societies are not so relevant to their everyday lives, underlying religious beliefs about human worth and how to relate to other people and the Earth are still important parts of their lives. And people-to-nature values have traditionally been the role of religion in most societies.

Christianity as a religion stemmed from the life, teachings, and death of Jesus of Nazareth (the Christ, or the Anointed One of God) in the 1st century AD. It has become the largest of the world's religions. Geographically the most widely diffused of all faiths, it has a constituency of more than 2 billion believers. Its largest groups are the Roman Catholic Church, the Eastern Orthodox churches, and the Protestant churches; in addition to these churches there are several independent churches of Eastern Christianity as well as numerous sects throughout the world. It has been part of the great diversity of humankind where there are many different religions and belief systems that have developed like Animism, Buddhism, Hinduism, Islam, Jainism, Taoism, and many more.

As a tradition, Christianity is more than a system of religious belief. It also has generated a culture, a set of ideas and ways of life, practices, and artifacts that have been handed down from generation to generation since Jesus first became the object of faith. Christianity is thus both a living tradition of faith and the culture that the faith leaves behind. The agent of Christianity is the Church, the community of people who make up the body of believers.

The Christian community is said to be a distinct community in the world, with a form of government in the Church, and a culture that can be derived from Biblical principles. However it is not a closed community but it interfaces with the world. The field of Christianity is the world. In earlier generations, Christians have interfaced with local communities simply by living "Christianly" in those communities. Christians interfaced with their non-Christian neighbours on a daily basis and if they were living "Christianly", then their love, good deeds, service and devotion became what the world saw like that which took place among the tribal *Khasi* people of Northeast India in the 19th century. The Missionaries (Welsh Mission followed by the Catholic Mission) came to these Hills in 1841 with an evangelistic commitment where they were ignorant about primal cultures. Their main aim was to liberate the people from bondage to what they regarded as superstition. It broke down centuries-old superstitions and inculcated the spirit of progress on scientific lines. They tended to make a distinction between the religious (what they frequently referred to as "superstition") and the non-religious elements in their culture. And this was done through education. Thus, in the blaze of western influences, the

Khasis learned to discard the traditional cloak and almost kept pace with the progress of the society on modern lines. This evangelical work brought change in Religion and finally in their Culture.

Today, things are different. The 21st Century Christians have self-consciously withdrawn from the world. People have become more individualistic and isolate themselves from the people around through cars, homes, entertainment and so on. This creeping cultural isolationism, coupled with Christian's self-conscious withdrawal from the world have worked together to insure that Christians by and large have no real interface with the world. Christians can't rely on the mass media to present our public face to the world. The problem this poses for Christians is that the media gravitates to that which is dramatic and spectacular. Yes, the Christian way of sensitizing the teachings of Christ has gain momentum in the present decade particularly through the media, yet this has to be looked into that it does not turn into any political slogan. As James Davison Hunter points out in his book "Culture Wars," the media gravitates to the extremists in any issue. Even when they have the best of motives, the media only lends itself to a one-dimensional portrayal of Christians. Christians have got to "go public" in other dimensions - building cultural capital through pursuing excellence in every sphere of culture rather than withdrawing into their own safe, evangelical enclaves. And they've got to "go public" by letting their light shine in such a way that others may see their "good deeds" and praise their Father in heaven. But whether living together Christianly with other non-Christians or reaching through the media, Christian interface definitely has had its sway in traditional Culture.

Church history demonstrates that one of the constant struggles of Christianity, both individually and corporately, is with 'Culture'. Where should Christianity stand? Inside the culture? Outside? Ignore it? Isolate themselves from it?

Should Christians try to transform it? Theologian Richard Niebuhr provided a classic study concerning these questions in his book *Christ and Culture*. Even though his theology is not always evangelical, his paradigm is helpful. It includes five views.

First, he describes the *"Christ Against Culture"* view, which encourages opposition, total separation, and hostility toward culture.

Second, the *"Christ of Culture"* perspective is exactly the opposite of "Christ Against Culture" because it attempts to bring culture and Christianity together, regardless of their differences.

Third, the *"Christ Above Culture"* position attempts "to correlate the fundamental questions of the culture with the answer of Christian revelation."

Fourth, *"Christ and Culture in Paradox"* describes the "dualists" who stress that the Christian belongs "to two realms (the spiritual and temporal) and must live in the tension of fulfilling responsibilities to both."

Fifth, *"Christ the Transformer of Culture"* includes the "conversionists" who attempt "to convert the values and goals of secular culture into the service of the kingdom of God."

It is true that the decisive thing is the regenerative power of God. Leave aside conversion and propagation, Christian values that Christ has taught like the attitude of love, hope, forgiveness, patience, kindness, self-control etc can all be laid open and shared through open dialogues and advocacies with others belonging to other faiths and religion but who share the same religious values. This is what we talk and remind ourselves when it comes to discussion on unity in diversity from religious point of view. The superiour-inferiour category that labels the other person as an inferior when he differs in language, culture or religion and the right- wrong category convinces the person that his own way of life is right and the other person's way of life is unsatisfactory or wrong should be erased. For instance the line that divides between the Christian Khasi and non- Christian Khasi should be deleted. This has brought differences in their attitude towards their culture. The former will be more inclined to the Christian Culture, which is the western culture and the latter to the traditional Khasi culture.

International Demonstration Effect—the process of foreign cultural penetration are already posing a serious threat to the traditional Khasi cultural identity and are alienating the youth from their traditional cultural moorings. There are certain symptoms of a deepening malaise that reflect the new dangers arising from the breakdown of the traditional moral order and the lag in the reconstruction or building of a new moral order. The unbridled acquisitiveness of *"the new rich"* and their flaunting of their new wealth acquired through total disregard for means and methods arouse envy of the deprived section. The unbridled avarice of the *'haves'* cannot but arouse the vehement envy of the *'have-nots'*. Both are the product of an acquisitive and amoral society. The emergence of the "new middle class" which was once upon a time a classless society straightly denotes the existence of the "new rich". So we remember Oliver Goldsmith's unforgettable words: "Where wealth accumulates, men decay!" In the emerging situation, there is the existence of the so-called *'elite culture'* and *'mass culture'*. The 'elite culture' is followed by those who refrain of practicing all the basic elements of Khasi traditional culture and who wish to maintain only those aspects that suits their so to say standard of living, lifestyle and degree of achievement. These are not necessarily the "new rich class" but lets say the educated section, the cream of the society, the 'elites'- that particular segment of the society that Yogendra Singh keeps on mentioning in his book, "*Modernization of Indian*

Tradition". Of course I wouldn't say that they constitute a large section, maybe only a fraction from the entire Khasi Society. But their attitude in response to their culture is one of a *"Separation Syndrome"*, separated from the mass culture, which I mean that culture which the entire populations of the society who are not the elites follow. This elite culture has been built up by these small segment and has surfaced the traditional culture, which to them is a little outmoded and backward, and does not go along with their standard, degree and level of achievement. They seem to shy away when it comes to live by their Khasi standards.

While focusing our minds on this, I would like to quote Sumitranandan Pant when he says,*"It is not the question of politics which faces the world today: It is that great cultural problem which is before the world!"*

If we bring culture and Christianity thus into close union—in the first place, will not Christianity destroy culture? Must not art and science be independent in order to flourish? We answer that it all depends upon the nature of their dependence. Subjection to any external authority or even to any human authority would be fatal to art and science. But subjection to God is entirely different. Dedication of human powers to God is found, as a matter of fact, not to destroy but to heighten them. To the Christians, God gave those powers. He understands them well enough not bunglingly to destroy His own gifts. In the second place, will not culture destroy Christianity? Is it not far easier to be an earnest Christian if you confine your attention to the Bible and do not risk being led astray by the thought of the world? We answer, of course it is *easier*. Shut yourself up in an intellectual monastery or seminary, do not disturb yourself with the thoughts of unregenerate men, and of course you will find it *easier* to be a Christian, just as it is easier to be a good soldier in comfortable winter quarters than it is on the field of battle.

Missions today demand a change of life that allows one to sere the other person as valid and to relate to that one in the same way that God directly through his own culture. If Christ is the transformer of Culture, members of a group or community must identify him as one of their own, a Christ that understands and knows their Culture. They should rediscover Christ within their own Culture and within their own tradition, the Christ of faith that symbolizes freedom, peace and justice.

We may recall that in reply to Tagore's charge that Indian nationalism under Gandhi's leadership was tending to promote blind anti- Westernism; Gandhi made the following statement which in a large way constitutes our national credo on culture. This credo is, however, violated in practice everyday, every hour and every minute. He says,

> *"I do not want my house to be walled on all sides and my windows to be stuffed.*
> *I want the culture of all lands to be blown about my house as freely as possible.*
> *But I refuse to be blown off my feet by any. I refuse to live in other people's houses as an interloper, a beggar, or a slave".*

Again

> *"No country can become a nation by producing a race of imitators....*
> *I want to write many new things, but they should all be written on the Indian state".*

Further

> *" The Indian culture of our times is in the making.*
> *Many of us are striving to produce*
> *a blend of all the cultures, which seem today to be in clash with one another.*
> *No culture can live if it attempts to be exclusive".*

During India's cultural reconstruction, Nehru had created an impressive infrastructure in the form of the three

Academies- The *Sangeet Natak Academy*, The *Lalit Kala Academy* and The *Sahitya Academy* supported by a chain of State Level Academies which played an important role to spread the cultural fragrance in and around the region and how to make young people aware of the cultural etiquette, cultural exchanges, cultural inter-connection and cultural preservation.

Whether the society throws up a creative synthesis of the best of traditional and the modernity, these will depend on choices made and options exercised by the present generation on the basis of awareness of the cultural link between their past, present and the future. Not only are individuals responsible, but it is the task of the cultural policy makers, the 'collective representatives' as Durkheim calls to generate at one end awareness of cultural roots and moorings and to promote at another end a critical and positive attitude towards the impact of cultural and religious forces from outside. Christian interface will continue and traditional communities like the Khasi community for instance must find a path of modernization and revitalization suited to its own cultural roots as well as new cultural challenges. No doubt, it must also create new content and forms of culture corresponding to the needs of its growth and development in this scientific and technological age. May it contradicts the words of Yeats when he said, *"the great song is dying out from the lips of the people."*

Christianity has played an important part in the rapid social change of recent years and has come to be recognized as a powerful social influence. To neglect it in considering the social integration of the nation would be quite impossible. At the same time, however, Christianity is undeniably an imported religion. So there is the need to synthesize the two through the development of effective cultural symbols. Cultural integration, rather than being based on cultural identity, is more easily achievable then on the basis of externally oriental political symbols such as anti-Communism and anti-Capitalism; or social symbols like anti-corruption, anti-poverty and anti-exploitation which are the issues of the day.

REFERENCES

Alasuutari, Pretti. 1995. *Researching Culture: Qualitative Method and Cultural Studies*. New Delhi: Sage Publications.

Barclay, Harold B. 1986. *Culture - The Human Way*. Canada: Western Publishers.

Barnic, Martin. 1983. *A Sociology of Contemporary Cultural Change*. Oxford: Basic Blackwell.

Benedict, Ruth. 1980. *Patterns of Culture*. London: Routledge and Kegan Paul.

Brown, Ina Coriwene. 1963. *Understanding Other Cultures*. N.J.: Prentice Hall.

Chattopadhyaya, D.P. 1973. *Societies and Cultures*. Bombay: Bharatiya Vidya Bhandar.

Cherian, M.T., *Hindutva Agenda and Minority Rights A Christian Response*, Bangalore: Centre for Conteporary Christianity, 2007.

Datta, Amlan, *The Gandhian Way*, Shillong:North Eastern Hill University Publication, 1986.

Dennett, Daniel C. 1995. *Darwin's Dangerous Idea - Evolution and the Meanings of Life*. New York: Simon and Schuster, Rockfeller Center.

Despres, Leo A. 1975. *Ethnicity and Resource Competition in Plural Societies*. Paris: Mounton Publishers, The Hague.

Done, Michael R. (ed.). 1988. *The Real and Imagined Role of Culture in Development: Case Study from Indonesia*. Honolulu: University of Hawaii Press.

Downs, Federick S. 1994. *Essays on Christianity in North-East India*. New Delhi: Indus Publishing Company.

Ember, Carol, R. and Ember, M. 1977. *Cultural Anthropology*, 2nd Edn. New Jersey: Prentice Hall Inc., Englewood Cliffs.

—— (Ed.) *Christianity is Indian – The Emergence of an Indigenous Community*, New Delhi:ISPCK, 2000.

Fine, Gary Alan (1989), "The Process of Tradition: Cultural Models of Change and Content" in Graig Calhoun (ed.). *The Studies in Comparative Historical Sociology*. Greenwich, Conn: JAJ Press.

Garg, Pulin K. and Indira J. Parikh. 1955. *Crossroads of Culture: A Study in the Culture of Transcience*. New Delhi: Sage Publication.

Harold B. Barclay. 1986. *Culture: The Human Way*. Calagry: Western Publishers.

Harris, Marvin. 1975. *Culture, People and Nature: An Introduction to General Anthropology*. New York: Harper & Row Publishers.

Herskovit, J. and Melville. 1971. *Cultural Anthropology*. New Delhi: Mohan Primlani, Oxford and IBH Publishing Co. and Melville.

Hedlund, Roger, E., Ed. *Missiology for the 21st Century – South Asian Perspective*, Chennai: ISPCK/MIIS, 2004.

Inglis, Fred. 1994. *Cultural Studies*. Blackwell Publishers, Oxford, UK and Cambridge, USA.

—— *India: the Grand Experiment*, (Surrey: Pippa Rann Books, 1997).

Johnston Hank and Klandermans Bert (ed.). 1998. *Social Movements and Culture: Social Movements—Protest and Contention*, VCL Press.

Johnston, Ronald L. 1975. *Religion in Society, Sociology of Religion*. New Jersey: Prentice Hall, Englewood Cliffs.

Jeyachandran, L.T., "Chak De India:The Christian and National Building," *Engage*, April 2008.

Kirpal Prem., *Culture and Development*. New Delhi: Har-Anand Publications, New Delhi.

Kroeber, A.L. 1952. *Nature of Culture*, Chicago: University of Chicago Press.

Lessa, William A. 1972. *Reader in Comparative Religion: An Anthropological Approach*. Third Edition. New York: Harper and Row.

Lienhardt, R.G. "Religion" in Shapiro A.L. (ed.). 1971. *Man, Culture and Society*. London: Oxford University Press.

Malinowski, B. 1944. *A Scientific Theory of Culture and Other Essay*. Chapel Hill: University of North Carolina Press.

Mukherjee, R. 1991. *Society Culture Development*. New Delhi: Sage Publications.

Mukherjee, Ramakrishna. 1995. *Society, Culture, Development*. New Delhi: Sage Publications.

Mangalwadi, Vishal (2001), *The Quest for Freedom and Dignity*, Mumbai:GLS Publishing.

—— *1997. Missionary Conspiracy, Letters to a Postmodern Hindu*, 2001 New Delhi:Good Books.

Mathew, C.V., 2001. *The Saffron Mission*, New Delhi: ISPCK.

Raj Sunder, E., 1998. *The Confusion Called Conversion*, New Delhi:TRACI Publications.

Rundell, John and Mennoll Stephen (ed.). 1998. *Classical Readings in Culture and Civilization*. New York & London: Routledge

Sen, Amartya, 2006. *Identity and Violence – The Illusion of Destiny*, London:Penguin.

Sanyal, B.S. 1962. *Culture: An Introduction*. New Delhi: Asia Publishing House.

Singh, Yogendra. 1991. *The Sociology of Culture*. Moscow: Progress Publishers.

Thomas, Julian. 1996. *Time, Culture and Identity: An Interpretive Archaeology*, London and New York: Routledge.

16

Genetical Concepts of the First Biblical Man and Woman on Earth

—D. Marngar

Introduction

The earliest known written record describing a great Flood is the *Gilgamesh Epic*, written about fifty centuries ago, or about 3000 BC. Other ancient records have been found that the present lists of either 8 or 10 kings that ruled in the region of ancient Sumeria after kingship descended from heaven until the Flood. The oldest known of these antediluvian kings lists were written perhaps as early as 2,000 BC. Different king lists and translations variously recorded that the first man lived sometime between 453,600 and 222,600 years before the Flood.[1]

The contents of the antediluvian kings lists and the *Gilgamesh Epic* are reflected in the Biblical Genesis accounts of the creation of the first man and the list of 10 descendants and 8 patriarchs from Adam to the time of Noah and the Flood. Authorship of Genesis is traditionally attributed to Moses about 1,000 BC, but was probably written and heavily edited from the 9th through the 5th centuries BC.[1]

In the book of Genesis it was written that "God created man in his own image, in the image of God created he him; male and female created he them." (Genesis 1:27)

"And Jehovah God formed man of the dust of the ground, and breathed into his nostrils the breath of life; and man became a living soul" (Genesis 2:7).

Family Tree as described in the Bible

Name: Adam - First Patriarch[2, 3, 4]

Created by God: God created Adam on the sixth day of Creation -

(4004 BC) in the Garden of Eden, as reckoned by Bruce G. Armstrong and Irish theologian James Ussher in 1650 AD

Events

(4004 BC) – Adam and Eve expelled from Eden on the tenth day of creation.

(3874 BC) – Adam was 130 years of age when Seth was born

(3769 BC) – Adam was 235 years of age when Enosh was born

(3679 BC) – Adam was 325 years of age when Cainan was born

(3609 BC) – Adam was 395 years of age when Mahalaleel was born

(3544 BC) – Adam was 460 years of age when Jared was born

(3382 BC) – Adam was 622 years of age when Enoch was born

(3317 BC) – Adam was 687 years of age when Methuselah was born

(3130 BC) – Adam was 874 years of age when Lamech was born

Death

(3074 BC) – Adam dies at the age of 930 years

Patriarch: 930 years, from 4004 BC to 3074 BC.

Pre-Adamite hypothesis or **Pre-Adamism**[5]

It is the religious belief that humans existed before Adam, the first human being named in the Bible. Advocates of this hypothesis are known as "preadamites", as are the human-like creatures believed by them to have existed before Adam.

History and Development of Hypothesis[5]

Theophilus of Antioch and an Egyptian pagan Apollonius, argued that the world was 153,075 years old. The most serious early challenge to biblical Adamism came from the Roman Emperor Julian the Apostate who, on his rejection of Christianity and conversion to Theurgy, a late form of Neoplatonism, accepted the idea that many pairs of original people had been created, a belief termed co-Adamism or multiple-Adamism.

1655 La Peyrère argued that Paul's words in Chapter 5, verses 12-14 of his Epistle to the Romans should be interpreted such that "if Adam sinned in a morally meaningful sense there must have been an Adamic law according to which he sinned. If law began with Adam, there must have been a lawless world before Adam, containing people". Thus, according to La Peyrère there must have been two creations: first the creation of the Gentiles and then that of Adam, who was father of the Jews. The existence of pre-Adamites, La Peyrère argued and explained Cain's life after Abel's murder which, in the Genesis account, involved the taking of a wife and the building of a city. This account of human origins became the basis for 19th century theories of polygenism and modern racism.

Some Pre-Adamite theorists held that Cain left his family to master an inferior tribe described variously as "nonwhite Mongols", "Black Races" or "beasts of the field". Pre-Adamites also claimed that Cain took a wife from one of the inferior pre-Adamite peoples. The idea that Cain's mark was blackness arose in eighteenth century Europe, and was popularized in 19th century America by the founder of Mormonism Joseph Smith.

Recent genetic research on variations in Y-chromosomes over time place the most recent male-male ancestor of all men living today at sometime between 270,000 and 15,000 years ago.[6]

How do Y chromosomes and Mitochondrial DNAs fit into the Biblical Framework?

Intriguingly, in light of current scientific knowledge, the *Bible* seems to mention DNA itself: "Thine eyes did see my substance, yet being unperfect; and in thy book all my members were written, which in continuance were fashioned, when as yet there was none of them" (Psalm 139:16), as well as its recent potential to record both the time and the places where people lived: God "has made of one blood every nation of men to dwell upon the whole face of the earth, having determined ordained times and the boundaries of their dwelling" (Acts 17:26).

Humans have 23 pairs of chromosomes, including one pair of 'sex chromosomes' which are XY in males and XX in females. Thus the Y chromosome is passed down only through the male line, from father to son. The scientists from eight countries have drawn up a genetic family tree of mankind by studying variations in the Y chromosome of more than a thousand men from different communities around the world. [7] [25] The Y chromosome is one of the two sex chromosomes (X and Y) which only men carry (women carry two X chromosomes). It was found to be consistent with the biblical teaching that we come from one man, Adam.[25]

Females have no Y chromosome, but an analogous test can be performed on them — it's only through the female line that mitochondrial DNA is transmitted. The mtDNA evidence is consistent with all humans being descended from a single woman as the Bible teaches, although it doesn't actually prove that there was ever only one woman in existence.

Rebecca L Cann, Mark Stoneking and Allan C Wilson— in analyzing DNA from the energy producing compartments of the human cell known as the mitochondria, have discovered that this genetic material, inherited through the ages, provides "new perspectives on how, where, and when the human gene pool arose and grew." [8]

Deoxyribonucleic acid (DNA) contains codes which direct the cell to form the proteins that serve as the foundation for our bodies. Certain portions and sequences of the DNA are called genes which, besides maintaining our bodies' daily activities also determine our heredity: height, skin pigmentation, and eye color down the generations, the transmissions of traits that keep the race or species going for thousands or millions of years. DNA is in fact the blueprint for life itself.[8]

The role of DNA in the mitochondria (the power plants of the cell) is much more limited but nonetheless vital: it codes for key components of our energy production system, i.e., it is a piece of coded information in the mitochondria the purpose of which is to extract energy from food molecules suspended in the cytoplasm outside the nucleus.[8, 9]

While it is the nuclear DNA that determines what the next generation will look and act like, the mtDNA, densely packed with its own group of genes, has two principal characteristics that make it more valuable in studying genealogy:[8, 9]

(a) It is simpler and maternally inherited, allowing a geneticist to look straight into the female past, and

(b) It provides a magnified view of genetic diversity because of mutations - changes in the tiny biochemical configurations that occur as a matter of time - accumulate much faster in mtDNA than in the nucleus, giving each individual a "signature" that can be compared with others.

Whatever population has accumulated the most mutations—is the most divergent among each other - can be assumed to be the oldest. The longer a population has existed, the more mutations. The geneticists claim that every existing human can be traced back to a very special colony of humans from Africa. The oldest maternal lineage leading to modern day humans had been discovered - everyone has recent African roots.[9]

Methodololgy

Y Polymorphism and mtDNA Analyses

As you may know, a person is made up of 23 pairs of chromosomes or 46 (44 + XX, 44+XY) in total: half from mom, half from dad. Of these 23 pairs, a female would have a pair of XX chromosomes, which signifies the female gender. The male would have an XY pair, signifying the male gender. In males, unmatched X and Y chromosomes exchange DNA only at the ends of the two chromosomes (pseudoautosomal regions).[10, 25]

Chromosomes are composed of DNA, which itself is composed of 4 nucleotides: A (adenine), T (thymine), C (cytosine) and G (guanine). These letters, ATCG, are the ones we follow. Currently there are 2 genetic methods of finding out if you are related to someone who may be an ancestor, whether living or dead.

1. The first method is "Y polymorphism:"[11] In many cultures, we have always traced our ancestors back in time by following the paternal line. In order to do this genetically, we must follow the Y chromosome. Polymorphism is a term to show that mutations do occur in the Y chromosome, as can happen with other chromosomes. Note that the Y chromosome for the most part does not change (except for a small part of the pseudoautosomal regions). Different combinations of polymorphisms are known as haplotypes. Thus we are able to look at these changes and establish a genetic relationship between 2 living people (or 1 living, 1 deceased; or 2 deceased). This Y polymorphism test is relatively new, and studies regarding the frequency of different combinations of polymorphisms are even newer.

2. The second method is called mitochondrial DNA or mtDNA analysis:[12] This method involves the analysis of DNA found in the mitochondria, not the nuclear DNA of the nucleus in the body's cells (thus not the 23 pairs). You must note that in using this method, you are tracing ancestors through the maternal, not paternal, line. This is because mitochondrial DNA is passed from the mother to her children.

In both methods you look for the most recent common ancestor (MRCA) of the 2 individuals. The assumption here is that the number of nucleotides (ATCG) differing in 2 individuals increases on average in relation to the temporal distance from their last common ancestor. In other words, the closer in time, the higher the number of matching nucleotides.

In the Y polymorphism method. There are 4 chromosome changes that do occur from generation to generation, and these are known as *markers*:[6, 13, 25]

- *indels*: these are insertions or deletions of the DNA at particular locations on the chromosome. An example is the YAP (Y chromosome alu polymorphism).

- *snips*: these are single nucleotide polymorphisms in which a particular nucleotide is changed (like A is changed to G). Since snips and indels (stable alus) are very rare, they also are known as unique event polymorphisms (UEPs).
- *microsatellites*: these are *short* sequences of nucleotides (example: ATCG) which are repeated over and over again a number of times in tandem. Changes sometimes do occur, however, and the number of repeats may increase or decrease.
- *minisatellites*: these are *longer* sequences of nucleotides (example: ATCG) which are repeated over and over again a larger number of times in tandem. Changes sometimes do occur, however, and the number of repeats may increase or decrease.

Because all of the markers (indels, snips, microsatellites and minisatellites) are joined one to another along the entire length of the Y chromosome (except for the pseuodoautosomal regions), a haplotype constructed from a number of different markers actually documents the history of the Y chromosome.

To find the most common paternal ancestor, the team drew up a genetic family tree of mankind. They mapped small variations in the Y chromosomes of 1,062 men in 22 geographical areas, including Pakistan, India, Cambodia, Laos, Australia, New Guinea, America, Mali, Sudan, Ethiopia and Japan.[14]

Results

Y-Chromosome - Y and mighty[15]

"There has been almost a century of ignorance and misunderstanding of it," says David Page of the Whitehead Institute in Cambridge, Massachusetts, who is currently working on a major study of the Y. "It has been regarded as a wasteland but I see it more as a natural park with as many unusual features as Yosemite or Yellowstone." Right now, these quirks are providing answers to such very big questions as: where did we come from? How did we develop language?.

Y's power to shock has only recently been revealed. There have been reports on the way it can be used to track down the "ancestral" Adam, the one man from whom all males are descended, a theory put forward that it is a gene on the Y that accounts for man's ability to speak.

These ancient events around its birth conferred on the Y one of the special features responsible for its current stardom: it appears only in males. Any egg that was fertilised by Y-carrying sperm became male; eggs that got the X stayed female. That is why the Y is a unique source of information about the male line. It's a genetic version of those famous biblical begats.

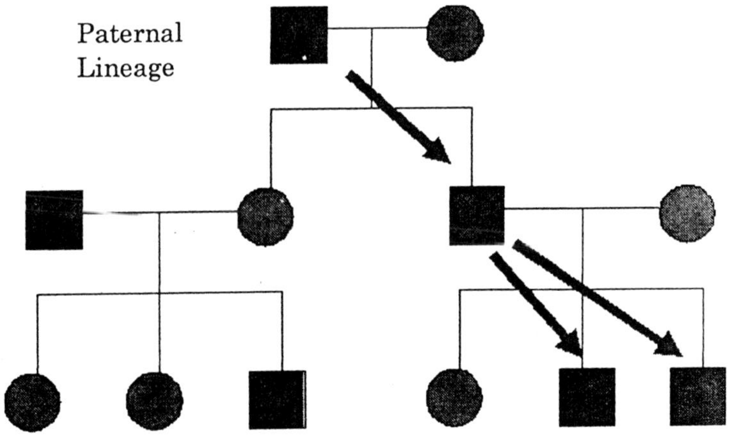

The Jewish priests[16, 25]

A study in collaboration with Karl Skorecki, a nephrologist

at the Rambam Medical Centre in Haifa, and Mike Hammer, looked at Jewish priests (*Cohanim*; singular *Cohen*). Cohanim are not the same as Rabbis; the latter are appointed functionaries while members of the priestly class inherit their position through the male line. In biblical tradition, Aaron, the brother of Moses, was the first priest: God awarded the priesthood to him - and his sons. In other words, the priesthood passes with the Y chromosome and there is no legitimate way in which a non-priest can become a priest. We reasoned that if oral tradition had been faithfully maintained, with the priesthood being passed, by and large, from father to son throughout the generations, island of Y chromosomes of Jewish priests would have been created within, but separated from, a sea of non-priests.

By measuring the differences in the mutations that have crept into the Y, researchers had shown that the males of two different ethnic groups are more or less related to a common ancestor. The bigger the differences, the longer they have been separated. Some of the results, reported last few years, were surprising. For instance, the Lemba are the black, Southern African, Bantu-speaking population whose oral tradition says they were originally Jewish. According to their stories, they were once craftsmen who lived in the Yemen. The men would travel south to trade but when a disaster struck back home, some of the men took local wives and settled down. Researchers reported that the pattern of mutations on the Y chromosomes among men of the Lemba was close to that found among a Jewish priestly group known as the Cohens. Similar research suggests that the Israelis and the Palestinians came from a common stock around 7,800 years ago.[25, 27]

Information from mtDNA Analysis

The female equivalent of the Y-genetic information passed only from mother to daughter - is known as mtDNA. This is the DNA of the mitochondria, the powerhouse of every cell. For a few years there has been broad agreement that the mitochondrial Eve lived around 143,000 years ago, which seems to make nonsense of the 59,000 years ago that Nature Genetics reported for the "Y-Adam."[17]

"Mitochondrial DNAs from 147 people, drawn from five geographic populations, have been analyzed by restriction mapping. All these mitochondrial DNAs stem from one woman who is postulated to have lived about 150,000 to 200,000 years ago...."[17]

The age of "Eve" (the name for the one African woman whose mtDNA had been traced down the ages) has been set at between 140,000 and 200,000 years (her median age rounded to 200,000). She was almost certainly a highly evolved descendant of an African erectus, and her offspring spreading out of Africa perhaps 90,000 to 180,000 years ago to take over the world - although it is possible that the migration may have occurred as recently as 21,000 B.C. [18]

A science journal, *Nature Genetics*, recently published a new set of variations (haplotypes) on the Y and it confirmed that modern humans had originally migrated out of Africa, and reported that if the dates were correct, the genetic Eve, the one from whom all humans are descended, was 84,000 years older than the genetic Adam, as measured by the Y.[19]

What "mitochondrial Eve" and "Y-chromosome Adam" really represent are really statistical entities called the Most Recent Common Ancestor, or MRCA, meaning the last shared relative. As such, they exquisitely confirm the Biblical account. Since at the great flood, all people living at that time were dead except 8 people alive, the males on the ark were Noah and his three sons, thus all should have had identical Y-chromosomes. The process of tracing the MRCA for men is ended here and could not proceed further because of no other men carrying different mutations on their Y chromosomes are alive in this great flood. The four women, however (Mrs. Noah, Ham, Shem, and Japheth), ostensibly not related to one another, would therefore trace their maternal lineages back to the Biblical Eve. The MRCA of the men, then, WAS Noah, but the MRCA of the maternal lineage was NOT Mrs. Noah, but Eve - who did (according to both science and the Bible) live considerably before her statistical counterpart, Noah.[26]

Sufficient hereditary material was extracted and purified from samples of placenta to compare the intricate variations between and among peoples of Asian, European, African, Australian and New Guinean descent. The mitochondrial DNA - "mtDNA" - offered a wholly unique attribute that could not be found elsewhere: it was inherited only maternally, from the mother. Except for occasional minor mutations, this type of DNA was passed intact from great - grandmother to grandmother to daughter with virtually no input from males and thus no mixing - no blending of father's and mother's genes - that would jumble, complicate, and thereby obscure its history.[12, 26]

It survived the generations over millennia without being adulterated by recombination. For that reason mitochondrial DNA - as opposed to nuclear DNA where such blending does occur - is a powerful new tool "...for relating individuals to one another."

Mitochondrial DNA is a convenient tool because it is much smaller and simpler than the DNA in a cell's nucleus. The DNA in a cell's mitochondria has already been fully mapped and found to contain only 37 genes, all of them inherited solely from our mothers, "...so you are connected by an unbroken chain of mothers - whether you are a son or a daughter - back into the past, and what we are interested in doing is building up a genealogical tree that connects those maternal chains."[12, 26]

African Origin or Out of Africa Model

Adam was black and lived in Africa 50,000 to 100,000 years ago, according to scientists who have detected traces of his genes in the DNA of modern man.[20, 21]

Taken together with earlier results on the evolution of women, the studies carried out by geneticists in the United States and at Cambridge University indicate that the whole of humanity may be descended from a small tribe of about 10,000 people, some of whom migrated out of Africa within the past 100,000 years or so.[22]

After almost a decade of study, two international teams have found the genetic trail leading to Adam, and it points to the same time and place where mitochondrial Eve lived. The genetic trail is so clear that it allows researchers to compare the migration patterns of men and women tens of thousands of years ago. It even pinpoints the living men whose Y chromosomes most resemble Adam's: a few Ethiopians, Sudanese, and Khoisan people living in southern Africa, including groups once known as Hottentots and Bushmen.[22]

The Stanford researchers so far, they have found 93 new polymorphisms in the Y chromosomes of men from around the world. And when the team started sorting these polymorphisms into a phylogenetic tree, they found one particularly ancient marker, called M42. In its most ancient form, shared by other primates, this marker is an A, or adenine. Today, it is found only in Africa, in just a few of the 900 males they had scanned- 15% of the Khoisan, and 5% to 10% of the Ethiopians and Sudanese contained this marker A. These men must have inherited this ancient form from a common ancestor. The data further show that sometime in the past 100,000 to 200,000 years, this M42 site underwent a mutation-a change from A to T (thymine) in one of Adam's descendants. While men with the A stayed in Africa, some of the Africans with the T left the continent and spread around the globe. Today, "all men outside of Africa, as well as most African men carry the T said Underhill. [23]

Meanwhile, another team headed by geneticist Michael Hammer at the University of Arizona, Tucson, surveyed another non-coding region of the Y chromosome in 1544 men worldwide and found the same pattern. The DNA sequences varied among individuals, but Hammer found that the variants cluster into 10 major groups, known as haplotypes, which occur in different frequencies in different populations.[24]

Haplotype 1A, defined by an A at a particular site, appears to be ancestral because the A is found in chimpanzees, and Hammer's team found that in humans, it occurs only in some Africans. "It's at the highest frequency in the Khoisan," he says- the same population fingered by Underhill's team. Although the ancient form of 1A persisted in some groups in Africa, it also underwent a change to a G (guanine) 150,000 to 200,000 years ago in one descendant of Adam's. Like the T in Underhill's site, this form was carried out of Africa when men moved away and replaced other males around the globe.[24]

Both sets of results bolster the so-called Out of Africa model of human origins. Underhill says: "I think this speaks persuasively for an Out of Africa origin for modern humans."

Eve and the Out-of-Africa theory

Mitochondrial Eve is believed to have lived in Africa she is sometimes referred to as African Eve, an ancestor who has been hypothesized on the grounds of *fossil* as well as DNA evidence.[22] According to the most common interpretation of the mitochondrial DNA data, the titles belong to the same hypothetical woman. Family trees constructed on the basis of mitochondrial DNA comparisons show that the living humans whose mitochondrial lineages branched earliest from the tree (*L1*) are prevalent among the *San* and the *Mbuti* people.

Researchers therefore reason that all living humans descend from Africans, some of whom migrated out of Africa and populated the rest of the world. If the mitochondrial analysis is correct, then because mitochondrial Eve represents the root of the mitochondrial family tree, she must have predated the exodus and lived in Africa. Therefore many researchers take the mitochondrial evidence as support for the "*single-origin*" or Out-of-Africa model.[22]

The Mitochondrial DNA provides another support for the *Out of Africa hypothesis* in the form of gene diversity. One finding that is not subjected to interpretation is that the greatest diversity of mitochondrial DNA sequences exists among Africans. This diversity is believed to have accumulated because humans have been living longer in Africa than anywhere, although the same relative diversity can also be explained if just more people lived in Africa than in other regions—an interpretation of the past that all evolutionary models also accept, even those that contradict the African-origin theory, such as *Multiregional evolution*.[22,23]

Some modern-day men living in what is now Sudan, Ethiopia and southern Africa are believed to be the closest living descendants of the first humans to set out on that great journey tens of thousands of years ago.

The Y chromosome in the Study of Human Migration and Prehistory[25]

Genesis, chapter 5, records "the generations of Adam": Adam begat Seth, Seth begat Enosh, Enosh begat Kenan... down to Noah of the great flood (Table 1). Translated into modern genetic terms, the account could read "Adam passed a copy of his Y chromosome to Seth, Seth passed a copy of his Y chromosome to Enosh, Enosh passed a copy of his Y chromosome to Kenan"... and so on until Noah was born carrying a copy of Adam's Y chromosome. The Y chromosome is paternally inherited; human males have one while females have none. What is more, the Y chromosome of a father passes to his son is an unchanged copy of his own.

Table 1
Before the flood: the generations of Adam according to the book of Genesis

Names	*Date of Birth from] Creation (BC)*	*Date of Death from Creation (BC)*	*Age till the date of death (Years)*
Adam	0	930	930
Seth	130	1042	912
Enosh	235	1140	905
Kenan/Cainan	325	1235	910
Mahalaleel	395	1290	895
Jared	460	1422	962
Enoch	622	987	365
Methuselah	687	1656	969
Lamech	874	1651	777
Noah	1056	2006	950
Shem, Ham, Japheth	1556	-	-

Genetics has confirmed the Bible's (long discredited) claim that Noah's family populated the entire world, putting to rest the widespread theory that humans evolved simultaneously in several places. Analysis of Y- and mitochondrial chromosomes also confirm after Noah, the population grew, dispersed into northeast Africa, and gathered in the Middle East shortly before dispersing into the rest of the world, also matching the Biblical account of events between the times when eight people exited an ark and when the entire human population, 70 strong families, gathered at a plain in Shinar to build a tower.[26]

Next, God destroyed the tower and scattered the peoples. Numerous global cultures remember this event in legend, and, again, DNA analysis confirms it. Genetic and archaeological evidence demonstrate that, shortly after Noah, humans - in a sudden and rapid exodus—filled the globe. Scientists speculate endlessly as to what led these ancient humans to migrate en masse in this "Great Leap Forward": the Bible provides the answer. DNA evidence can now detail the movements of these early fathers with some precision.[26]

Interestingly, both genetic and linguistic data reflect a trifold division of humanity about the time that Ham, Shem, and Japheth would have existed, with one group (Ham and his descendants) going west into Africa and east along the coasts into the south Pacific, one group (Japheth) colonizing Europe as well as central and northeast Asia, North America and South America, and the last (Shem) remaining largely in the Middle East.[26]

Ancient original settlements that are found in the Basque area of France, the Australian archipelago, and the Kalahari Desert area of Africa, almost assuredly comprised of the families of the sons and grandsons of Noah.[26] This fact, and evidence of small bands of cousins left along the way, both confirms and provides a mechanism for another Biblical assertion: "Those were the three sons of Noah, and from them came the people who were scattered over the earth" (Genesis 9:19).

Genetics and Human Migration Patterns[28]

Much discourse is emerging from scientific circles detailing the results of genetic testing in relation to human migration patterns. These studies attempt to show the distribution of ethnic genetic codes over certain geographic areas in relation to time.

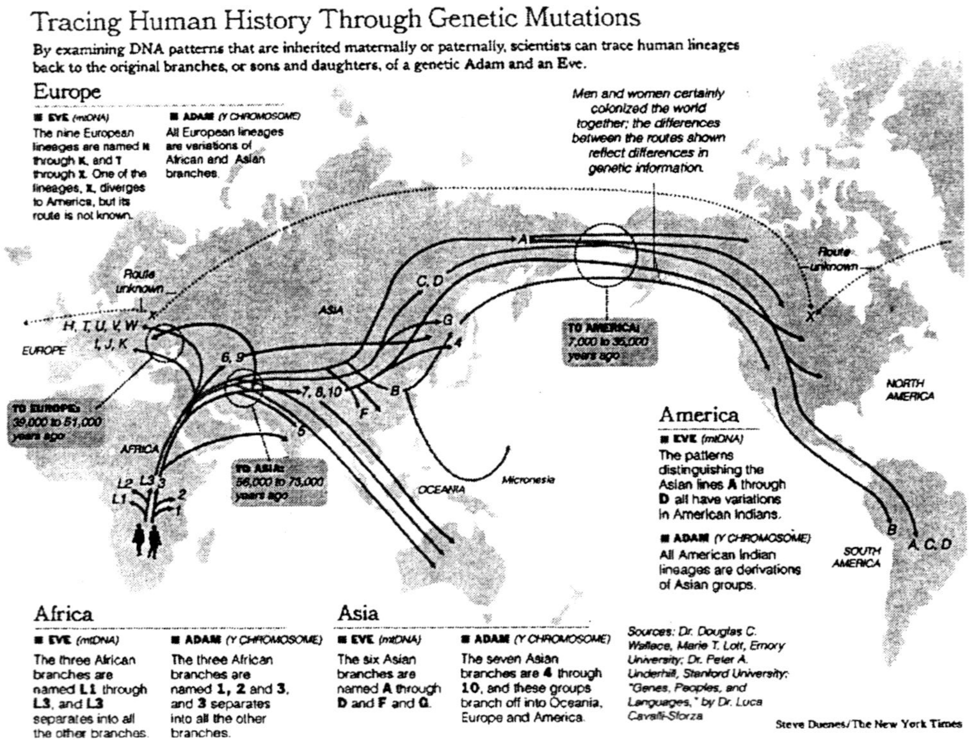
Tracing Human History Through Genetic Mutations
By examining DNA patterns that are inherited maternally or paternally, scientists can trace human lineages back to the original branches, or sons and daughters, of a genetic Adam and an Eve.
Europe
EVE (mtDNA)
The nine European lineages are named H through K, and T through X. One of the lineages, X, diverges to America, but its route is not known.
ADAM (Y CHROMOSOME)
All European lineages are variations of African and Asian branches.
Men and women certainly colonized the world together; the differences between the routes shown reflect differences in genetic information.
Route unknown
X
H, T, U, V, W
I, J, K
EUROPE
TO EUROPE: 39,000 to 51,000 years ago
AFRICA
L2 L3 3
L1 2 1
6, 9
ASIA
7, 8, 10
5
TO ASIA: 56,000 to 73,000 years ago
C, D
G
4
B
F
A
OCEANIA
Micronesia
TO AMERICA: 7,000 to 35,000 years ago
Route unknown
NORTH AMERICA
SOUTH AMERICA
B
A, C, D
America
EVE (mtDNA)
The patterns distinguishing the Asian lines A through D all have variations in American Indians.
ADAM (Y CHROMOSOME)
All American Indian lineages are derivations of Asian groups.
Africa
EVE (mtDNA)
The three African branches are named L1 through L3, and L3 separates into all the other branches.
ADAM (Y CHROMOSOME)
The three African branches are named 1, 2 and 3, and 3 separates into all the other branches.
Asia
EVE (mtDNA)
The six Asian branches are named A through D and F and G.
ADAM (Y CHROMOSOME)
The seven Asian branches are 4 through 10, and these groups branch off into Oceania, Europe and America.
Sources: Dr. Douglas C. Wallace, Marie T. Lott, Emory University; Dr. Peter A. Underhill, Stanford University; "Genes, Peoples, and Languages," by Dr. Luca Cavalli-Sforza
Steve Duenes/The New York Times

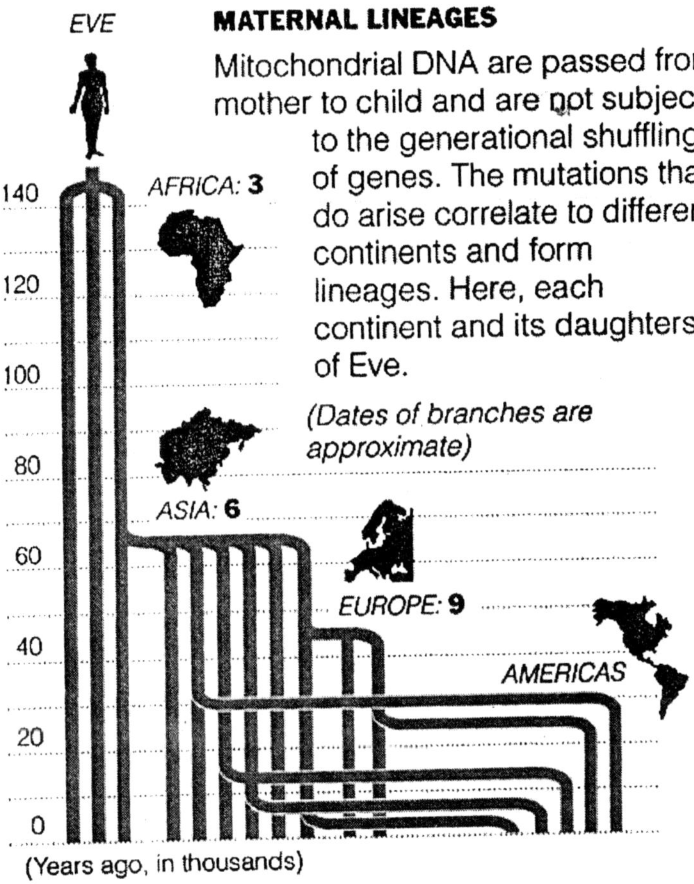
EVE
MATERNAL LINEAGES
Mitochondrial DNA are passed from mother to child and are not subject to the generational shuffling of genes. The mutations that do arise correlate to different continents and form lineages. Here, each continent and its daughters of Eve.
(Dates of branches are approximate)
AFRICA: 3
ASIA: 6
EUROPE: 9
AMERICAS
140
120
100
80
60
40
20
0
(Years ago, in thousands)

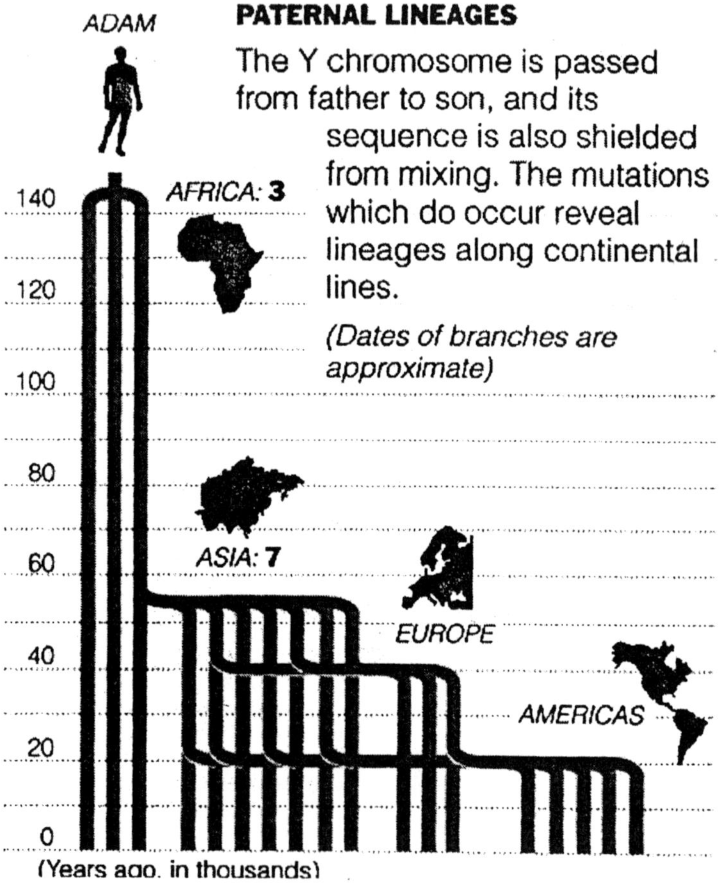
PATERNAL LINEAGES
The Y chromosome is passed from father to son, and its sequence is also shielded from mixing. The mutations which do occur reveal lineages along continental lines.
(Dates of branches are approximate)
ADAM
AFRICA: 3
ASIA: 7
EUROPE
AMERICAS
140
120
100
80
60
40
20
0
(Years ago, in thousands)

Scientists have now identified the human lineages of the world descended from 10 sons of a genetic Adam and 18 daughters of Eve. This ancestral human population lived in Africa and started to split up 144,000 years ago. This time period is when both the mitochondrial and Y chromosome trees first branch out.

Analysis of DNA from many ancient skeletons and mummies is performed on the mitochondrial DNA, or mtDNA. This "ancient" DNA is often degraded and present in very small quantities. mtDNA offers the best chance of isolating DNA from ancient samples because it is small and is present in the cell with many copies.[28]

Daughters of a Genetic Eve[28, 29]

Dr. Douglas C. Wallace and his colleagues at the Emory University School of Medicine in Atlanta constructed a world female genetic tree based on mitochondrial DNA. He found that almost all American Indians have mtDNA that belong to lineages he named A, B, C and D. Europeans belong to lineages H through K and T through X. The split between the two main branches in the European tree suggests that modern humans reached Europe 39,000 to 51,000 years ago, Dr. Wallace calculates, a time that corresponds with the archaeological date of at least 35,000 years ago.

In Asia the ancestral lineage is known as M, with descendant branches E, F and G. In the Americas are lineages A through D. In Africa there is a single main lineage, known as L, which is divided intc three branches. L3, the youngest branch, is common in East Africa and is believed to be the source of both the Asian and European lineages.

Dr. Wallace's mitochondrial DNA lineages are "haplogroups" but known as "daughters of Eve," because all of the lineages are branches of the trunk that stems from the mitochondrial Eve.

Dr. Wallace is now exploring the root of the mitochondrial tree. In the March 2000 *American Journal of Human Genetics*, he and colleagues identify the Vasikela Kung of the northwestern Kalahari desert in southern Africa as the population that lies nearest to the root of the human mtDNA tree. Another population that seems almost equally old is that of the Biaka pygmies of Central Africa.

Universal Maternal Ancestor can be found for all the members of any population. The example traces the lineages of 15 females in a stable population. In each generation, some maternal lineages proliferate and others become extinct. Eventually, by chance, one maternal lineage replaces all the others.

Figure. Determination of the MRCA through mitochondrial DNA[30]

Conclusion

"We are all Africans at the Y-chromosome level and we are really all brothers," Dr. Underhill said. Dr. Wallace remarked that since he started working on mitochondrial DNA in the late 1970's: "What I have found astounding is that it clearly shows we are all one human family. The phylogeny in Africa goes back to the origins of our species, but later is touching Europe and Asia, saying that we are all closely related."[23]

A historical document carried in the blood of everyone alive today - DNA. Tiny spelling mistakes—changes in the DNA sequence - that occurred in the past can give us clues about genealogical relationships. If two people share a change, then they are likely to share an ancestor. If we look at the spelling mistakes carried by people all over the world, we find that ultimately all of us share a common ancestor. In the case of the male line, defined by a piece of DNA in the Y-chromosome, this analysis allows us to trace back to a common male ancestor for everyone alive today. In other words, Adam.[18]

Every piece of DNA in our bodies can be traced back to an African source. The Y-chromosome traces back to eastern or southern Africa, around 60,000 years ago. The present-day inhabitants of Ethiopia, Sudan and southern Africa carry the clearest signals of our earliest ancestry, signals that have been lost in the rest of us. So they give us a glimpse of our 60,000 year-old Adam. The San Bushmen of the Kalahari - who in many ways are a composite model of facial features from people all over the world - give us a portrait of Adam and his fellow early humans.[18]

Y-chromosome gives us two very important clues to the question of how we populated the world. First, it shows us our most recent common ancestor (Adam). This man lived in Africa around 60,000 years ago. The significance of this date is that it means that all modern humans were living in Africa until at least that time. In other words, within the past 60,000 years - only about 2,000 generations - our species has populated the entire planet. Clearly, we are all very closely related. The second clue provided by the Y-chromosome concerns the routes we followed in our migrations around the planet. The male line gives us the best view of the routes followed. So, the Y - a piece of DNA that really doesn't do much more than to make men - men - is one of the best historical documents ever written. Women also have a female history written in their mitochondrial DNA, showing the path to Eve around 150,000 years ago.[18]

It's interesting that both genetics and the *Bible* show that there is a common origin of humanity. According to genetic data we come from a single male ancestor. In the *Bible* too it is mentioned that there is a single male Adam and single female, Eve. We don't equate the results one-to-one with the biblical story, of course, because if you count back through the generations described in the *Bible*, Adam should have existed in 4004 BC, and our Adam existed 60,000 years ago. Also, our Adam and Eve weren't the only people alive at the time, just the lucky ones who left descendants down to the present day. But it is nice to know that we arrive at the same general conclusion: we're all related.[18]

Whether or not genetic prehistory is suitable material for a modern origin myth, it is about to be made available to a wider public. In general, there is more and more agreement among paleoanthropologists, archaeologists, geneticists and historians about the details of our past. We suppose one thing that some people still find hard to accept is that we left Africa so recently, and blitzed our way around the world, but it does seem to have happened like that.

REFERENCES

1. "Antediluvian King Lists", *Connections of Chaos*, 2003.
2. "Antediluvian Patriarch Lists", *Connections of Chaos*, 2003.
3. "Apocrypha and Pseudepigrapha", Religion Library, Art Galore! Book Gallery, 2003.
4. "Adam and Eve Genealogy Pages", *Connections of Chaos*, 2003.
5. Genetic Ancestors of all Humans", *Connections of Chaos*, 2003.
6. Jobling M. A. and Tyler-Smith C. 2003. The Human Y Chromosome: An Evolutionary Marker comes of Age, *Nature Reviews Genetics* 4, 598-612
7. Cavalli-Sforza L.L. and Cavalli-Sforza F. 1995. *The Great Human Diasporas: the History of Diversity and Evolution*, Addison-Wesley Publishing Co., Reading, MA
8. Cann R.L., Stoneking M, and Wilson A.C. 1987. Mitochondrial DNA and Human Evolution, *Nature* 325: 31-36,
9. Wilson A. C. and R. L. Cann. 1992. "The recent African genesis of humans", *Scientific American*. Vol 266 No 4.
10. The Y Chromosome Consortium. 2002. A Nomenclature System for the Tree of Human Y-Chromosomal Binary Haplogroups *Genome Research*, Vol. 12, Issue 2, 339-348.
11. http://ybase.org/statictics.asp
12. Gibbons A. 1998. "Calibrating the Mitochondrial Clock," *Science*, Vol. 279, January 2, p. 29.
13. Zegura S.L., Karafet T.M., Zhivotovsky L.A. and Hammer M.F. 2004. High-Resolution SNPs and Microsatellite. Haplotypes point to a single entry of Native American Y chromosomes into the Americas. *Molecular Biology and Evolution* 21, pp.164-175.
14. Jobling M.A. and Tyler-Smith C. 1995. "Fathers and Sons: the Y Chromosome and Human Evolution," *Trends in Genetics*, 11, pp. 449-456
15. Jerome Burne. 2001. Y Chromosome Y and Mighty. Guardian, August 18, (http://www.guardian.co.uk/archive/article/0,4243, 4240155,00.html)
16. Skorecki, K. et al. 1997. "Y-Chromosomes of the Jewish Priests," *Nature*, 385, 32.

17. Michael H. Brown. 1987. Mitochondrial DNA and Human Evolution, "The Search for Eve" *Nature*, January 1.
18. Spencer Wells. 2002. *The Journey of Man, A Genetic Odyssey*, Princeton University Press.
19. Genetic Adam Never Met Eve BBC News, 30 October, 2000.
20. Genetics & Genealogy: Article #2, Genes Reveal Adam Came Out Of Africa. Tom Wilkie, Science Editor, *The Independent*: Thursday, 23 November 1995.
21. Gibbons A. 1997. "Y Chromosome Shows That Adam Was an African", *Science*, Vol. 278, 31 October, p 805.
22. Chris Stringer. Evolution: Out of Africa and the Eve Hypothesis. *Genetics & Genealogy*, Article # 20
23. Underhill, P et al. 2000.Tracing the dispersal of human populations by analysis of polymorphisms in the non-combining regions of the human Y-chromosome. *Nature Genetics*; 26: 358-361.
24. Hammer, M et al. 2000. PNAS 97:6769-6774.
25. Bradman Neil and Thomas Mark. The Y Chromosome in the study of human Evolution, migration & prehistory.The Centre for Genetic Anthropology of University College, London, in *Genetics and Genealogy*, Article # 14
26. Wendy Wippel. The History of the World in the Molecules of Life. *Personal Update NewsJournal*, September 2006.
27. Nicholas Wade. In DNA, New Clues to Jewish Roots. *The New York Times*: May 14, 2002
28. Nicholas Wade. The Human Family Tree: 10 Adams and 18 Eves, *New York Times*, May 2, 2000
29. Sykes, Brian, *The Seven Daughters of Eve*. Norton; New York, 2001.
30. home.nc.rr.com (Determination of the MRCA through mitochondrial DNA).

17

Seminar Recommendation and Resolutions

We, teachers, scholars, research students, resource persons and all participants hailing from different parts of the country and having met together in Shillong for a two day national seminar from 14-15, October, 2008 organized by the Synod College on the theme: CHRISTIANITY – NATIONAL INTEGRATION, submit the following statement, recommendations and resolutions before the nation, academic institutions, political leaders, the church and people at large for deliberation, adaptation and implementation.

Statement

That we are proud of our country India for its rich and diverse cultural resources, ancient civilization and its heritage. Its spirit of tolerance was unique through out its age-old history and resulted in multi cultural situation. Christianity in India, which originates in the 1st century through Christ's doubting disciple, St. Thomas, grows in the vicissitudes of India's integrative cultural environment. Christianity, therefore, is a vital and integral part of the nation's history.

That Christianity has taken and continues to take active participatory role in building the people and the nation through its multi-dimensional ministries that became evident in the establishment of a wide network of educational institutions, medical services and humanitarian activities among people irrespective of caste, class, creed, language, gender or region. Christian missions have involved in helping the poor and needy, identifying with the marginalized, participated in rural reconstruction, taken care of the orphans and the outcasts.

That through out its presence in the country, Christianity always stands for people's justice, peace, truth and non-violence. It believes in equality, liberty and human rights. It also works for the liberation of the dalits, tribals, women and backward communities. Through numerous educational institutions, it engages in shaping the destiny of the youth of the country.

That Christianity stood by the country and actively involved in the freedom movement, fought for political freedom from colonial rule and strongly endorsed the country's unity and integrity. It participated in building a secular, democratic and a People's Republic country. At the threshold hold of the new millennium, Christianity vows to fight against poverty, fundamentalism, militancy, communalism, casteism and against gender inequality.

Recommendations and Resolutions

That given its commitment and role in nation building, the National Seminar upholds and calls for the promotion of Christian values of love, peace, justice, equality, tolerance, communal harmony and non-violence.

That Christian Churches should continue to work selflessly for the upliftment of the poor, the rejected, the alienated and the oppressed. That they should continue to fight against illiteracy, poverty, caste system, class distinction and social discrimination.

That Christianity should strengthen and broaden its active involvement in the promotion of awareness and preservation of our national heritage and also the caring and tending of our habitat and its biodiversity-ecology, nature and environment.

That there should be a well dynamic plan in developing and preserving of indigenous literatures and native Christian historical research and study and should at the same time espouse high philosophical ideal for the country's simultaneous growth and advancement in faith and science.

That given the pluralistic cultural context, Christianity should seek and promote inter-religious dialogue, peaceful co-existence with and mutual respect for people of other faiths, traditions and ideologies.

That Christians should become aware, respond and involve themselves and be pro-active in the public domain and in the politics of the country. We should stand in solidarity with those who are being persecuted, discriminated or oppressed because of their faith and should have the courage to denounce the persecution of Christians and other minorities.

Christians and churches in the country should realize that the impact of globalization could be witnessed in several Christian institutions, especially in the spiraling rise of tuition fees, further widening between the 'haves' and 'have-nots' thereby creating a division in the society. We should, therefore, strengthen our educational institutions, to equip them to face the challenges of globalization and to inculcate through education the values of human beings and citizenship.

That Christianity should also stand united in drawing the attention of the Government about the reality that Christianity and other religious groups in India are in minority and that it should ensure, protect and implement the minority rights of them all.

That Christianity should hold fast in the pursuit of truth and excellence, raising our standard and the standard of the nation in the eyes of the world.

Last but not the least, we reaffirm the prophetic role of the Church and Christians in India and make a renewed commitment to address the importance of national integration, to voice for the plight of the voiceless, to work for all round development of the country, to seek for empowerment of the marginalized sections in the society and to campaign against anti-national elements, destructive forces, oppressive and divisive structures.

Index